Democracy and Election

Democracy and Elections in Africa

STAFFAN I. LINDBERG

The Johns Hopkins University Press
Baltimore

2   4   6   8   9   7   5   3   1

The Johns Hopkins University Press
2715 North Charles Street
Baltimore, Maryland 21218-4363
www.press.jhu.edu

Library of Congress Cataloging-in-Publication Data
Lindberg, Staffan I., 1969–
Democracy and elections in Africa / Staffan I. Lindberg.
p. cm.
Includes bibliographical references and index.
ISBN 0-8018-8332-6 (hardcover : alk. paper) —
ISBN 0-8018-8333-4 (pbk. : alk. paper)
1. Elections—Africa. 2. Democracy—Africa. 3. Africa—Politics
and government, 1960–   I. Title.
JQ1879.A5L55 2006
324.96'0329—dc22   2005024560

A catalog record for this book is available from the British Library.

To Kasha and Omma

Contents

Tables and Figures

Preface

This book contributes to both the comparative study of democratization and the understanding of African politics in several ways. Since Michael Bratton and Nicholas van de Walle's (1997) influential *Democratic Experiments in Africa* there has been no comprehensive study of African elections and democratization. This work attempts to fill that gap. Its relatively positive message about the prospects of democracy in Africa, based on empirical analysis of observable election data on the continent up till June 2003, may surprise some scholars as well as policy makers.

This volume focuses on the democratic qualities of elections, the core institution of liberal democracy, in newly democratizing countries. Developing an original data set with 16 variables on a universe of 232 African elections, this study examines the relationship between elections and democracy and provides evidence that elections improve the quality of a democracy. It refutes several established hypotheses in the field and shows that there is no general negative trend in either the frequency or the quality of elections in Africa and that elections are neither the end of a transition process towards democracy nor merely formal procedures. Rather, the analyses show that the inception of multiparty elections in a country instigates liberalization and that repetitive electoral activities create incentives for political actors by fostering the expansion and deepening of democratic qualities in the society. Complete breakdowns of new electoral regimes, when they occur, typically happen shortly after first elections; by the second or third elections, regimes are highly likely to survive.

The study also shows that a sequence of elections not only contributes to increasing the democratic quality of a political regime but also broadens and deepens civil liberties in the society. Demonstrating this impact of repetitive elections as an "imported" institution over diverse contexts in Africa makes available a new understanding of the role of elections in democratization, as a set of factors with causal effects, and is an important theoretical contribution of this book. It makes a methodological contribution in its development of a panel-group time series and a new type of lagged time-series analysis as a way of assessing the effects of repetitive elections on the level of democracy in a society. In policy terms, the results support the international community's current focus on elections as an effective means of positive change, and they refute the pessimism about the export of institutions.

The larger theoretical argument made in this book — that repetitive elections, even when flawed, are one of the important causal factors in democratization — speaks to the resurfacing recognition among scholars that Rustow (1970) had an important point when he argued that democratic behavior produces democratic values and not the other way around. Adding another component to this thesis, this book shows how the creation of incentives and disincentives by new institutions such as elections fosters democratic behavior that in turn leads to a more democratic culture.

In the preparation of this book, an invaluable source of inspiration, data, insights, and stimulation were the people I met and worked with in the Parliament of Ghana from 1999 to 2001, when I served as a consultant to Parliamentarians for Global Action's West African program. I had an office in the heart of the legislative structure and worked closely with staff, honorable members of Parliament, and ministers. Through daily dealings in Parliament, I was afforded an invaluable political anthropologist's view into one of Africa's most successful emerging democracies. Many of the MPs were generous with interviews and explanations of the layers of politics in Ghana. The interaction with everyone from cleaners and drivers to MPs and the Speaker of the Parliament generated more professional and personal returns than any acknowledgment such as this could do justice. I am so grateful to so many, and I hesitate to identify particular individuals in fear of not expressing my equal appreciation of others. Special thanks, though, go to two who have become my Ghanaian parents: the Honorable Alhaji A. Salifu and the Honorable Theresa A. Tagoe.

Numerous senior colleagues have also fed this project, especially at conferences where early versions of some parts of this book were presented, for example, African Studies Association annual meetings, International Studies Association annual conferences, European Consortium for Political Research's workshops in 2000, American Political Science Association meetings, the conferences on democracy and democratization in Chile in 2002 and Uppsala in 2004 (thanks, Axel Hadenius, for inviting me), and the conference on electoral authoritarian regimes in Mexico in 2004, hosted by CIDE and the National Endowment for Democracy and organized by my friend Andreas Schedler. I am also deeply grateful for the support of all my colleagues at the Department of Political Science, Lund University. While at Lund, I conducted related studies, including research on the Swedish preparations for UN world conferences during the 1990s. Special thanks go to Kristina Margård and Mats

Sjölin, who read the entire manuscript and provided a wealth of useful comments, and to Magnus Jerneck, who has been invaluable in his support through the years. Thanks also to the Swedish International Development Agency, SAREC, for two major grants in support of the project, to the Crafoord Foundation for its grant, and for Lund University's financial support of conferences and related fieldwork trips.

Some parts of Chapters 2, 3, and 4 had their preliminary expression in an article based on an earlier and limited version of the data set. I acknowledge permission to reproduce parts of that article, which was published in the *Journal of Commonwealth and Comparative Politics.*

I am grateful for the rich comments provided by the external reviewers who read the manuscript for the Johns Hopkins University Press and for the fine copyediting supplied by Anne Whitmore. I also thank the many other excellent scholars who read all or parts of the manuscript and/or related articles. Among them are Daniel Altman, Michael Bratton, Matthijs Bogaards, Patrick Chabal, Roger Charlton, Michael Chege, John F. Clark, Ruth B. Collier, Michael Coppedge, Steven Fish, Axel Hadenius, John Harbeson, Liisa Laakso, Ken Mease, Gerardo Munck, Andreas Schedler, Stephen Snook, Richard Snyder, Fredrik Uggla, Leonard Villalón, Nicholas van de Walle, and Lucan Way. Goran Hyden has been an enthusiastic critic and a constant source of encouragement. I wish to extend my thanks to both him and his wife, Mama Melania. K. C. Morrison gave freely of his valuable time, reading the whole manuscript, offering many valuable comments, and partnering with me on a project on political clientelism. Joel Barkan graciously agreed to review and comment extensively on an earlier form of the manuscript, for which I am deeply beholden. Winifred Pankani has with excellence assisted me on the clientelism project and has read the manuscript several times, contributing far beyond what anyone could ever expect. You are my fiercest critic and my greatest support.

I dedicate the labor of this book to my daughter, Omma, and my precious wife, Kasha.

Democracy and Elections in Africa

CHAPTER ONE

Introduction

This book is about how and why political systems develop the different qualities that characterize regimes as democratic, semidemocratic, or authoritarian. Such differences in political systems have been an object of study at least since Aristotle formalized the distinctions among monarchy, oligarchy, and anarchy. Many qualities of political regimes warrant closer inspection, but this study examines a very precise set, one that is of unique interest for the greater amount of freedom it provides for the people in the world: democratic qualities.

To speak of democratic qualities implies that we know what democracy is. While there are many views on what democracy is—or ought to be—a common denominator among modern democracies is elections. Partly, this commonality is a consequence of the practical concerns, recognized by James Madison (1789/1961, 81–84), Thomas Jefferson (1816/1903–1904), and John Stuart Mill (1861/1958, 212–218), that larger democratic political systems require representative government (Seligson and Booth 1995, 6). But elections are also and more importantly an institutionalized attempt to actualize the essence of democracy: rule of the people by the people. Every modern definition of representative democracy includes participatory and contested elections perceived as the legitimate procedure for the translation of rule by the people into workable executive and legislative power. Elections alone are not sufficient to make a democracy, yet no other institution precedes participatory, competitive, and legitimate elections in instrumental importance for self-government (cf. Bratton and van de Walle 1997). By studying the electoral processes—the campaign, polling day, the immediate response to results, the acceptance or rejection of the outcome by various groups—we study the mechanism of translating people's power to rule into governmental power as vested in systems of representative government. My approach focuses on three dependent variables—participation, competition, and legitimacy—as democratic qualities of elections. Operationalized well, these variables are empirically observable in actual electoral behavior and can measure de facto regime qualities.

THE ROLE OF ELECTIONS

My overall purpose in this book is to demonstrate the significance of elections, as the realization of rule by the people, in fostering democratization in Africa. I argue that elections in newly democratizing countries do not signal the completion of the transition to democracy but rather foster liberalization and have a self-reinforcing power that promotes increased democracy in Africa's political regimes. Elections also facilitate the institutionalization of and deepening of actual civil liberties in the society and are a causal variable in democratization. This is *not* to say that elections are the only important factor in expanding civil liberties and democracy; however, they have so far not received adequate recognition in the literature.

In pursuit of this overall purpose, a necessary first step was to create a comprehensive empirical data set of all elections in Africa from 1989 to 2003. The second research objective was an empirical chronicling of the democratic qualities of the elections, which would make it possible to test over time a set of empirical generalizations on the development of African politics that emanates from Bratton and van de Walle's (1997) seminal contribution.

Objective number three was to evaluate different methodological approaches to the study of elections as they relate to democracy, in order to show the limitations and fallacies inherent in some approaches. The literature on transitions to democracy and on elections in Africa hypothesizes about the development of the democratic content of elections after first or so called "founding" elections. The fourth objective addressed this second set of hypotheses and tested an alternative generalization about the power of elections: their self-reinforcing and self-improving quality.

The final objective of the study was to develop a theoretical framework of causal links between the power of elections and further democratization in a society. This framework of the democratizing power of elections is corroborated by five tests and constitutes an addition to the literature on comparative democratization. Lastly, I reflect on the implications of this new evidence for the established theories of transition to and consolidation of democracy in the Third World.

There are several benefits to pursuing these five interrelated objectives in a single coherent study. It allows for inquiry into some of the core hypotheses in the field of democratization. After O'Donnell and Schmitter's seminal work, *Transitions from Authoritarian Rule* (1986), it was assumed that any country moving away from authoritarian rule could be considered as transitioning towards democracy. By the mid-1990s, however, discussions of "hybrid regimes," "electoral authoritarianism," and "virtual democracy" had taken center stage (e.g., Archer 1995, Collier and Levitsky 1995, Joseph 1997, Przeworski 1988), negating the transition paradigm (Carothers 2002a). The earlier enthusiasm was replaced by a pessimism that soon also permeated policy making in Europe and Washington. This study challenges such pessimism, providing empirical evidence suggesting that movement from dictatorial rule to a competitive electoral regime tends to lead to further democratization and, eventually, democracy.

The evidence of this study calls into question another assumption: since Rustow's famous article (1970) it has been largely accepted that regime transition unfolds in stages, wherein "founding" elections in a country signify the genesis of a new democratic phase. The empirical analysis presented in this book shows that first elections are not necessarily founding but are most often a step in the transition towards democracy. In Africa, democracy tends to take root after a sequence of three electoral cycles. Importantly, the empirical evidence testifies that after third elections regime breakdowns occur only in very rare instances. This finding emphasizes the need for the international community to sustain support to transitional countries over an extended period, typically 12–15 years.

Finally, the role of elections in democratization has been the subject of debate in recent years. A growing number of scholars (whose analyses tend to be based on a small number of cases or case studies) have argued against the importance of elections and have criticized the current international emphasis on electoral practices. The analysis presented in this book indicates that elections in Africa have in fact had a causal impact, improving the quality of democracy there. The process of holding an uninterrupted series of *de jure* participatory, competitive, and legitimate elections not only enhances the democratic quality of the electoral regime but also has positive effects on the spread and deepening of civil liberties in the society. In the final analysis, the causal effect of elections in this regard is attested to while controlling for other well-known factors in a multiregression analysis.

WHY AFRICA?

There are at least three specific reasons to study the democratic qualities of elections in Africa rather than another place. First, authoritarian regimes dominated the political landscape of Africa until the end of the 1980s. The political changes of the early 1990s created an air of "demo-optimism" in political science circles. Within a few years, however, the political liberalization and optimism turned into "demo-pessimism," notably in authors like Joseph, who saw "virtual democracies" rather than true democratization (Joseph 1997, 1998). Other scholars predicted that things would quickly return to the usual "big man," neopatrimonial, clientelist, informalized, and disordered politics that had previously characterized African politics (e.g., Ake 1996, Chabal and Daloz 1999, Chege 1996, Mbembe 1995, Villalón 1998).

Some dissenting voices, like Wiseman (1999), have taken the naysayers to task for being excessively pessimistic. Because of the discordant views, the democratization field is fraught with contradictory hypotheses based on disparate approaches using various conceptualizations of democracy. The debate on democratization in Africa has even been likened to a "dialogue of the deaf" (Chabal 1998). In my view, part of the problem is that political scientists working on Africa pay too little attention to careful conceptualization of dependent variables, clear delimitation of hypotheses about the relationships between cause and effect, and/or rigorous measurement and compilation of comparable data. The study of political change in Africa still suffers from inadequate theoretical specification, methodological rigor, and, perhaps most of all, insufficient collection of data suitable for comparative analysis. Consequently, not enough cumulative work has been done.[1]

One strategy for addressing this state of affairs is to conceptualize and collect comparative data on partial regimes (Schmitter 1992) rather than on the "bundled wholes" (Collier and Adcock 1999) of overarching concepts like democracy and neopatrimonialism. A growing number of scholars have already called for such disaggregated data, to facilitate insights into the specific parts of politics in Africa. For example, Herbst (2001) stresses the lack of adequate specification of indicators for assessing each theory. Chabal (1998), Gibson (2002), Mahmud (1996), and Wilson (1994) all ask for more precise specification of a tractable dependent variable and more rigorous measurement. This book offers a step in that direction. Competitive elections constitute a partial regime in unbundled political regimes. An election is a phenomenon that can be conceptualized and measured in relatively unambiguous terms, with highly valid indicators and reliable data for comparative analysis. The present research provides three precise dependent variables, measured using eleven indicators for a nuanced analysis. In addition to increasing the robustness of the subsequent analysis, this precision provides several more opportunities for other researchers to use each of the dependent variables or indicators on either side of the equation for their own purposes. For example: Under what circumstances do opposition parties participate in electoral processes? What factors facilitate or prevent alternations in power? What is the effect of electoral systems on competition in Africa?

Does higher political competition cause increased political corruption? And so on. The study of the characteristics of African multiparty elections as a partial regime produces extensive data, generates variables, and solves puzzles in our field. The strategy is not a panacea but contributes to understanding political development in general and regime change and democratization in Africa in particular.

In response to the political changes of the early 1990s, many Africanists became "transitologists," proposing models, analogies, ideal types, and actor-oriented theories based on the new events. These authors seem to have followed the general move from structural determinants of democratization towards actor-oriented analyses (cf. Osaghae 1995; Schmitter and Santiso 1998, 71). This move is not inappropriate, but it is unsatisfactory. Actors *do* have power, and their subjective interests, goals, and calculations influence outcomes. Yet, not *every* course of action is available to either old or new rulers and opposition groups in transitional states.[2] Institutions generally have built-in incentives for the actors occupying and using them. Repetitive electoral cycles create new path dependencies by providing new incentives for political actors. The role of elections in forging new behavioral patterns among dominant political actors and the masses in Africa is an understudied area. This study examines two ways in which electoral institutions affect actors' behavior. Chapter 4 analyzes how the self-reinforcing power of repeated electoral practices leads to more consecutive democratic elections. Chapters 5 and 6 reveal that repetitive elections have a positive impact on democratic qualities in society, rather than being—at best —merely a reflection of it.

The comparative study of elections and democratization in Africa is still dominated by the pioneering work of Bratton and colleagues (Bratton 1997, 1998; Bratton and Posner 1999; Bratton and van de Walle, 1996, 1997). This study seeks to extend the scope of their work, making possible the evaluation of earlier research and furthering our understanding of elections and democracy in Africa. I build on Bratton and colleagues' data but have consulted a wide range of additional sources to fill in missing values, double-check data entries, and correct errors. Including more recent elections brings an additional 150 cases into play and presents results based on 232 observations. In an important methodological distinction, the present analysis controls for free and fair elections when measuring the variables, in an effort to eliminate distortions caused by election results that were partially manufactured, something not done in previous studies. Finally, this analysis introduces the use of a time-series panel-group comparison and lagged time-series analysis to the study of African elections, to mitigate selection bias. Thus, the results presented here should be less biased and permit more reliable conclusions about the frequency, democratic qualities, and trajectories of elections in Africa.

In comparing the 44 countries holding elections in Africa between 1989 and 2003, my deliberate strategy has been to stick to disaggregated measures—the ten indicators of the three dependent variables and the additional control variable for free and fairness. I believe this to be a strength on both methodological and empirical grounds. Methodologically, a model that combines three dimensions and eleven indicators into one index would be extremely complex. Any variation in the rules of aggregation and combination would eventually affect the indexing, making the results extremely sensitive to the choices of the researcher (Munck and Verkuilen 2003). With disaggregated measures, however, these problems do not occur. Empirically, the detail of the analysis and the wealth of data presented improve the soundness and robustness of the theoretical conclusions and provide more opportunities for other researchers to use them as dependent or independent variables.

ON REGIMES

As a starting point, it is appropriate to define the term *political regimes*, often referred to as the "rules of the game": a set of rules that determine the distribution of political power. Regimes differ from governments in that a government is the person or group that exercises executive power while a regime is the regulatory and institutional framework of their rule (cf. Fishman 1990). Nevertheless, regime transitions are, more often than not, the effects of new governments. Regimes also differ from states, in that a state as a locus of power consists of territory, a set of fundamental institutions necessary to the existence of a state, and the idea of a state (Buzan 1991; and compare with: Buzan, Jones, and Little 1993; Hall 1986; Mann 1986; and Tilly 1990, 1993). The state is what one rules, regimes are how one rules, and government is the group of individuals who rule. In short, regimes are the rules governing the distribution of power and the relationships between the agents of power in polities.

Generally, the concept of political regime is used to differentiate between democracies and nondemocracies (e.g., Collier and Adcock 1999; Linz and Stepan 1996), as well as to distinguish between different forms of democracy, such as parliamentary and presidential (e.g., Cheibub and Limongi 2002, Linz 1990, Mainwaring and Scully 1995, Stepan and Skach 1993) or liberal and illiberal (Diamond 1999; Karatnycky 1999). The concept is also typically employed to delineate subtypes of regimes, both authoritarian and democratic (e.g., Collier and Levitsky 1997; Diamond 2002; Diamond, Linz, and Lipset 1989; Schedler 2002a). But this book is a study of elections as a presumed necessary instrument of representative democracy and a part of the political system as a set of central institutions. In this sense, it is a study of a partial regime, a subset of the rules of the game in the sense originally formulated by Schmitter (1992).

A regime as a set of rules is both constitutive and regulatory. The constitutive rules establish the distribution of power by constituting the actors and institutions on which rights and obligations are conferred. In political democracies, this translates into equal political rights for all citizens, rights of associations including political parties, and institutions such as electoral management bodies, presidential office, legislatures, and judicial bodies of abjuration. The rules also establish the areas of competence for actors and institutions, both imposing constraints by delimitation of capacities and providing opportunities by assigning rights and means of power. For example, citizens may vote for president and members of parliament in a democracy but not for the board of directors in a company. The latter power is assigned to another set of actors constituted to be known as shareholders, among whom rights are not equal but relative to economic investment. A supreme court may be given the power to be the final arbitrator of electoral disputes but not the right to issue electoral laws and regulations. As these examples show, what are sometimes referred to as "mere procedural" rules are in fact highly political issues of power distribution. When elections are institutionalized, new actors are created and power is distributed in new ways, which goes a long way towards explaining the contentiousness of electoral rules negotiations in many places in Africa.

The regulatory rules delimit the processes actors and institutions have to follow and how they resolve conflicts. Citizens cannot vote just anywhere, on any issue, or by any means. The regulation of political decision-making processes typically does not give voters the right to veto decisions made by the executive. The procedures regulate how citizens can and must exercise their political power. In these ways, institutions, it has been argued, both constrain actors' capabilities and scope of choice (e.g., Bates 1989, Moe 1990, North 1990) and expand individual choice (e.g., Ostrom, Schroeder, and Wynne 1993). Actors have room to maneuver, and their subjective interests, goals, and calculations matter for outcomes, but within limits not of their own choosing. Regime change is about breaking old patterns and establishing new ones, even if this alteration has to occur in the context of the old structure and in the face of established patterns of behavior. Electoral processes are part of regime change, and insights gained in the study of democratization might be useful in other instances of institutional change.

ON ELECTIONS AND DEMOCRACY

The unit of analysis in this book is elections that *de jure* have allowed for equality of political participation and free competition, making them formally legitimate elections. Needless to say, rights of participation and competition may be legally permitted but not effectively enforced, and procedural legitimacy may exist in law but not in fact. The realization of these essential democratic qualities is not in constants but in variables. Equal participation, free competition, and legitimacy are democratic qualities that a political system may or may not have to varying degrees. In scientific jargon, the political system is the ontologically given object and democracy is an attribute expressed in certain qualities. For analytical purposes, the political system of any country may be endowed with these three qualities in degrees ranging from zero to a theoretical maximum. This study focuses on the democratic qualities of elections, specifically for legislative and executive offices, as actualized or effectively enforced political rights. The object of examination is the variation of these qualities among the elections studied.

To obtain a full empirical spread, we are required to include all units that potentially have these qualities in any degree. That is why the minimum criterion for inclusion as a case is *de jure* participatory, contested, and legitimate elections. No claim is made that such elections constitute a democracy; making such a claim would be to fall into the trap of the electoral fallacy (Karl 1986, 9). Elections may coexist with systematic abuse of human rights, the disenfranchisement of parts of the population, and other very undemocratic practices. Nevertheless, holding *formally* participatory and contested elections is a key necessary condition for those elections to be democratic and the political system to be a representative democracy.

The indicators include the accomplishment of free, fair, and peaceful elections in which opposition parties participated, the outcome was acceptable to all parties, and no antidemocrats contested for power. Occasional turnovers, though not necessarily in the short term, provide further evidence of incumbents' willingness to adhere to the rules of democracy, while breakdowns of regime indicate a complete depletion of legitimacy among crucial actors. The winning candidates' and parties' shares of votes and seats are indicators of the level of competition; voter turnout is a measure of popular participation. Chapter 2 provides a full discussion of these indicators of the realization of participation, competition, and legitimacy as democratic qualities. Together these election traits and outcomes and the actors' behavior provide a good measure of how democratic a political system is, because these events put the control of power at stake.

PREINDEPENDENCE AND POSTINDEPENDENCE ELECTIONS IN AFRICAN NATIONS

The continent of Africa contains 53 countries, of which five are in Northern Africa: Egypt, Libya, Tunisia, Morocco, and Algeria. These countries are normally excluded from analyses of Africa because of their distinctly different sociocultural characteristics and political history. The remaining 48 states, those in sub-Saharan Africa, constitute the geographical setting for the empirical analysis in this book.[3] The histories of elections in these countries differ in many respects.

The literature on contemporary elections and democratization in Africa is still relatively thin compared to that of southern Europe and Latin America. Yet, as has been pointed out elsewhere (Hyden, Leslie, and Ogundimu 2002), Africa had its first wave of democratization in the late 1950s as countries engaged in struggles for national independence. But the history of elections in Africa started even before that. Already from 1848, a few "assimilated" Africans in Senegal were able to vote for a *député*, a parliamentary representative to the French national assembly (Hayward 1987, 1). In one of the very few comparative studies of the pre- and postindependence elections in Africa, Ruth Collier (1982) shows that the few elections held before 1945 were highly exclusive affairs conducted among small elites in a few major cities. The first elections to legislative councils in British colonies, including Ghana, Kenya, Nigeria, and Sierra Leone (Jordan 1969, Price 1967) and Zambia took place in the 1920s. It took until the 1950s for the same to happen in, for instance, Malawi, Tanzania, and Uganda (Collier 1982). With the exception of Senegal, the situation was different in the French colonies, which were administered as a group and, following the recommendations of the 1944 Brazzaville Conference, were legislatively to be one with France, so self-government was dismissed even as a possibility in the distant future (Morgenthau 1964). However, from 1946, Africans in the French colonies voted, both in elections to assemblies in France (subject to restrictive eligibility criteria) and to local government councils. The French colonies actually experienced no fewer than seven territorywide elections before the introduction of universal suffrage, whereas most British colonies had had only one or two. Almost all of both countries' colonies held national elections based on universal suffrage before independence. Except for Guinea and Gabon, the French colonies held two such elections; a majority of the British and other colonies held one prior to independence (Collier 1982, 37, 44–45).

These preindependence attempts at competitive elections were carried out under the auspices and design of the colonial powers, from whose perspective it was a form of "tutelary" democracy that Africans were expected to learn as a precondition for independence. The preindependence leaders, such as Kwame Nkrumah, Kenneth Kaunda, Julius Nyere, Leopold Senghor, and Jomo Kenyatta, however, were not ready to accept the extended timetable for learning that the colonial powers had in mind. They forced an acceleration of the process that led to the holding of national elections much earlier than had originally been intended. The important element for our purpose is that these initial elections were generally carried out in a peaceful manner; they were fairly free and fair; and the outcomes were never generally disputed. In most cases, suffrage was universal; there were normally no restrictions on candidature or party (Cowen and Laakso 2002, 4); and the first generation of African nationalists could claim the legitimacy of having been duly elected in competitive elections. These elections were also transitional, in that a new system of government and administration was being established; and according to some early observers (e.g., MacKenzie and Robinson 1960), they did contribute to a new legitimacy in the eyes of both the colonialists and the African nationalists.

This first wave of electoral democracy in sub-Saharan Africa was short-lived, however.[4] Once in power, the leaders of the new nation-states approached the double tasks of national development and national integration by insisting on national uniformity, which set in motion a reversal towards autocracy across the continent that lasted for almost 30 years. Despite this trend, Uganda was the only postindependence civilian regime to suspend elections altogether. In some countries, such as Guinea, Mali, Ivory Coast, and Rwanda, regular one-party elections were held more or less as a result of de facto dominance (even if this dominance in several instances was shattered later). In other countries, such as Benin, Gabon, Chad, Niger, Ghana, and Congo, one-party rule was created coercively and proved to be a lot less stable (Collier 1982, 104–109). Ogendo (1999) makes the interesting observation that even hard-line autocrats made an effort to use the country's constitution to legitimize their takeover of power, and the laws of the land were not treated as completely irrelevant even though countries in Africa ended up with "constitutions without constitutionalism." Constitutions were viewed as instruments; there was no real commitment to them as ends in themselves. More than 20 one-party regimes were rapidly formed across Africa, by election, merger, or coercion, and the era of military coups was initiated with the 1960 coup in what is today referred to as Democratic Republic of Congo (DRC) (Collier 1982, 104–105). Unlike now, African elections in the 1960s and 1970s were often followed by regime breakdown. The 1966 Ghanaian coup that removed President Kwame Nkrumah from power was in part a response to the electoral manipulation that played a role in his monopolization of power (Austin 1975, 4). In Burundi the 1965 elections leading to a clear Hutu victory were followed by one coup attempt and two coups within 18 months (Lemarchand 1970). Similar developments took place in other countries, for example Nigeria (O'Connell 1970) and the DRC (Young 1965). Soon the most African nations were in the hands of authoritarian governments and, except for brief interludes in some countries, remained under nondemocratic control until the first years of the 1990s.

Most of what we know about African politics was produced during this authori-

tarian period, and this is reflected in the naming of mainstream concepts like "clientelism" (Lemarchand 1972), "neopatrimonialism" (Medard 1982), "prebendalism"
(Joseph 1987), and "rentier state" (Bates 1981). Despite the reversals after the first
wave of multiparty elections, there was variation in the way nationalist leaders approached the task of governance and some interesting experimentation with how political contestation could be combined with a desire for national unity and the existence of a single-party system. It was no coincidence that Tanzania's president, Julius
Nyere, took the lead in this effort. His ruling party, Tanganyika African National
Union (TANU) had won all seats in the preindependence election in 1960, rendering the first parliament without official opposition. A constitutional review committee was appointed in 1964 to make recommendations to parliament for legalizing a
one-party system and to organize competitive elections within its auspices based on
the single-member district formula, to occur a year later. The first national election
under this new formula, in 1965, was generally met with a lot of excitement and sat-
isfaction (Cliffe 1967). Variations of this semicompetitive approach to legislative
elections, in which the voter could choose among several candidates approved by
the ruling party, were later introduced in several other African countries (Nohlen,
Krennerich, and Thibaut 1999, 6): Kenya (1969), Zambia (1973), Sudan (1974), Zaire
(1977 and again in 1987), Malawi (1978), Mali (1979), Ivory Coast (1980), Sierra
Leone (1982), Togo (1985), Ethiopia (1987), Central African Republic (1987), Comoros (1987), and Cameroon (1987). Only a few countries continued multiparty
elections from independence: Botswana, Mauritius, and Senegal.

   Academic observers like Hayward (1987), Collier (1982), and Bayart et al. (in Hermet, Rose, and Rouquij 1978) enthusiastically proclaimed these as steps towards "political development." Hayward (1987, 16), for example, showed how the semicompetitive nature of one-party elections in Kenya, Tanzania, Nigeria, Sierra Leone, and
other countries led to the unseating of many incumbent MPs by disgruntled voters.
According to Hayward, these elections offered people a choice. To Almond and
Coleman (1960), one-party rule was a functional response to the challenges of political development in the African context. The most positive interpretation came
from Naomi Chazan (1979), who referred to this type of elections as an "African-
derived formula for constructive popular representation." It was, she argued, suitable
for a country lacking an opposition party but needing competition and accountability. Richard Sklar (1983) espoused a similar optimism when he cited the semicompetitive one-party elections as evidence that the continent was moving, albeit incrementally, towards more competitive political systems. However, other authors,
such as Ansprenger (1997) and Thibaut (1998), dismissed the elections because they
never delivered the results their advocates had promised. For instance, these elec-

tions never allowed voters a choice of who should rule or a chance to influence national policy directions. Most critical among the early observers perhaps was Zolberg (1966), who detailed governmental manipulation of electoral processes in West Africa.

Nevertheless, the prevalence of this trend towards semicompetitive elections cannot be dismissed as only an elite formula for staying in power, because these were not merely "plebiscitary" events by which elites recreated the existing order. As Hyden and Leys (1972) noted in a comparative study of such elections in Kenya and Tanzania, they gave the local electorate an opportunity to oust those leaders who breached their trust or failed to deliver "pork" to their constituents. In this specific respect, the formula worked to legitimize those in power, but equally importantly the system as a whole. Voters preferred to have some one who could represent them in the capital in a persuasive manner and by doing so secure benefits for them. It seems that—at least to some extent—voting was meaningful to them.

CONTEMPORARY AFRICA'S TRACK RECORD

There are indications that this approach to the electoral act did not change with the coming of multiparty elections in the 1990s. The few studies available on voters' motivations seem to indicate that people's votes are still based on their area of residence rather than on policy preferences. Barkan's (1995) study shows that the more agrarian the society, the higher the geographic concentration of the vote,[5] that rural voters in particular seem to continue to choose representatives based on how good they are as "patrons" of their respective community or constituency. A couple of empirical studies of the multiparty elections of the 1990s (e.g., Lindberg 2003, Wantchekon 2003, Wolf 2003) corroborate the persistence of *personalized* patron-client relations in electoral politics in Africa. It is not clear how much this preference for patron over policy at the constituency level is an effect of national policy issues' being increasingly influenced by international financial institutions and the donor community or is part of a "parochial" political culture in which dependency on someone with the right political connections is prevalent (Almond and Verba 1963), or derives from something else. Regardless of the cause, this voting behavior provides an electoral logic that is not as much the case in other countries, where national elections are primarily about policy choices. The most notable effect of this voting style is the proliferation of political parties and the difficulty of uniting the opposition in standing against the government party during elections. Each geographical area is treated as an independent base, where politicians compete for a (sometimes single) seat with little or no regard for what is happening in other con-

TABLE 1 *Number of parties registered in last parliamentary election*

Country	Parties (Yr.)	Country	Parties (Yr.)	Country	Parties (Yr.)
Angola	18 (1992)	Gambia	6 (2002)	Niger	19 (1999)
Benin	35 (2003)	Ghana	7 (2000)	Nigeria	30 (2003)
Botswana	7 (1999)	Guinea	18 (2002)	Sao Tome and	
Burkina Faso	30 (2001)	Guinea-Bissau	11 (1999)	Principe	9 (2003)
Burundi	6 (1993)	Ivory Coast	10 (2000)	Senegal	61 (2001)
Cameroon	42 (2002)	Kenya	40 (2002)	Seychelles	4 (2002)
Cape Verde	5 (2001)	Lesotho	19 (2002)	Sierra Leone	10 (2002)
Cent. Af. Rep.	29 (1998)	Liberia	16 (1997)	South Africa	16 (1999)
Chad	42 (2002)	Madagascar	41 (2001)	Sudan	8 (2000)
Comoros	10 (1996)	Malawi	11 (1999)	Swaziland	N/A (1998)
Rep. of Congo	100 (2002)	Mali	12 (2002)	Tanzania	13 (2000)
Djibouti	8 (2003)	Mauritania	16 (2001)	Togo	25 (2002)
Eql. Guinea	13 (1999)	Mauritius	20 (2000)	Uganda	N/A (2001)
Ethiopia	50 (2000)	Mozambique	15 (1999)	Zambia	15 (2001)
Gabon	36 (2001)	Namibia	8 (1999)	Zimbabwe	7 (2000)

stituencies or at the national level. Parties are often personal vehicles pursuing clientelistic platforms (Monga 1995, 365; Wantchekon 2003). Taken together, this emphasizes person over party and has resulted in a prevalence in African countries of political parties that are one-person operations.

As Table 1 illustrates, the number of parties is typically high in competitive elections in contemporary Africa. These numbers represent neither "effective number of parties" (Laakso and Taagepera 1979) nor "relevant parties" (Sartori 1991) but merely the number registered to contest in elections, and thus they do not give substantial information on competitiveness or the nature of the party system in these countries. They nevertheless provide some food for thought on the political context in Africa.

The emphasis on person rather than party in Africa is a probable reason why so many elected autocrats managed to stay in power in the 1990s. By 1997, almost half of the 48 autocrats from pre-1990 Africa were still in executive office as a result of some kind of elections (Baker 1998). These incumbents, even though elected, are not necessarily interested in transforming old structures, since their rule—even as leaders of democratically elected governments—is dependent on old and often clientelist structures of governance. Thus, we have reason to be skeptical about both the credentials and the function of competitive elections in the contemporary African context. We need to critically examine the empirical realities of these elections in the established tradition of comparative politics before we can accurately assess their democratic qualities and the value of holding them as part of a democratization process. Locating this study within the theoretical core of comparative politics makes available a set of new and interesting cases for examination by the field.

Of the 48 sub-Saharan countries, 44 held *de jure* contested elections between 1989 and 2003. The Democratic Republic of Congo, Eritrea, Rwanda, and Somalia lack a record of contested elections. The DRC when it was Zaire degenerated into a predatory, extractive state (Clark 1998) under President Mobutu, collapsing into anarchy around 1995–1996. Insurgent leader Laurent Kabila temporarily restored some degree of peace in the vast country and gave it its new name. The DRC's mineral-rich eastern areas were the site of Africa's first continental war, involving armies of at least eight different nations and an unknown number of private military forces during the late 1990s and early twenty-first century. Eritrea seceded from Ethiopia in 1994 after successfully defeating the military might of Addis Ababa in a civil war. The young state represents one of the very few exceptions to the stability of borders in Africa since independence. Its rule by the People's Front for Democracy and Justice has so far been harsh and evidently nonliberal, and elections of the sort investigated in this book have not been contemplated there.

Rwanda was the scene of horrific acts leading to genocide and almost inconceivable crimes against humanity in 1994. After a long mediation process involving both unilateral and multilateral actors, the country held contested elections, but they occurred shortly after the end of this study's range, on 25 September 2003. The incumbent president, Paul Kigame, won by a landslide, with 95 percent of the votes, in a process that, according to the European Union team of observers, was marred by irregularities. The main opposition candidate, Faustin Twagiramungu, petitioned the Rwandan Supreme Court in protest, but his petition was dismissed, and the court later confirmed the official results.

Devastated by civil war, foreign occupation, and ecological crises, Somalia has not been able to resurrect central, much less civilian, rule since the dramatic changes there after the Cold War, concluding with a U.S.-led invasion, disastrous consequences, and ensuing anarchy. The northern part of the country, Somaliland, has proclaimed sovereignty, although the international community has so far refused to recognize it as a sovereign state. Nevertheless, it is receiving assistance from numerous bilateral donors in rebuilding efforts that include the holding of presidential and parliamentary elections on 14 April 2003. In those polls, the incumbent and self-declared president, Dahir Riyale Kahin, faced a strong opposition challenge. The main challengers were Ahmed Muhammad "Silaanyo" of the Kulmiye Party and Faisal Ali "Warabe" of the Justice and Welfare Party (UCID). The accuracy of the results was hotly disputed, but the constitutional court of the self-declared republic confirmed the incumbent president as the winner of the presidential election. In the interest of unambiguous application of the selection criteria (discussed in the methodology section of Chapter 2), the Somaliland elections have not been included in the present analysis. The northeastern part of what was once Somalia—Puntland—is claiming regional autonomy, and the leadership seems to be in some kind of authoritative control, but contested elections are not on the agenda. Somalia proper, the southern part, which includes the capital, Mogadishu, is still ruled by militias and warlord factions of the four main clans. While there is some amount of order and authority at the local level, no central authority has been reestablished, despite several attempts supported by the international community.

An overview of the occurrence of elections in these 44 countries is presented in Table 2. The countries are grouped by how many successive elections have been held without a breakdown of the electoral cycle. For example, Ghana's most recent executive and legislative elections were the third successive elections without a breakdown of the electoral cycle; hence, it is placed in the "Three Elections" category. This emphasis on an unbroken series of elections is central to the main arguments in this book, supported empirically by the analyses in Chapters 4 and 6. Further, I apply a definition of first elections inspired by Bratton and van de Walle (1997, 196), in which the office of the head of government and/or seats in the legislature are openly contested following a period when contested and participatory politics had been denied.[6] In the table, an asterisk marks countries where a coup, civil war, or similar event occurred after the country had successfully held elections, interrupting the series of elections. In five countries (second column), the electoral

TABLE 2 *Length of most recent succession of elections as of 1 July 2003*

No Elections	Broken Down Still	One Election	Two Elections	Three Elections	Four or More Elections
DRC	Angola*	Comoros*	Chad	Burkina Faso	Benin
Eritrea	Burundi*	RoC*	Eql. Guinea	Cameroon	Botswana
Rwanda	CAR*	Guinea-Bissau*	Ethiopia	Cape Verde	Madagascar
Somalia	Ivory Coast*	Lesotho*	Gambia*	Djibouti	Mali
	Liberia*	Niger*	Guinea	Gabon	Mauritius
		Sierra Leone*	Malawi	Ghana	Senegal
			Mozambique	Kenya	Zimbabwe
			Nigeria*	Mauritania	
			South Africa	Namibia	
			Sudan	Sao Tome and	
			Swaziland	Principe*	
			Tanzania	Seychelles*	
			Uganda	Togo	
				Zambia	

Note: Abbreviations: DRC = Democratic Republic of Congo, CAR = Central African Republic, RoC = Republic of Congo.
   *Indicates that a coup, civil war, or similar event interrupted the electoral process at some point during the period studied.

process as of 1 July 2003 had broken down after one or more elections had been held, and elections were not taken up again during the period studied; these states are therefore placed in a separate category.[7] Table 2 serves only to introduce the empirical field and does not purport to provide evidence for the arguments in the following chapters. Rather, it facilitates the outline of the contents of the remaining chapters.

As recorded in Table 2, quite a few African countries — 33 of them — have held not only first but also second elections, and 20 have managed even third elections, while seven have concluded a series of at least four successive elections. Reading contemporary literature on African politics in general and on democratization in particular, one would not expect these facts. Even Africanists seem insufficiently aware of the spread and frequency of contested elections in Africa, perhaps in part because the comparative literature on elections and democratization in Africa is limited; hence, the need to provide an overview and some basic empirical details.

OUTLINE OF THE BOOK

Chapter 2 addresses what democracy is and how we can identify measurable democratic qualities present in elections to varying degrees. For present purposes, democracy is understood to mean self-government by a sovereign people. I argue that at least three dimensions are necessary instruments for the realization of self-government: equality of political participation, freedom of political competition, and legitimacy of the idea of self-government. These dimensions constitute the three central democratic qualities that we look for in elections. They are not the only important dimensions, but they are necessary for the realization of self-government. Elections are understood as periodic and *de jure* participatory, contested, and legitimate institutions used to select representatives to the executive or legislative branches of government. The extents to which the three qualities are realized in practice in elections are the three dependent variables used in Chapters 3 and 4. Chapter 2 also details the methodology of this study, down to nitty-gritty details of data collection and processing.

Chapter 3 takes the initial steps in the empirical analysis from the perspective of developments over time and reveals that, contrary to what the literature suggests, the number and frequency of elections in general, and free and fair elections in particular, are not on the decline. Second, the democratic quality of elections in Africa is also not on the decline. Both popular actors' and key actors' participation in elections have been relatively stable over the period studied and at higher levels than has been previously reported. The level of competition leaves room for substantial improvement but remains stable. While legitimacy is the only dimension with signs of a statistically significant improvement over time, the changes are still fairly small and do not indicate a general acceptance of the rules of the game. I contend that analyzing elections this common way—simply over time—has limited analytical value, and an alternative approach is proffered in the succeeding chapter.

Chapter 4 explores the theoretically interesting question of the self-reinforcing power of repetitive elections and makes the argument that an uninterrupted series of *de jure* participatory and competitive elections—no matter what their initial quality—has led to successive elections of identifiably higher democratic quality in Africa. This finding is not trivial, particularly in light of the prevalent Afro-pessimism, which tends to degrade the value of elections. The very nature of elections as a procedural regime with real effects on the distribution of power induces a self-improving power, making them a worthwhile exercise in and of themselves.

The literature on African politics has produced hypotheses based on the differences among the various countries. Chapter 4 also tests these hypotheses by introducing a new kind of panel-group time-series comparison. This comparison reveals that the "latecomers" among electoral regimes in Africa started from less promising positions and that their first elections were generally less democratic than those of "older" generation countries. However, the trend towards a steady improvement of the democratic qualities of elections is found in all groups as they hold successive elections. The comparison thus further corroborates the conclusion that the mere holding of *de jure* participatory and competitive elections tends to be self-reinforcing and improves with greater experience. The socialization of actors into the rules of a new set of institutions seems to redirect and reformulate actors' behavior, making it more and more in accordance with democratic expectations over successive electoral cycles. The impact of these "imported" institutions in Africa is constant across very different contexts.

Another reflection that might be inspired by Table 2 relates to instances in which the electoral cycle has broken down completely. While regime survival is used as an indicator of the legitimacy of competitive elections in this book, it is also a dependent variable in its own right with its own research tradition. The findings on breakdowns presented here provide food for thought, as a vast majority of complete breakdowns happened at an early stage of these transition processes, shortly after first elections had been held. When regimes survive two elections, they are highly unlikely to break down, as far as can be discerned from the track record so far. The implication is that if these countries can be supported in completing three electoral cycles, the internal dynamics will change to augur well for a more stable polity.

In sum, Chapters 3 and 4 address hypotheses in the existing literature where previous studies of competitive elections in Africa carried out by Bratton and colleagues

(Bratton 1997, 1998; Bratton and Posner 1999; Bratton and van de Walle 1997) held the following: (a) Aside from helping some new regimes to survive, elections did little, and the frequency and quality of elections is on the decline. (b) Late "founding" elections (those held after 1995) as well as second elections are generally worse than earlier attempts in terms of participation, competition, and legitimacy. (c) Fewer turnovers resulted from second elections, and in this regard African politics is said to be returning to a "normality" of dominant parties and personalities in the "big man" form of politics. While those conclusions were warranted by data available at the time, the present analysis, based on a longer period and many additional cases, challenges these findings on several accounts. There is no general negative trend in either the frequency or the democratic qualities of elections in Africa. Analyzing trends over first, second, and third elections shows that there is a significant improvement in democratic quality, in particular as countries hold third elections. While the cited authors noted that turnovers were uncommon in second elections, current evidence shows that alternations of power have been nearly as common in third elections as in first ones. Hence, the pessimism in this regard should also be reconsidered.[8]

Chapter 5 goes into largely uncharted terrain. Table 2 suggests that there is a relationship between democracy *writ large* and greater experience with elections. Is there such a thing as democratization by elections, as our colleague Andreas Schedler (2002b, forthcoming) has suggested? For sure, there are inherent dangers of a certain amount of both tautology and colinearity in such claims. Elections are a key defining characteristic in almost every theory of democracy, and most measures of democracy and political freedom rely heavily on electoral indicators. These theoretical and methodological difficulties are discussed in Chapter 5 in the course of reviewing the main theories of democratization. The chapter outlines a new theoretical framework of plausible causal links between the repetition of elections and improvement of democratic qualities in society outside of the political system. The causal links are summarized in a set of general hypotheses with unambiguous empirical implications suitable for evaluation.

Then, Chapter 6 uses five alternative tests to evaluate these hypotheses. In order to gauge the independent explanatory power of repetitive electoral cycles on democratization, I offer a new measure of the effects of elections for a lagged time-series analysis. Five alternative empirical tests indicate (a) that an uninterrupted repetition of elections tends to be associated with an increase in real civil liberties in society such that at the time of second elections they are better than at the time of first elections, and so on, (b) that improvements in civil liberties in society tend to occur as effects of holding elections rather than in periods before or between elections, and (c) that none of the globally well-known causes of democracy act as intervening or other independent variables erasing the explanatory power of elections. The empirical results thus provide support for both the main hypothesis and the causal links suggested in the theoretical framework, fitting *almost two-thirds of all countries* in Africa. In periods before and between elections, changes in the level and spread of democracy *writ large* have been marginal and often even negative. However, in conjunction with elections, substantial improvements in democratic qualities in society are recorded, opening up a new understanding of the role of elections in democratization as a set of factors with causal effects. Such a perspective has been inadequately addressed in theories of democratization so far.

Finally, Chapter 7 sums up the main findings of the study and places the findings in the broader context of democratization studies. Reflecting beyond what can be empirically evidenced, it seems likely, from incidental accounts and in combination with other studies, that in Africa liberalization does not occur first, leading to pressures that result in elections. Rather, decisions by ruling elites to instigate elections have resulted in political openings, increased civil liberties, and societal pressures. The civil society mobilization and popular protests posited by Bratton and van de Walle (1997) have in fact had no effect on the spread of civil liberties. There is no evidence that a previously harsh regime is beneficial for the successful installation of democracy in African countries nor that different kinds of hybrid regimes are generally the institutional outcome on the continent. But the transition paradigm that protracted transitions tend to be beneficial for democracy seems to get some support from empirical analysis. Also, Islam seems to have no significant negative effects on democratization in Africa, prompting the thought that part of the means to achieve democracy in Islamic countries may be found on this continent. In addition, Chapter 7 questions the methodology of mainstream consolidation studies and challenges the field to unbundle and disaggregate the dependent variable. Elections as a partial regime may well be consolidated *and* stabilized long before other partial regimes and may also be an independent variable causing other partial regimes to consolidate. For example, when an electoral regime stabilizes, it affects citizens' attitudes, both through the learning and adaptation of partaking in these practices and through forming expectations that some kind of democratic elections will prevail. Citizens' attitudes towards elections and democracy being another part of consolidation are then partly caused by the holding of repetitive elections. In this vein, it seems that the practice of elections, having a say in government and being part of the political community, may contribute to a remedy for the disengagement from the state so common in Africa over the past 30 years. As it did in the West over a long period of time, representative procedures and inclusion feed the sense of citizenship and provide powerful symbols of peaceful coexistence and collaboration.

A related issue is the export of institutions; this book lends support to the more optimistic view that "Western" institutions may well be successfully transplanted to function in intended ways, although with local variations. Electoral institutions and rights may therefore also contribute to controlling corruption, by furthering civil liberties and providing actors with incentives for improving checks and balances in their own self-interest. At the very least, it seems that repetitive elections have made a great contribution towards ending neopatrimonial—although not clientelistic—politics in Africa, and this might well be one of their major achievements.

The policy implications of this study are also discussed in the final chapter. If the democratic qualities of elections tend to improve when countries manage to make it to third or fourth elections, irrespective of how they started, it provides a strong case for continued aid and support for electoral processes in developing countries. Almost no breakdowns occur after second elections have been held. Once the electoral cycle is established, it seems that a critical mass of actors get their interests vested in preservation of electoral politics. Renewed authoritarian rule is no longer attractive in terms of costs and benefits. This is further evidenced by the observation that all coups and similar incidents in Africa during the 1990s were followed by an immediate concession by the new ruler(s) to hold elections. If successive elections not only improve their own democratic qualities in terms of actors' behavior during the elections but also contribute to the spread of democracy in the society, the case becomes even stronger for support to keep the electoral process going at any cost. This perspective puts elections at center stage, not only as a necessary component or indicator of democracy, but also as a cause of democratization. In a nutshell, elections will, more often than not, be the way to democracy.

CHAPTER TWO

On Democracy and Elections

Studying frequencies of and trends in specific democratic qualities of elections obviates the need to make awkward decisions about the point at which an election becomes fully democratic or when real democracy has been attained in a particular country. Nevertheless, a few conceptual clarifications are in order, to ensure a correct reading of the following empirical analysis. *Qualities* as a scientific term simply denotes characteristics that in principle can be either positive or negative. Adding the adjective *democratic* is a refinement that requires specification of the defining value(s) of democracy. Based on the identification of this core value, the essential attributes we call democratic qualities can be deduced. Following the classic rules of mutually exclusive definitions, specifying what democracy is necessarily involves clarifying also what it is not. In the following pages, this is considered from four approaches. Is democracy an object in itself or an attribute? I argue that it makes more sense to view democracy as an attribute of the political system than as an object in itself. Second, it is argued that in the present context it is preferable to use a degree approach rather than a dichotomy between democracy and nondemocracy. Third, every empirical definition of democracy necessarily must be based on a normative justification, and the baseline in this book is a deliberately "thin" understanding of representative, liberal democracy that can travel across sociocultural contexts. The fourth approach involves identification of a definition of democracy that lends itself to attribution and graduation. Anticipating the argument, the core value of democracy is understood to be self-government and the three necessary attributes are equality of political participation, free political competition, and procedural legitimacy.

In general, I recognize that there is no necessary link among a particular term, like *democracy*, the conceptual construct in the mind, and the empirical phenomenon to which it refers.[1] These relationships have been discussed at length already by scholars like Pierce (1958), Ogden and Richards (1923), and de Saussure (1915/1974).[2] While our conceptualizations always condition our observations—if we define swans as white birds the category will lack the black Asian variants of swans—the consequence is that we need more, not less, precise and explicit specifications of concepts. Hence, the inclusion of a little elaboration on democracy and its qualities.

Good empirical research must rely on observation—preferably systematic and comprehensive—if we wish to make valid causal inferences that speak to the empirical implications of the theory (cf. King, Keohane, and Verba 1994; Brady and Collier 2004). In this sense, Popper's proposition that empirically falsifiable theories are the evidence of robust scholarship (Popper 1953/1999, 57 ff.) is still an appropriate guiding tool, and the definition of democratic qualities we use must lend itself to empirical evaluation. Still, the way we choose to frame and define our study object in a sense shapes the data collection and processing. For example, *elections* is a term used to denote various concepts that in turn refer to a mass of phenomena in the world. If we are to believe cognitive psychology (e.g., Dawes 1995, 81–83; Høyrup 1995, 9–12; Piaget 1972; Rosenberg 1995, 123), our concepts are formed in a perpetual reflexive process involving encounters with empirical phenomena and our own reactions to these phenomena. The more encounters we have had with a particular type of phenomena—election-related phenomena, for example—the more are our percepts influenced by expectations based on our earlier encounters (e.g., Garfinkel 1984; Giddens 1982; cf. Flyvbjerg 1991, 64–65). In other words, our concepts contribute to the construction and recording of even as "purely" empirical phenomena as elections. The protection against the dangers of relativism is clear and precise specification of concepts and theories followed by empirically sound, relevant, and preferably (if possible) systematic data collection. In specifying our concepts we lay open the prerequisites of our study, and in demarcating and operationalizing our theory we clarify its descriptive or causal claims, as well as what would falsify our statements. These are additional reasons for a slight exploration of the concept of democracy within the limited scope of the research objectives: to descriptively chronicle and analyze elections in Africa with a view to engaging comparative theories of democratization.

MAKING A CONCEPTUAL CHOICE

Elections are one of many ways of choosing leadership and disposing of old governments in a political system. As a core institution of representative democracy, elections are supposedly the means of deciding who should hold legislative and executive power. Yet, elections also take place in countries that are not fully democratic; and the "democraticness" of elections can be characterized by the degree to which they display certain democratic features, in a range from zero to a theoretical maximum. If we agree that some political systems can be more democratic than others, then "democraticness" becomes an attribute that the political system is endowed with. This reasoning translates into viewing democracy as an attribute of the political system, the latter being the object of study.[3]

An essentially different view is to approach democracy as an object in itself. For example, identification of a specific regime type conceptualized as democracy is done using characteristics that are defining of, and hence exclusive to, that particular regime type. That implies democracy to be something with object-like characteristics in need of definition. Such is the logic of classical concept formation (Collier and Mahon 1993; Coppedge 2005; Munck 2001b; Sartori 1984; Schedler 2001a). If a certain attribute, or its value, is not exclusive to a particular concept, it cannot be used as a defining characteristic and should therefore not be included in the definition. For instance, it makes little sense in this approach to say that democracies are defined by political competition, since competition in a broad sense is a characteristic of most political systems. The frequency of coups, insurgencies, and toppling of governments is clearly indicative of the fierce competition in authoritarian contexts. The form of political competition that could be said to be a defining feature of democracy would need a more precise and unambiguous specification. If by *political competition* we mean the struggle for the highest executive or legislative office, in a democracy this struggle is channeled through a specific kind of electoral processes. Those processes are constituted by a particular set of rules governing candidate, party, and voter eligibility criteria, political rights of speech, association and information, electoral management bodies, the electoral system, district boundaries, campaign contributions, voting requirements, rules for complaints and abjuration, and so on.

It can also be argued that democracy is characterized by political participation of a particular kind. Political participation in democracies—as distinct from nondemocracies—is based on the notion of citizens' political equality. Individuals who so wish should be able to form a political party and contest in elections on the same conditions as everyone else. All citizens of age and mental sanity should be able to cast their vote based on the principle of one person, one vote. In social scientific jargon: the sovereignty of the people should be distributed equally. Just as unspecified political competition is not defining for democracy, political participation in a general sense exists in most systems of rule. In nondemocracies, however, it is characterized by exclusion or patron-client or other unequal relationships. Conversely, when it comes to defining authoritarian regimes, the use of coercion is probably not a good indicator, because it is an aspect of most democracies as well, a fact that is often ignored in concept formation and empirical classification. There are many examples of inadequate specifications of democracy and authoritarianism in the literature on democratization (cf. Munck 1994, 2001b). Approaching democracy as an object requires an unambiguous specification of the defining attributes.[4]

Such is the principal difference between approaching democracy as an object in itself and conceptualizing democracy as a quality or a set of qualities that a system of rule potentially has and that can be found in various degrees. The approach here is to treat democracy as an attribute of the political system, where self-government translates into a set of qualities—equal political participation, free political competition, and procedural legitimacy—that a system of rule potentially has to varying degrees.

Definitional discussions in the literature on the empirical study of democracy are also frequently in terms of a controversy between those who define democracy in terms of kind or of degree, whether democracy and nondemocracy are best conceptualized as a dichotomy or as two ends of a continuum (cf. Collier and Adcock 1999). It should be recognized that this debate is a false one on one level. Any study has to make a distinction between those phenomena that are objects of analysis and others that are not. Hence, the researcher always has to make a decision on differences in kind, such as what kind of regime can potentially be a democracy and what cannot and should therefore be excluded from the analysis (cf. Munck 2005). Within that class of objects defined as units for analysis, however, further choices can be either of the kind-type or the degree-type. Scholars like Alvarez et al. (1996), Huntington (1991, 11–12), Geddes (1999), Linz (1975, 184–185), and Cheibub et al. (1996) rather vigorously argue in favor of a dichotomous approach. Speaking about democracy as a matter of degree is, in Sartori's words, a "stultifying" exercise in "degreeism" (1987, 184). Sartori's concern with conceptual stretching was to defend the meaning of democracy against the so-called democracy professed by leaders of authoritarian systems of rule. Fearing the dilution of democracy by ascription to it of nondemocratic characteristics, Sartori's followers suggest rigid demarcation of what democracy is, and is not.

While these concerns are certainly valid, is the question of a dichotomous versus a graded conception of democracy an ontological and therefore a fundamental issue, or is it merely a methodological choice to be made in relation to a specific research focus? I certainly would argue the latter, as did Levitsky and Adcock (1999) in their call for methodological, rather than philosophical, justifications. It is possible, and I would argue preferable, to work with a graded measure of democracy and use that graduation to establish and defend a particular cut-off point between two or more regime types. When the distribution of cases along a continuum is known, the sensitivity to errors generated by certain cut-off points can be assessed; while if one starts out with only a dichotomy, such a test cannot be performed and the role of the classification criteria in producing the results will remain unknown. In addition, scholars can certainly agree on basic defining characteristics of democracy, excluding purely authoritarian systems without necessarily having to agree on the cut-off points.

Alvarez et al. (1996) go even further than Sartori in arguing that there are no borderline cases or intermediate categories. Their argument is that, given a theoretically grounded definition of democracy, precise operational rules, and the necessary empirical information, the classification of regimes as democratic or nondemocratic will be unambiguous; technical difficulties in classifying empirical examples do not validate the theoretical conclusion that democracy is a dichotomous phenomenon. That is certainly true, but what Alvarez et al. fail to recognize is that the same argument negates their own justification for their approach: that all regimes can be unambiguously classified as either democracy or nondemocracy on the basis of systematically generated empirical observations does not validate the theoretical argument for a binominal classification, since concepts can never be verified empirically.[5] While deductions are validated by their logical consistency and inductions are validated by their empirical applicability over a large number of cases, the validity of the specification of a concept and its internal characteristics lies in its ability to address the research question. Thus, what is important is the ability of a dichotomous or a graded concept of democracy to engage in the kind of analysis the researcher sets. The real test of the usefulness of a conceptual construction is its ability to be operational in empirical analysis.

Other scholars, like Dahl in his formulation of polyarchy (1971, 2, 8; 1989, 316–317) and later Bollen and Jackman (1989, 612–618), Coppedge and Reinicke (1990), and Diamond (1996, 53), posit that democracy is a matter of degree and that most countries fall somewhere along the continuum between the poles of full democracy and complete nondemocracy. There are two main variants of this argument. The first ranks countries along a single indexed continuum while the other situates them based on subordinate categories, from partial to total democracies, sometimes referred to as "diminished subtypes." The two variants are similar in that they treat democracy not as an either-or concept but as one of extent.

The literature on democratization in the Third World is rich with variations on the theme of diminished subtypes. Collier and Levitsky (1995) reportedly stopped counting at 550 when they were reviewing the literature in the 1990s. Examples include "limited democracy" (Archer 1995, 166), "restricted democracy" (Waisman 1989, 69), "protected democracy" (Loveman 1994), and "tutelary democracy" (Przeworski 1988, 60–61). Some labels can be misleading, since they are negations, for example Joseph's "virtual democracy" (1997, 367–368). Collier and Levitsky (1997), like Schedler (1998), place diminished subtypes on the conception classification scheme based on a dichotomous approach and organize them on the ladder of generality.[6] I disagree with this approach and posit that subtypes such as these are a matter of degree; they simply have less of one defining attribute and are therefore neither full democracies nor fully authoritarian but somewhere along the continuum between democracy and nondemocracy.[7] Diamond's recent (2002) typology is typical, ranging from closed authoritarian to full democracies with four intermediate categories, an instance of degreeism that we naturally associate with ordinal variables. We know that there is a difference between the categories and that there is a range from lowest/worst to most/best, but what we do not know is the exact distance between these categories.[8]

The other kind of degreeism works not with categorizations but with continuous indices. This approach has been used by, for example, Bollen (1979), Coppedge and Reinicke (1990), Freedom House (2004), Marshall and Jaggers (2001), Hadenius (1992), and Vanhanen (1997). Each democratic attribute is measured and quantified according to predefined thresholds, then combined according to some formula, usually additive, more rarely multiplicative.[9] Several variations would be possible, depending on whether democracy is conceptualized as having one, two, or more dimensions; the consequences of the choice are far-ranging.[10] Take the widely debated issue of equality of political participation. Perfect equality would require equal opportunities for all individuals and would have to take into account known and unknown personal abilities and psychological orientations as well as factors like education, work, place of residence, parents' backgrounds—which are known to affect participation—not to mention race, class, gender, and age. We know this to be impossible. Opportunities of political participation are not perfectly equal (some would say they are not even close) in the established democracies, yet these countries are still considered democracies. A dichotomous conceptualization of equality of political participation that does not acknowledge these limitations is a useless anaytical tool, as no country in the world would be considered a democracy and there would be no variation in the dependent variable to explain. Rather, equality of political participation is typically conceptualized as equal formal rights and popular participation operationalized in terms of degrees; and voter turnout is used to indicate the level of actual participation, under the assumption that everyone would vote if they had the same opportunity. Even though there are other options, the choice of indicator(s) must be justified by its ability to yield relevant analysis. In this study, for example, the level of political participation is measured by three indicators: voter turnout (popular participation), share of opposition parties contesting elections (opposition participation), and whether old authoritarian leaders participate in the contest (known antidemocratic leaders' participation).

In sum, for those favoring a dichotomous view, regimes cannot be half-democratic, while those in the degree camp find democratic attributes to be variables with shades of grey that nondemocratic regimes may also have in some measure. Methodologically, the dichotomous approach set the minimum standard of how much of these characteristics must be present for a political system to be a democracy. If x_1, x_2, and x_3 are present, the polity in question is classified as a democracy. These are absolute requirements, whether the operational definition of democracy is a minimal or a more extensive one. Both approaches need to specify the defining characteristics of democracy, to avoid unfocused, pointless empiricism.[11] Degree approaches tend to specify ranges of each defining characteristic without specifying cut-off points. A cut-off point can be identified while keeping graded measures, and many researchers do so. I prefer the graded approach because it brings more information to bear on the theory than does the dichotomous approach and it is also more sensitive to the shades of grey that always exist in the real world, and democratization is a process—a regime becomes increasingly democratic. The study of such a process requires a graded measure that can capture not only the divide between democracies and nondemocracies but, more important, the differences in degrees of democratic qualities among less-than-full democratic political systems.

In addition, the research questions guiding this inquiry direct interest to what degree the elections in Africa have acquired democratic qualities, not whether they can be classified as fully democratic or not. The even more general question whether the political system can be classified as democratic or not is outside of the scope and intent of this inquiry. Following the argument made above, the definition of what is "democratic" that we look for in studying these elections should lend itself to attribution and graduation.

DEFINING DEMOCRACY

Studies of elections, democratization, and transition tend to avoid debating normative democratic theory, and even a cursory reading of the comparative literature seems to confirm that many follow Sklar's (1996, 26) suggestion that "political science is not moral philosophy; it does not prescribe the ends of political action; it is concerned with finding adequate means for achieving politically defined ends." The normative question of which model of democracy is preferred—direct or representative, elitist or participatory, neoliberal or social-democratic, thick or thin—is generally not addressed (cf. Merkel 1998, 33). One prominent exception in the debate on democratization in Africa is the late Claude Ake, who engaged in extensive normative discussions as a point of departure for his empirical work (e.g., Ake 2000). While most scholars take a stance on liberal elitist democracy without further philosophical discussion, pragmatic reasoning, rather than the Sklarian stance above, seems to cause the majority quickly to decide that Dahl rather than Rousseau and Mills rather than Habermas supply the most appropriate point of departure. There are at least three pragmatic reasons for this choice.

First, the democracies of the world are, to a greater or lesser degree, elitist, liberal, and representative. There simply are no direct democracies—save the frequent referendums in Switzerland—or variants of discursive or participatory democracy. The democratizing countries strive towards what the established democracies are, and it probably would seem awkward to many of them to implement elitist liberal democratic practices as opposed to, say, discursive ideals.

Second, political theory is a sophisticated subdiscipline that requires specialized skills that few of us in comparative politics have mastered. Third, most of our efforts are spent on descriptive and causal theory that rarely questions long-term ideological goals; hence, it is no accident that it is in discussions of how established democracies can be deepened or broadened that normative theory has played a more active role. The more prevalent and pressing problem in democratizing countries—epitomized in Africa—is not how to perfect democracy but how to establish a system that at least comes close to being a minimal democracy. This book is accordingly limited in philosophical ambition: to explicate the normative basis for its empirical analysis. What we are concerned with here is the empirical existence of democratic qualities in political systems in general and in these systems' electoral institutional expressions in particular. Hence, a representative liberal democracy, rather than a model direct or participatory democracy, is the most relevant frame of reference.

Third, taking a less orthodox but normative stance here, the definition ought to be applicable over a wide range of sociocultural and economic contexts in order to counter the risk of ethnocentrism—implicit or otherwise—an especially important concern with regard to politics in Africa. Like Bratton and van de Walle (1997) and Chege (1996), I believe that concepts, models, and theories developed in the West by Westerners or based on the study of Western countries can and should be applied to politics in Africa. There is no reason to assume *a priori* that these theories and concepts cannot be used to understand African politics. Likewise, theories and concepts that are of African origin might prove useful in the study of the West or Asia. For example, Hyden's theory of the economy of affection (Hyden 1983), developed to grapple with African realities, is proving applicable to societies outside of Africa (Hyden 2005).

The empirical applicability of a concept or a theory is ultimately an empirical question. Contrary to what many tend to think, the Western democracies cannot be captured in one model that fulfills exactly the same functions and provides the same meaning across societies. Taking the ten most common features of existing modern democracies and making a crude dichotomous distinction for each, we get 2^{10} = 1,024 possible configurations (Rothstein 1998, 135; cf. Schmitter and Karl 1991; Lijphart 1984). A few severely simplified examples suffice to clarify this point. The vision of representative justice and governing ability in proportional versus majoritarian electoral systems (e.g., Lijphart 1984; Lijphart and Waisman 1996) is one example of how democracy may serve different emphases. The general differences between how presidential democratic systems and parliamentary ones function and which one is better for democratic survival is another (e.g., Bernhard 1999, Cheibub and Limongi 2002, Easter 1997, Linz 1990, Linz and Stepan 1996, Mainwaring 1993). Whereas democracy in the United States, for example, is widely accepted as the solution to the problem of tyranny, in Sweden and the Netherlands, for example, it is integrated with a much broader social agenda and popular empowerment. In the United States, a voter turnout of 50 percent of registered voters is considered adequate; but in Sweden, where all citizens are registered as voters automatically, such a result would amount to a national political emergency. One need only consider these and other equally significant variations in the way democracy is perceived and practiced in countries like the United States, Sweden, France, Italy, and Britain to see that any empirical definition of democracy must be fairly "thin" or abstract.

In sum, use of democracy as a variable attribute of political systems should include an empirically oriented definition of representative liberal democracy that is general enough to apply to a variety of contexts but specific enough to discriminate against clearly nondemocratic political systems and to facilitate an unambiguous operationalization.

Self-Government as the Most Fundamental Value

What then is the core of liberal representative democracy and which are the principal democratic attributes necessary for its realization? I propose that the most fundamental value of representative liberal democracy is self-government. There seems to be no substantial disagreement on this matter in political theory. This is not to deny that there are other democratic values as well but to say that self-government, the freedom of individual citizens to rule over themselves through a concerted collective process, is logically the most fundamental of the democratic values. The word *democracy*, after all, means rule by the people. In translating self-government into observable characteristics, the question becomes, What key instrumental dimensions are necessary to its realization?

The right to self-government, as Dahl reminds us, is neither a trivial nor merely a procedural right (Dahl 1989, ch. 12). It effectuates a substantive distribution of power and autonomy to both the individual citizen and the people as a collective. The very procedures of liberal representative democracy are therefore creating freedoms and distributing power equally, in the sense of "one man, one vote." Hence, I agree with Dahl that even the narrowest procedural definition of democracy entails integral substantive rights and freedoms. By implication of this argument, the distinction between procedural and substantive definitions of democracy collapses. Yet, an approach that sets out to measure the democratic qualities of elections must, at the minimum, specify how such democratic qualities are defined. Accordingly, let us turn to the specific justification for the focus on political participation, free competition, and procedural legitimacy.

Political Participation

In a democracy, the people should rule over itself, that is, the people are sovereign. This sovereignty must be distributed equally, because unequal distribution of sovereignty implies that some segments of the people are *not* sovereign. This idea of sovereignty-cum-equality is what Locke referred to when declaring that all men are, or ought to be, considered equal as political beings (Locke 1689–90/1970, 322).[12] Dahl calls the same thing the "idea of intrinsic equality" (1989, 85). Leaving aside the definition of "the people," it follows logically that rule by the people requires equality of political participation.[13] As Ake (2000) noted, it is the equal opportunity to be part of the decision-making process rather than the approval of each substantial decision by everyone, which satisfies the right to self-government.[14]

Equality of participation is, thus, a core dimension of democracy because it is a requisite of self-government as the expression of the sovereignty of the people.[15] For a political system to have the potential to be democratic, it must legally provide for political participation based on equal distribution of sovereignty, provide equal shares of legal political freedoms for all citizens. Equal legal opportunities for participation, in terms of suffrage, organization of political parties, and their right to participate as contestants in elections, are therefore criteria for inclusion of elections as units of study having the potential of realizing democratic qualities. In principle such participation involves the people as individual voters and the people as organized political groups, or parties. Participation in elections in transitional political systems such as the ones examined in this study includes the additional aspect of participation by known antagonists to elections and democratization, in the form of previous authoritarian rulers. Operationalizing exactly what equal opportunity of political participation entails with regard to elections is undertaken later in this chapter.

Competition within the System

As Sartori (1987, 30) reminds us, the etymological understanding of democracy discussed above leaves out the other side of the coin: rule of the people is exercised *over* the very same people. This is no easy equation; several formats for translation of rule by the people into a rule over the people have been envisaged. However, in order to be workable, any modern form of national democracy must be representative.[16] In modern democracy, which married liberal rights with republican obligations and responsible leadership, representation became grafted upon democracy (Hindess 2000). In this understanding of democracy, a particular kind of vertical accountability takes on paramount significance (Schedler 1999), making free competition a core issue and creating voter choice, without which it is impossible to hold representatives accountable. While it can be argued on theoretical grounds that the necessary political competition can be achieved in *de jure* one-party systems (Macpherson 1968, 37), this has not been the case in the real world. At minimum, for people to have a choice there must be at least two alternatives. While choice in a two-party system is limited, as long as the legal provisions do not prevent more parties from engaging and as long as other restrictions or practices, such as threats or intimidation, do not seriously undermine the process, there are *de facto* no constraints on the potential for choice. But, as a necessary condition, legal provisions must allow for political competition under a representative formula. While more competition is not always better, a low level of competition indicates that the potential for this democratic quality to contribute to the realization of self-government has not been fulfilled.[17]

In sum, to rule, the people must have procedures for making decisions that are mutually binding on all members of the polity. This requires some form of government, which in a complex modern democratic polity entails representation of the people. This representation cannot be limited by geographical, socioethnic, or other forms of functional representation in one-party systems. Individuals or groups aspiring to represent the people and assume the function of government—or legislature—must be subjected to competition. Thus, the fundamental value of self-government as individual and collective freedom translates not only into equality of political participation but also into free political competition allowing the people to exercise its sovereign discretion to rule.[18]

Again, since this study is not concerned with classification into democracies and nondemocracies, there is no need to establish cut-off points for exactly how much political participation and competition is needed. A rule of thumb is that more political participation is better and there should be at least two competitors. The legal existence of political competition under *de jure* multiparty politics provides an eligibility criterion for making a valid observation of an election with the potential for this democratic quality. Similarly, the legal provisions for equal political participation are a qualifying criterion for inclusion of an election in the analysis. Thus, the understanding of democracy envisaged in this study descends from Schumpeter's basic definition (1947, 269), which has been refined by scholars such as Riker (1986, 25) and Huntington (1991, 29). The most widely accepted extension of Schumpeter's definition is Dahl's (1971, 1–7) concept of "polyarchy." Most of the contemporary comparative work on democratization is conducted in reference to Dahl. Scholars like Bratton and van de Walle (1997), Diamond, Linz, and Lipset (1989), and Reilly (2001), for example, build on Dahl's definition. The meaning of democracy for the purposes of this book is understood along the same lines, as self-government requiring not only equality of political participation but also free political competition. What needs to be added is a third dimension concerned with legitimacy.

Legitimacy

Legitimacy has been debated for millennia, as in Plato's discussions on justice and Aristotle's distinction of monarchy, aristocracy, and democracy. Weber's (1958) frequently cited ideal-type construction of traditional, charismatic, and rational-legal legitimacy is concerned primarily with the causes of legitimacy, which is not our subject here. The same debate frames the discussion of Lipset's (1959) distinction between procedural legitimacy and legitimacy produced by government effectiveness, and their mutual relationship. For present purposes, legitimacy is analyzed as an attribute of self-government and not the reason for its existence. The very essence of democracy as rule of the people is that it is somehow exercised *by* the people. There are many other kinds of legitimacy, yet this understanding is peculiar to democracy, hence "democratic legitimacy."[19] When the people manifest their desire to rule themselves by established procedures, self-government is legitimate. If the people of a country do not support the idea of self-government, modern liberal democracy cannot thrive there, since there is little prospect of coercing a people to rule themselves. This means that, as an attribute of democracy, legitimacy is in the eyes of the beholders, dependent on the views of that country's people, political parties, and power elites rather than on the judgment of the observer. This kind of legitimacy may also be referred to as "real" as opposed to "formal" legitimacy. In adopting this view of legitimacy, I side with Linz (1988) and Diamond (e.g., 1990), even if my conceptual argument is slightly different from theirs.

The principally different notion of objective, or formal, legitimacy, such as Nagel's (1991, 35), is based on the judgment of the observer that the people have "no grounds for complaints." Hence, it is not the people's views but the supposedly distant observers' assessment of the country's political procedures and processes that is being evaluated. It is a most unsavory approach. Cast in Nagel's terms, the communist system in the Soviet Union was fully legitimate, because some Russian researchers and leaders would concur that the people had no grounds for complaint. This seems counterintuitive to the general understanding of legitimacy. More importantly, such an objectivist view is authoritarian and fails to recognize the sovereignty of the people, seriously undermining the notion of self-government, and can be used to justify morally unacceptable systems of rule.

One of the most prominent recent political thinkers launched the idea of contextual understanding of legitimacy; Beetham's (1991, 16) argument is about the use of power in general, not about legitimating a particular regime. Yet, his tripartite definition—the exercise of power is legitimate if it is in accordance with existing rules, if these rules can be justified by shared beliefs, and if there is evidenced consent to the arrangement—is arguably in every practical sense also subjective. The first requirement is one of lawfulness, which is beside the point here. When it comes to systems of rule, constitutions are made to reflect what the actors consider a legitimate regime; hence, they cannot be used to evaluate whether the same system is legitimate. The second part effectively depends on the third requirement, consent. If there is no consent, there must be a lack of shared beliefs about how power should be distributed and exercised. In essence, Beetham's definition depends primarily on the subjective evaluation of the people.

In sum, at the core of the democratic self-government system is the principle that the people participate in selecting representatives who govern and are held accountable for their actions through political competition. Yet, these two central democratic qualities are not enough, because their existence builds on a fundamental assumption of legitimacy. In order for the people to exercise rule over themselves, the people must consider the peaceful solving of conflicts and competing interests by self-government to be appropriate and desirable.

Three core instrumental dimensions have been identified as necessary for the realization of self-government: equality of political participation, free political competition, and legitimacy of the idea of self-government. The discussion has until now been kept abstract for a distinct purpose. This definition of self-government allows for wide sociocultural variation: elected officials may include chiefs, priests, or other "traditional" authorities; constituencies may be different ethnolinguistic groups; there may be women political representatives or women may be discriminated against; there may be special consensus rules of decision making or not; elections may be more or less frequent; the system may be unitary or federal, presidential or parliamentary, proportional or majoritarian; and so on.

As this book is not primarily about democracy but a study of elections, the frequency and trajectories of their democratic qualities in terms of political participation, competition, and legitimacy become central. By analyzing elections as the central institution of representative democracy, we can potentially learn much about the system as a whole. However, a claim that the level of democracy *writ large* has a strong and positive relationship to the quality of elections has to be substantiated by empirical analysis, the object of Chapter 6. The discussion below presents a definition of elections and the justification for an exclusive focus on elections as the unit of analysis in this study and then operationalizes the democratic qualities of elections. For the purposes of examination and possible replication, technical clarifications and specifications of the unit of analysis, data collection and processing, sample characteristics, and data documentation are discussed in some detail.

OPERATIONALIZING DEMOCRATIC QUALITIES OF ELECTIONS

What constitutes the unit of analysis in this study is relatively straightforward. Elections are concrete occurrences with institutional expressions, rules, and regulations. They are well documented, can be observed directly, and are tangible, in the form of indelible ink, ballot papers, boxes, election officials, voters, and so on. Existing forms of democracy are representative and use periodic elections as the mechanism for selecting the individuals and groups—political parties and their candidates—who will enjoy legislative and executive power for a limited period. Thus, a necessary component for any aspiring representative democratic system is the institutional guarantees for holding periodic and contested elections to the executive and legislative branches of government.

Following the argument in the first half of this chapter, the electoral institutions must by law guarantee equality of participation and free competition. If those democratic qualities are ensured, periodic elections should be regarded as legitimate by voters and political elites. "Periodic" implies that the elections are held at constitutionally designated intervals. For the purposes of this study, I regard an election as starting about six months before polling day, when campaign activities pick up—and illicit activities as well. Also, the election is not viewed as stopping with polling day or even the announcement of results, but only after either all parties and main candidates have accepted the results or disputes have been settled by appropriate agencies—typically the judiciary—and possible demonstrations and protests have subsided. Because in the present study the disputes and resolutions often took up to three months after the elections, the elections effectively lasted for about nine months in total.

In short, the unit of analysis in this study is *de jure* participatory, contested, and legitimate periodic elections.[20] The realization of the level of actual participation, contestation, and legitimacy of these elections are the dependent variables. Operationalizing participatory, contested, and legitimate elections, we find that each of the three dimensions in turn has three or more aspects. Each of these aspects has a separate indicator with a theoretical range from zero to full—the variations with which this book is primarily concerned.

Freedom and Fairness of Elections as a Variable

Another fundamental issue in new electoral regimes is the extent to which the election process is free and fair according to international standards, as documented by domestic and international observers. This variable creates an important distinction between whether processes are acceptable or not. It also conditions other variables; manipulation of election results through coercion or fraud invalidates indicators like voter turnout, the winner's share of votes and legislative seats, and alternation in power. The distinction between free and fair processes and flawed ones is therefore crucial from a methodological stance. One could argue that this variable should have been included as an indicator of competition, since it might seem counterintuitive that unfair elections can be competitive at all; but they can. There are, for example, a few instances in Africa in which genuinely unfair elections have effectuated an opposition win: the presidential and parliamentary elections in Ivory

Coast on 22 October and 10 December 2000, the executive elections in Madagascar on 16 December 2001, the parliamentary elections in Malawi on 15 June 1999, and the constituent assembly elections in Namibia on 11 November 1989 are cases when electoral irregularities affected the results but there was still an alternation in power. Even though the "menu of manipulation" is wide (Schedler 2002a), trying to cheat is one thing and doing it successfully is sometimes quite another, although serious irregularities do not usually coincide with turnovers. Yet, we should and will capitalize on the opportunity to keep such relationships open to empirical analysis, rather than constraining ourselves with theoretical assumptions. It is also quite possible that manipulated or outright fake elections can be a sign of high levels of competition; just because competition was not allowed to play out in the election results does not mean it was not there. In Zimbabwe, for example, there has been an inverse relationship between the level of real competition and the trustworthiness of official results. The more competitive the struggle for political power in Zimbabwe, the more unfair and violent the suppressive means applied by President Mugabe and his regime. In such cases we cannot take the election results as indicative of the level of competition that was present but must keep in mind that unfair elections might indicate high levels of actual competition in the political system.

We must also recognize that irregularities, manipulation, and fraud are not only sins of incumbents. Opposition parties in Africa are notorious for their tit-for-tat strategies, and on many occasions manipulations might cancel each other out, but there is no well-documented method for gauging such claims on a comparative basis in large-N analyses. While there is no such thing as a flawless election, human and technical errors being unavoidable, irregularities must not alter or determine the outcome. We are therefore well advised to treat the freedom and fairness of elections (a) as indicating whether the electoral process was acceptable or not; (b) as a control variable when measuring indicators such as turnout and share of votes and seats, since their values will be affected by whether elections were free and fair or not; and (c) as an aspect of the empirical puzzle of Africa's recent election history. Although it is a given that the freedom and fairness of elections is not completely independent of some of the other indicators, from turnout and opposition participation to peacefulness and losers' acceptance of results, the exact relationships remain empirical questions. For example, do opposition parties always contest free and fair elections or do they sometimes act undemocratically, crying foul to discredit the winner? Are breakdowns of regimes more likely after unfair elections?

The differentiation between free and fair elections and flawed ones is a necessary component of the analysis, having both substantial and methodological implications. Therefore, the freedom and fairness of elections is both analytically and methodologically necessary, in addition to the three main dimensions of this study. I delineate the freedom and fairness of an election in four ordinal categories: "No, not at all" when elections were wholly unfair and obviously a charade orchestrated by the incumbent regime; "No, irregularities affected outcome" when the elections had a legal and practical potential to be free and fair but there were numerous flaws and serious fraud that affected the result; "Yes, somewhat" when there were deficiencies either unintended or organized but they did not impact the outcome of the election; and "Yes, entirely" when elections were free and fair although there might have been human errors and logistical restrictions on operations. When distinguishing between flawed electoral processes and essentially acceptable ones in a binominal fashion, the first two categories are collapsed into "flawed" while the later two are grouped as "free and fair."

Quality 1: Political Participation

Political participation is a *sine qua non* of any kind of democracy. Rule by the people requires the people's participation, which is manifested in several ways in elections. First, in a representative system, popular political participation is exercised through voting. Equality of political participation in elections implies legal guarantees of universal suffrage, which may be limited by citizenship, age, or mental sanity. To be included in this analysis, an election must have taken place under regulated circumstances that in principle guarantee universal and equal suffrage. The percentage of an electorate that actually participated is used as an indicator of the realization of equal popular participation. Second, participatory elections imply that individuals and political parties have equal rights to exist and to field candidates. Empirically, the question is whether opposition parties and presidential candidates actually ran for office and thus realized their equality of participation. Finally, participation is also conditioned if known antidemocrats contest in the elections, either as individuals or as parties. Three indicators are used to assess these aspects.

1. *Voter turnout.* This classical indicator of popular participation is generally understood to be an important dimension of the quality of democracy (for a recent example, see Altman and Pérez-Liñán 2002). It has also been used as an indirect measure of popular legitimacy in many classical studies of established democracies (e.g., Lijphart 1999). Although context is likely to make a difference, a higher turnout is preferable from the vantage point of democratic quality as the realization of equal political participation. The people rule by selection of leaders through elections, hence, the larger the share of voters actually turning up for the polls the more pop-

ular power is actualized (there are no mandatory voting requirements in Africa). As a measure, the share of registered voters was used in preference to share of voting age population because in Africa population figures are often more inaccurate than voter registries. In a few cases, official turnout figures were radically inflated, for example Mauritania's executive election on 12 December 1997; in those cases observers' reported estimates were used as proxies.

2. *Opposition participation.* Participation by all political parties is only a given in established democracies. Whether opposition parties' participation is total or they effectuate a partial or total boycott, is used as indicator of the realization of political parties' equality of participation. It is assumed that—*ceteris paribus*—full participation of parties translates into higher democratic quality than if some or all parties boycott. Yet, we should not assume that this aspect of participation covariates perfectly with the other democratic qualities and the freedom and fairness of elections. On the one hand, opposition parties may participate even when elections stand no chance of being even remotely free and fair or legitimate. On the other hand, boycotts are occasionally staged in elections of relatively high democratic quality, with the aim of discrediting the ruling regime, when opposition parties stand no chance of winning. Such behavior nonetheless degrades democratic quality, and I take full opposition participation to indicate the presence of democratic quality in this aspect of equal participation. Opposition participation is measured here with three ordinal values: "Boycott" for total boycotts, "Partial boycott" for situations when one or more but not all of the main candidates (presidential elections) or parties (legislative elections) boycott the poll, and "Yes, all" for elections where all major political parties participate. The indicator records primarily the preelection period but also extends over election day itself.

3. *Autocratic guard gone?* In the context of new electoral regimes a third aspect is also central. The ostensible transformation of previously authoritarian rulers into democratic converts is a particularly interesting issue. One does not have to be a skeptic to wonder if the proverbial leopard could ever change its spots in a climate about which Baker (1998) noted that as of 1997 there were 20 former authoritarian rulers still in office under the guise of democracy. It seems reasonable to assume those who fought to prevent political liberalization will not willingly further it (Carothers 1998). This is also why students of democratization such as Diamond (1999, 60) include prodemocratic behavior among political actors as a requirement of consolidated democracies. From a pragmatic point of view, however, people generally fare better in terms of freedoms under benevolent rulers who, even if grudgingly and under pres-

sure, agree to some basic democratic rules. A dishonest but reformatory autocrat is likely to foster democracy more than an honest but staunchly repressive one.

This leads to an important theoretical issue to consider and evaluate through empirical analysis. Viewing the presence of former autocratic rulers as a threat to democracy builds on the premise that it is necessary for political leaders to believe in democratic values for them to introduce and further democracy, and thus the participation of nondemocrats is a negative feature. The second view, that authoritarian-minded rulers may further democracy through reform, implies that political actors do not necessarily always or even regularly act on value preferences but on the incentives offered by the institutions under which they operate. Using Dahl's (1971) language, leaders will enact a democratization process when the cost of repression is too high and if reform might help them maintain power. This becomes quite a puzzle for the empirical analysis if the participation of an authoritarian ruler and his associates is detrimental to the survival of the electoral regime and its democratic qualities, or if the electoral institutions, once in place, create incentives for prodemocratic behavior on the part of known antidemocrats.

Cases in this category are coded thus: "No" for elections where the presidential candidates or the leadership of one main party are previous authoritarian rulers, "Associates participated" when a candidate or the leadership of one main party are former close associates (ministers or similar) of the former authoritarian regime, and "Yes" when the main contenders do not have these close ties to a former authoritarian regime.

Quality 2: Competition

A decent level of electoral competition is central to the realization of self-government, which in a representative democracy builds on the accountability and responsiveness of elected representatives. To be included in the analysis, elections must have de jure allowed for formation and contestation of alternatives, the choice of rulers, and have provisions for alternations in power.[21] De facto electoral competition is likely to be low or nonexistent and alternations in power virtually absent in nondemocratic countries holding elections (Dahl 1989, Diamond 2002, Schedler 2002a, van de Walle 2002). To measure the variation in this dimension, four supplementary indicators are used: the winner's share of votes in presidential elections, the largest party's shares of seats in legislative elections, the second party's share, and the occurrence of alternations in power.

Several alternative indicators could have been used, and two in particular merit a brief comment. One of the most frequently used measures is Laakso and Taagepera's (1979) index of effective number of parties, a mathematical cousin to Rae's (1971) index of fractionalization. As shown by Pedersen (1980), Molinar (1991), and Bogaards (2004) and acknowledged by Taagepera (1999), the main problem with effective number of parties as an indicator of real levels of competition is that multiple distinct outcomes can be represented by the same number on the index and some of these can be very misleading. Bogaards's (2004, 185) example is Gabon, which had an effective number of parties at exactly 2.0 in the 1996 and 2001 legislative elections. This supposedly indicates a two-party system with a decent measure of competition, but the reality is that the ruling party won 70 and 71 percent of the seats, respectively, in these two elections. Taagepera (1999) gives examples of situations when the effective number of parties was three yet largest party acquired an absolute majority; at the same time, other party systems are more fractionalized but still score only 3.0. The reason for these misleading results is that the index combines two dimensions (size and number) that can vary independently, just as 16 can be the product of 4×4 as well as 2×8 and 1×16. The problem with the other main rival measure, the ratio of votes or seats won by the first and second candidate or largest and second largest party, is similar to the problem with the effective number of parties. The two quantities making the ratio can also vary independently, and there is a world of difference in competitiveness between an outcome in which the largest party gets 70 percent of the seats and the second party gets 30 percent and one where the largest party scrapes together 35 percent of the seats and the second party gets 15, although the ratio is the same. The 70:30 situation reminds one of Gabon and also South Africa, where the ruling party can do as they wish with no regard to the opposition, including changing the constitution. The second case is like the situation in Kenya, where competition is fierce. Hoping to avoid misleading results, I have chosen to base my analyses on uncombined, raw data on the main contestants' vote and seat shares, keeping these dimensions separate.

4. *Winner's share of the votes.* This variable measures the level of competition in executive elections. In a slight departure from Bratton and van de Walle's (1997) and Bratton's (1998) measure, I take figures from the first round of elections rather than the runoffs. The modification is motivated by a concern with validity. Many presidential elections in Africa demand an absolute majority and provide for two-round electoral systems. Since the runoff election is between the two most successful candidates from the first round, winning shares in the runoff tend to be inflated, while the figures from the first round are more representative of the actual level of competition. This choice also makes the figures comparable to executive elections in

countries such as Kenya which require only a simple majority. One could perhaps question if the closeness of the outcome is a valid measure of the level of competition of the electoral campaign, since the closeness of the outcome has been found in the established democracies to be mediated by the choice of electoral system. This objection does not apply to presidential races in Africa, and there are only five parliamentary systems[22] among the 48 states in sub-Saharan Africa. The closeness of the outcome is one of the most widely used indicators of the level of competition. The indicator measures the winning candidate's share of votes (first round) as a percentage of total valid votes.

5. *Largest party's share of seats.* This indicator measures the largest party's share of total seats in parliament. The share of votes has not been used for two reasons. First, the figures for share of votes are missing for more African elections than those for share of seats and even when available are likely to be less reliable, because of problems with voters' registries and counting and collation procedures, including irregularities. Second, the makeup of parliament is particularly important as an indicator of competition. A two-thirds majority in parliament typically gives the ruling party free rein to introduce changes in the constitution unilaterally. In such a situation, no bipartisan agreement on the rules of the game is needed, and incumbents in Africa have shown a tendency to exploit this advantage. Although the well-known phenomenon of dominant-party democratic systems exists in Africa (e.g., Botswana, South Africa), in general a low level of competition is taken as a sign of low democratic quality. As mentioned above, electoral systems are designed to mediate the proportionality between votes and seats. The most important effect of this is that proportional representation systems tend to produce multiparty as opposed to two-party systems and to decrease the winner's relative share of votes and seats. This effect is most prominent in proportional representation systems with medium to large multimember constituencies (MMCs) (see Bogdanor and Butler 1983; Downs 1957; Duverger 1954; Lijphart 1984, 1994, 1999; Lindberg 2005; Mair 1990; Powell 1982, 2000; Rae 1971; Sartori 1968, 1986, 1997; among others). Nevertheless, in all but one of the countries in Africa that use proportional representation systems with medium to large MMCs or pure proportional representation, historical cleavages predispose the electorate to support two main parties, nullifying the presumed effect.[23] Hence, the distortion of results by electoral systems should be insignificant. On the other hand, the disproportionality of the two-round absolute majority and plurality electoral systems can be expected to produce inflated legislative majorities, displaying lower than real levels of competition. There is therefore good reason to expect the share of seats indicator to underestimate rather than overestimate the level of competition. At the

same time, it provides information on the de facto competitiveness in African parliaments and offers the advantage of facilitating further discussions on legislative majorities and minorities.

6. *Second party's share of seats.* This additional indicator of competition in legislative elections measures the second party's share of total seats in parliament. Measuring the relative seat share of the winning party only has been criticized for not showing the strength or, perhaps more so, the weakness of the opposition in cases where the opposition is split among several parties. This indicator enlarges our picture of an election's competitiveness.

7. *Turnover of power.* This is perhaps the ultimate indicator of competition. If a de jure competitive electoral regime is truly competitive, it is likely at some point to result in alternations in power. Alternations in power are not a necessary condition for democracy or democratic qualities. Elections can be truly competitive without turnovers, and in some cases one party can rule for many electoral cycles. Yet, when a peaceful turnover of power occurs, we have unambiguous evidence that the election results have been accepted by the losing incumbent. As the empirical realities in Africa attest, alternations in power (whether executive or legislative) may occur even as a result of fraudulent elections. Electoral manipulation is not always sufficient to alter the outcome, and an alternation in power, manifesting institutionalized uncertainty[24] (Przeworski 1986, 57–61), remains an important indicator of the democratic quality of elections.

The use of turnovers as an indicator of competitiveness has been criticized, however. In Huntington's classical formulation, the "two-turnover test" has been used to infer consolidation of democracy after the first and founding election. Both for that purpose and to indicate competition as a democratic quality, whether the criterion is a single turnover or two, it is problematic if used without other indicators, because it is not sensitive to differences in electoral or party systems (Günther, Diamandouros, and Puhle 1995, 13; Schedler 2001a). Here it is used in combination with other indicators of competitiveness and this problematic aspect is therefore less significant. When alternations occur in a peaceful manner, it remains a sign of the realization of distributive authority of the people inherent in the expression "rule by the people." Elections are coded "No" if there was no turnover; "Half" if in executive elections there was an alternation in president and the new officeholder was an immediate successor to the former president or of the same party, or, in legislative elections, if there was a partly new coalition forming a majority in parliament; and "Yes" if there was a new president from a different party or there was a new party or coalition of new parties with a legislative majority.

Quality 3: Legitimacy

Legitimacy is perhaps the most obvious cut-off point between elections in democracies, nondemocracies, and hybrid regimes. Elections are not legitimate just because certain procedures have been used fairly but when the actors involved consent and testify to its legitimacy. Although legitimacy is often framed in terms of attitudes and sentiments, behavior is arguably the best indicator. If incumbents *say* they support democratic elections and will respect the rules of the game, that is great, but the real test comes when they lose an election. If they immediately accept the outcome, concede defeat, and honor a peaceful alternation in power, it testifies to the legitimacy of the election in their view. Similarly, opposition parties may appear democratic enough by their statements and programs, but if they refuse to accept the outcome of a free and fair election, the legitimacy of that election, regardless of its other qualities, is still inadequately established. If some elites resort to violent actions in response to the election results, legitimacy for them has no bearing. In the best of worlds, we would measure legitimacy in the view of both political elites and the electorate, but this has not been possible. We can measure elites' behavior, but we lack reliable indicators of voters' acceptance of the electoral process and its results, since that would require a kind of voter survey or behavioral data that does not exist in Africa—yet.[25] This is not a devastating drawback; there are good reasons to assume that political leaders and parties dispute election results to a higher degree than their voters or society in general. After all, their entire political life and status often is on the line. Therefore it is not unreasonable to use parties and their candidates as representatives of their voters and the collective of contesting parties as proxies for society in general, and the level of legitimacy as measured by elites' behavior should be a conservative measure that, if introducing any bias, would not overestimate the amount of legitimacy. Therefore, in this study, behavioral testimonies of elites' degree of acceptance of elections as the legitimate method of self-government is measured by three indicators: acceptance of the outcome, the frequency of alternations in power, and regime survival.

8. *Losers' acceptance of results.* Whether the losers accept the results indicates the extent to which political elites view elections as legitimate. In "normal" free and fair elections, we expect democratic-minded elites to accept defeat graciously—even if grudgingly—and to assume the position of a constructive opposition. Yet, in new electoral regimes losing parties may initially challenge the results, based on unsubstantiated rumors of irregularities, if many inexperienced and less-educated actors

are on the scene. Such a challenge may also be a tactic to gain political advantage, for example from the international community. Challenging accurate results can be a strategy used by "bad losers" seeking to undermine the political rule of their rivals, a posturing more likely to appear in transitional political systems when things are still in flux. Therefore, a challenge to the official results cannot be taken at face value as substantiating allegations of irregularities.

Opposition parties and presidential candidates may also accept defeat and the results of less than free and fair elections. This is more likely when opposition parties acknowledge that they would probably have lost even if the elections had been fully free and fair and when the incumbent engaged in "unnecessary" fraud. But it is also a possible strategy of opposition parties with a long-term perspective and expectations that are more moderate. If an electoral process is generally accepted as a substantial improvement on the past and there is a perceived prospect of future advancements, opposition parties may well accept defeat in the interest of peace and stability and in anticipation of a better chance at winning the next time around. Hence, the relationship between the freedom and fairness of elections and the losing parties' acceptance of defeat remains an empirically open question. Nevertheless, losers' peaceful acceptance is a critical test of the system's legitimacy. It is only when an election is free and fair and also the losers accept the results that we can speak of manifestly legitimate elections.

Losers' acceptance is measured using three ordinal values: "No, none" when none of the main losing parties accepted the outcome; "Some, or later" when either some or all losing parties rejected the results at first, as evidenced by public statements or file petitions, but within three months accepted them, or if some losing parties did not accept the results but others did; and "Yes, all immediately" when all losing parties conceded defeat immediately after the results were pronounced.

9. *Peaceful.* The second revealer of electoral legitimacy is the absence of politically related violence during the campaign and on election day. Relative peacefulness during the campaign and polling measures the legitimacy of an electoral contest as a means of allocating political power. Use of violence is a core symptom of failed institutionalization (Elster et al. 1998, 27; Schedler 2001a, 70–71). Assassination of political opponents, voter intimidation, attacks against the liberty and property of political adversaries, violence against elected officials or electoral administrators, riots, and ethnic or other forms of "social" cleansing are examples of serious politically motivated violence that prove that major actors do not see the elections as legitimate means of selection for the highest political offices. The three ordinal values used to described the subject elections' peacefulness are "No, not at all" when there was systematic and/or widespread politically related violence during the campaign,

on election day, or during the postelection period; "Isolated incidents" when there were nonsystematic and isolated incidents of violence or geographically limited outbreaks that, while disturbing and indicating insufficient levels of legitimacy, do not discredit the process entirely; and "Yes" for cases of entirely, or almost entirely peaceful elections. The last designation means that none of my reporting sources testified to instances of serious politically motivated violence during the election campaign period ahead of polling day, during voting, or in the immediate aftermath.

10. *Electoral regime survival.* A necessary element in an assessment of democratic quality is that electoral cycles continue. Coups, civil wars, or any reversion into autocratic rule following an election are evidence that the cycle of elections has broken down[26] and that key elite groups did not consider the election legitimate.

DATA COLLECTION AND PROCESSING

Information on the ten indicators of these three democratic qualities and of the freedom and fairness of elections was sought from many sources and used to code each of the 232 cases in the data set, the philosophy being the more sources, the better. The main concern has been reliability, to which there are two principal threats: biases in the sources consulted and subjectivity in the coder's scoring. Regarding the "noise" and contamination induced by sources, it is not always easy to determine, for example, if political violence was widespread or just isolated. When information is incomplete or the events surrounding election day were dramatic or chaotic, it can be a time-consuming task just verifying a simple thing like whether or not all opposition parties participated. In such cases, standard academic sources are more likely to lack definitive information. Reports from news agencies, like the BBC, IRIN News, and local newspapers accessed via AllAfrica.com, have been helpful in supplementing information and in filling in informational gaps. It is always best to have several independent sources to rely on; if they all agree, it is likelier the information is correct. If one or more sources disagree, the researcher will have to try to judge which is most reliable. This is a process similar to interrogation of one's interview or historical data in qualitative work: One questions the general character and reliability of the source, its reputation, and known liabilities, if any. Here, academic sources and independent institutes (such as IPU, IFES, and the Carter Foundation) are of higher value than information from diplomatic sources or multilateral organizations of which the country is itself a member. In addition, one looks for possible biases from interest in the specific case, and these are often found when neighboring countries send election observation missions.

Finally, the independence of each source must be evaluated. Naturally, even if ten "sources" report a particular piece of information but they all obtained it from a single source—such as the corrupt minister of justice, or the bitter and power-seeking opposition leader—we have in reality only one source. Researchers try to establish what the most probable and reasonable interpretation is, and in some instances it becomes necessary to seek more sources to make that judgment. In other cases—though very few in the present data set—one must give up and code the value as missing. For less than 5 percent of the 5,568 values entered in the data set of the 232 cases there have been only one or two sources. The majority of scores have been corroborated by at least five sources; a certain kind of reliability test was included already at the stage of data collection.

Using multiple sources and cross-checking information minimizes the net effect of filtering and contamination by bias in sources.[27] In order to counteract possible nonsystematic or systematic errors from coder's scoring, all data was collated in 48 country files. In addition to general political history, each country file contains a section on each election, with a coding scheme and extracts from all sources used and full references to each source for each piece of information. The country files run 6–20 pages in length and contain in all more than 500 pages of compressed country-specific information on elections and related events.

The procedure was to compile all the data in these country files and then code all the elections within a relatively short period of time.[28] The data was collected over the three-year period 2000–2002. While I took some data on 82 early cases from Bratton and van de Walle (1996) and Bratton (1998), I double-checked each coding in both the original and additional sources to ensure accuracy and consistency. That data set also had a larger number of missing values. For each of the 232 elections in the complete data set, information has been collected on the eleven indicators of democratic qualities and on additional background variables such as electoral system and share of women in the legislature, making the 5,568 observations. The author did all data collection and coding, which has advantages and disadvantages. The main advantage is that a single coder will be more likely to apply the scoring criteria consistently than will multiple coders. On the other hand, a double-blind coding procedure would allow cross-checking for reliability of scores and for inconsistencies in the scoring. No such intercoder reliability tests have been performed, for want of funds. The data set itself, the file information document, including a coder's translation, and the 48 background data files are freely available upon request from the author until the materials become available from Inter-University Consortium for Political Research, preparations for which are under way.

The data set contains 232 elections, of which 97 are presidential and 135 are parliamentary. Each of these two kinds of polls has been given the status of a case, even if polling took place on the same day. This was done for several reasons, one of which is to avoid introduction of bias into the data set, because those countries that hold executive and legislative elections on separate occasions would otherwise acquire double weight in the sample. A minority of countries' experiences would then bias the sample, unless they were perfectly representative, and conclusions might therefore be misleading. It is also the case that values sometimes differ on, for example, voter turnout and turnover of power, even if the two elections are held on the same day, and if collapsed, the data on general elections would distort the detailed data. Furthermore, presidential elections often involve a second round of voting at a later date, which might also cause the values of the different variables to fluctuate. The separate coding of presidential and parliamentary elections does not mean that two elections on the same day are coded as first and second elections; rather, sequential numbers are assigned to polls within each category, presidential and legislative.

Most of the indicators in the data set are ordinal or interval measures, and there are few missing values. (See Tables 3A and 3B.) The highest number of missing values represents 3.88 percent of the total sample. These few missing values are randomly distributed and induce no bias in the sample.

The indicators differ in the amount of information required to reliably code them. The percentage of votes won by the first and second candidate in a presidential race, for example, is a relatively "thin" and uncomplicated indicator. For sure, there can be disagreements between sources, falsified results, and contradicting claims of who actually won. Such disagreements between sources were relatively uncommon. There is very little interpretation and quantification involved from the researcher at the coding stage on such indicators. Other indicators are more complex in nature and require much more interpretative skill at the coding stage. Using specified and unambiguous coding criteria for each of the values in the indicators, the vast majority of cases were coded rather straightforwardly. Even so, a certain amount of interpretation is involved in judging, for example, if political violence — by far the most difficult indicator to code — was systematic and widespread or merely isolated when more than a few instances. Although politically motivated violence during the campaign, polling, or postelection process is typically something both academic sources, observation missions, and news reports cover, it is sometimes difficult to establish the extent and nature of its occurrences. When violence was reported, I have considered it nonsystematic unless proven otherwise. That should prevent overemphasizing the extent of violence. At the same time, the use of a middle category ("Isolated incidents") prevents creating too rosy a picture of the peacefulness of these elections.

Special mention needs to be drawn to how elections were coded as free and fair or not. While the initial coding was done using the four gradations described above,

TABLE 3A *Distribution on ratio indicators*

Indicator	Mean	Std. Dev.	Min.	Max.	N	Missing Values
Voter turnout %	63.5	17.65	20.0	97.0	223	9
Winning candidate's % of votes	60.4	19.30	21.0	99.0	95	2
Largest party's % of seats	67.0	20.62	17.0	99.0	131	4
2nd party's % of seats	17.7	12.44	1.0	47.0	130	5

TABLE 3B *Distribution on interval indicators*

Indicator	Value Label		Value	N	%
Free and fair?	No, not at all		0	13	5.6
	No, irregularities affected outcome		1	90	38.8
	Yes, somewhat		2	121	52.2
	Yes, entirely		3	8	3.4
Opposition participate?	Boycott		0	8	3.4
	Partial boycott		1	61	26.3
	Yes		2	163	70.3
Autocrats gone?	No		0	150	64.7
	Associates participated		1	51	22.0
	Yes		2	31	13.4
Turnover of power?	No		0	166	71.6
	Partial		1	23	9.9
	Yes		2	43	18.5
Losers accept outcome?	No, none		0	80	34.5
	Some, or later		1	76	32.8
	Yes, all immediately		2	74	31.9
		Missing		2	.9
Peaceful?	No		0	37	15.9
	Isolated incidents		1	141	60.8
	Yes		2	52	22.4
		Missing		2	.9
Regime survive?	No		0	36	15.5
	Yes		1	196	84.5

Note: Total N = 232.

in much of the following analysis the significant distinction is taken to be between elections considered acceptably free and fair or not according to the operationalization above. The most important documentation for such judgments has been mission statements and reports from international and domestic (if present) election observation teams. The main methodological problem with assessing these documents was the fluidity of the standards over time. What criteria observers have used and what irregularities count as more serious than others affect the findings of these teams (see, e.g., Elklit and Svensson 1997, Lehoucq 2003, Schedler 2002a). Some control for such inconsistencies has been provided in the use of other sources, such as *Election Watch, Keesing's Record of World Events,* and assessments of other academics who specialize in a particular country or region. In some countries, local think tanks and institutes provide additional information. Another problem was presented by the more politicized observation missions, such as those from the Organization of African Unity, then the African Union. These reports are often less reliable than others. Finally, independent observation missions did not monitor elections before 1990, and information has been derived from the alternative sources mentioned above. A complete listing of all sources consulted for the data and coding can be found in Appendix 1. All processing was done in SPSS 11.0.2 for Macintosh using standard techniques. In the calculation of means, the geometric mean was used instead of the arithmetic mean, the reason being that the geometric mean is not as sensitive to outliers and skewedness as its arithmetic cousin is (Blume 1974, Datton, Greenies, and Stewart 1998).

Transparency of data gathering, processing, and analysis makes inspection, and in the best of worlds replication, possible. Systematic data collection and analysis make evaluation of theories possible. Evaluation criteria will always be an issue to debate, but the fullest possible transparency in getting our results at least makes such discussions possible. In this spirit, as much of the empirical raw data and principles of interpretation as possible are included in this book, and what could not be included is available from the author upon request.

When it comes to making sense of collected data, interpretation is of the essence, regardless of the kind of data and the techniques used for processing. Voter turnout, for example, consists of relatively undisputable figures expressed as decimals or percentages with high reliability in most cases. It seems to have a high validity when used to measure the restricted sense of citizen participation in elections. However, the interpretation of turnout figures is another matter. First, which measure should be used, percentage of votes as share of registered voters, or eligible voting age population? Second, what is a "good" level of participation and what level should be called "low" or "unacceptable" participation? The data, no matter how solid or objective, never speak or tell us the story outright. Taking a bird's-eye view of politics necessarily limits the amount of information on each country one can digest and analyze. Country case studies have many important functions to fulfill in our quest to understand African politics better, but the proper testing of hypotheses and theories is not one of them.[29] With the present study, some predominant hypotheses in the literature on comparative democratization and African politics can be addressed.

One problem faced by all who have explored politics in Africa has been the lack of data. Yet, there is still a need to understand what can be generalized about African politics. This is not the place to dwell on the fortunes of qualitative case methodology and findings, but we need to know more about the complexities of individual nations in Africa and for this we need large-N analysis too. Systematic comparison across a larger number of cases may for now be the only possible way to show that some ideas are wrong. While some hypotheses that emanate from case studies or small-N comparisons are generalizable, others are not. No large-N study can do everything, of course, and the more complex the theories and concepts we try to test, often the less valid our quantitative indicators become. So, while we often wish to have a go at the big puzzles—like a finite answer to what creates a sustainable democracy—that seems neither practical nor possible. The strategy here has been to look at a very specific partial regime but to compare it across many countries. In short, this study seeks to solve a little piece in the big puzzle, but in the process it addresses theoretical puzzles and empirical hypotheses that are of a general concern to the comparative politics of elections and democratization.

To reiterate, democracy understood as self-government requires three qualities: equality of political participation, free political competition, and legitimacy of the idea of self-government. *De jure* participatory, competitive, and legitimate elections constitute the criteria for inclusion as a case in this study. The extents to which these three qualities are realized in practice are the three dependent variables measured by ten separate indicators of the electoral process in addition to judgments of the freedom and fairness of the elections. These indicators are assessed for the preelection campaign period through the postelection situation, where often the question is one of legitimacy. There is hardly any way to coerce people to rule in any meaningful way, and the voluntary principal-agent relationship between the people and its representatives cannot be established, or upheld, unless both parties in the relationship conceive of it as legitimate. In electoral terms, legitimacy means that the procedure for representation and sanctioning is conceived of as just, fair, and a good procedure in principle. That is exactly why observers worry when they see low political participation and disengagement from political competition in the established democracies. It is feared that such behavior signals a reduction in the belief in and support for democracy. In new democracies, and democracies-to-be, there are usually more radical expressions of disbelief in the idea of self-government, such as refusal to stand for elections, organized political violence, and violent overthrows of governments.

The ensuing empirical chapters use these indicators to probe some established hypotheses in the field. Chapter 3 disputes the purported decline in frequency and democratic qualities of elections in Africa. Chapter 4 details and analyzes developments over first, second, and subsequent elections, addressing the issue of socialization, or experience-based learning processes, resulting from institutionalization of electoral practices. The analysis strongly evidences a self-reinforcing power of repetitive *de jure* participatory, competitive, and legitimate elections and their tendency to improve in democratic qualities. Finally, Chapters 5 and 6 provide a theoretical framework of causal links and empirical evidence demonstrating that the mere repetition of *de jure* participatory, competitive, and legitimate elections—*regardless* of their qualities—contributes to democratization by leading towards higher levels of civil liberties in the society.

CHAPTER THREE

Elections in Africa over Time

Political liberalization in Africa has been interpreted in many ways since the world entered the post–Cold War era. Most scholarly accounts from the early 1990s triumphantly proclaimed a new era of democracy in Africa. Given the many significant changes that followed almost 30 years of gloom and stagnation, a certain euphoria was understandable. Except for Botswana, Gambia, Mauritius, and Zimbabwe, and to some extent Senegal, nondemocratic civilian or military regimes had ruled countries in Africa for much of the period since the 1960s. Economic failure, illustrated by always-low GDPs per capita, slumped further during the 1980s (van de Walle 2001). Corruption and embezzlement became rife, and in response societies disengaged from the state and the public realm and deepened their informal and personal ties, reviving social networks and extended family systems (e.g., Chabal and Daloz 1999), leaving rentier African states suspended in mid-air (Hyden 1980, 2000; Young, 1982). Ethnic fragmentation fanned by identity politics entrepreneurs ensued (Mamdani 1996), contributing to the implosion of states, including Rwanda, Liberia, Sierra Leone, and later Somalia, the Democratic Republic of Congo (DRC), and to a lesser extent Comoros and the Republic of Congo (RoC). Over a couple of years, political liberalization was introduced in more than half of the African states, and the rapid displacement of authoritarian regimes, like those in Benin and Zambia, as early as 1991 was heralded as a "second liberation" and a complete political renewal (e.g., Ayittey 1992, Hyden and Bratton 1992, Joseph 1992, cf. Bratton and van de Walle 1997). Within a few years half of the continent had held multiparty elections, giving credence to Huntington's assertion (1991, 174) that "elections are not only the life of democracy, they are also the death of dictatorship." This was the age of widespread Afro-optimism.

Several developments soon turned the tide. Dispute over elections in regionally important countries, like those in Kenya and Ghana in 1992, halted processes in Togo and Cameroon, and events in Nigeria caused concern. The failure even to initiate political transformation in Chad and the DRC, for example, fed these growing concerns. Zambia's second election, on 18 November 1996, was a disappointing contrast to its "best-in-class" first election, in 1991; while outright breakdowns of the democratization process in several countries, including Nigeria in 1993, Angola in 1992, and Gambia in 1994, served only to deepen this pervasive feeling that Africa was once again backtracking. Gambia's 1994 military coup was a special case in point. A relatively stable and prosperous democracy since 1982, the military overthrow of the government by General Jammah in 1994 was a particularly unexpected and devastating blow.[1] While scholars like Bratton (1998) argued that Africa had returned to neopatrimonial politics, others saw a continuation of disorder and destructive politics (Chabal and Daloz 1999), no change at all (Akinrinade 1998), political closure (Joseph 1998), semiauthoritarianism (Carothers 1997), or elections without democracy (van de Walle 2002).

Several students of comparative African politics sought to moderate the debate "between the extremes" (Chege 1996) and provide descriptions of the mixture of events taking African states in several directions simultaneously (Mbembe 1995). Cowen and Laakso's examination of 17 country case studies is a recent addition in this vein (Cowen and Laakso 2002). The single most influential comparative contribution, Bratton and van de Walle's 1997 study, was also an effort to provide an account of the multifaceted political developments in Africa while at the same time offering empirical generalizations. Their conclusion that African regimes had entered highly divergent paths of political development (1997, 98) still dominates the study of African politics.[2] I have investigated the robustness of their claims in a few preliminary analyses (Lindberg 2002, 2004a), and we must revisit them, because much of what is believed about contemporary African politics still relies on Bratton and van de Walle's analysis of events in a 5-year period, from 1990 to 1994. Using a 13-year time frame, from 1990 to 2003, and reflecting on events up to 1989 in selected countries, more robust conclusions can be drawn.

This chapter sifts through several hypotheses and lays a foundation for a more refined analysis in the later chapters. First, this chapter extends Bratton and colleagues' empirical research chronicling African elections and their democratic qualities.[3] The study of Africa is still suffering from a severe lack of empirical data and a lot still remains to be done to improve data gathering on African politics and its basic institutions. It is hoped that this book will be a step forward in that regard. Second, this chapter corrects some of the empirical generalizations from Bratton and van de

Walle's 1997 study that have become orthodoxy in the field. Generally speaking, their story was one of change, whereas this chapter speaks of continuity. My research indicates that discrepancies with their findings resulted from failure to control for freedom and fairness of elections, distorting results. Also, I obtained new and better data by studying a longer period. Third, while the analysis in this chapter uses chronological time as a referent, in much the same way as most other accounts do, in the end the usefulness of time as a scale is questioned. In the next chapter, the same qualities of elections are examined by referring to the number and progression of elections. The reader should note that unless specific sources are given for the empirical illustrations from various countries in this and later chapters, the data comes from the country files collated in this project.[4]

FREQUENCY AND NUMBER OF ELECTIONS

The first step in this empirical analysis of elections in Africa is to look at the distribution of cases over time. The data available to Bratton (1997, 72), Bratton and Posner (1999, 377) and Bratton and van de Walle (1997, 5) suggested that the number of African elections peaked in 1993 and then started to decline, and this finding has continued to influence the literature. Figure 1 shows disaggregated data for number of elections held and number of countries holding elections from 1990 through 2002. Over the 13-year period, the data refute the generalization of a decline in the frequency of elections.

As a general rule, on a continent where there have long been too few elections, more elections is better. However, too many elections in the same country can be a sign of instability and fragility of a nascent electoral regime. New elections can be brought on by unstable parliamentary coalitions, floor crossing, legislative-executive deadlocks, or presidential or parliamentary power plays. If unsuccessful, they can result in coups, followed by new first elections. All the same, constitutional but premature elections (early elections required by the dissolution of the legislature by the executive) are relatively scarce in Africa. Only a few governments have opted for this, among them Comoros in 1993, Republic of Congo in 1993, and Niger in 1995; and these premature elections were indeed signifiers of instability, for each of them was soon followed by a military takeover.

As Figure 1 shows, there is no continuing decline in the frequency of elections in Africa.[5] There are fluctuations but not a significant trend even if the regression lines suggest a slight increase in the number of annual electoral events. The decline posited by Bratton and colleagues was produced by the limited time frame of the data available to the authors at that time. The graph shows low electoral activity in

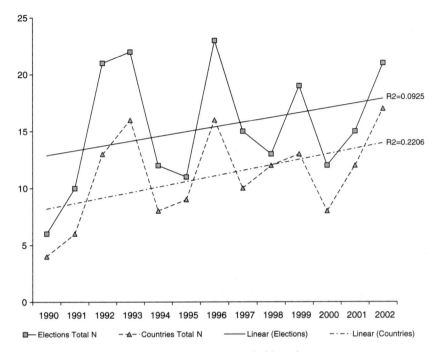

Fig. 1. Number of elections and number of countries holding elections, 1990–2002

1994 and 1995, the two last years of Bratton and van de Walle's (1997) study; but thereafter the frequency picks up again and a pattern seems to develop of one peak year followed by two years of low activity, then another peak year and so on. Many transitional elections in Africa occurred over a few years in the early 1990s, crowding elections together and creating these waves. Since African countries operate with different electoral cycles, this pattern is likely to change over time.

A similar observation can be made regarding the annual number of countries holding elections during this period, which we also would expect, given a normal distribution of elections over countries. Thus, the second curve not only strengthens the observation based on elections but also serves as an illustration of the relatively normal and equal distribution in the sample. The important thing to note here is that there is no overall decline in the number of elections or in the number of countries holding these elections. Rather than a decline, we see a slight increase over this period, commending a measured optimism, rather than pessimism, about the future of Africa.

Skeptics rightly argue that quantity is not the same as quality and one key characteristic of elections is freedom and fairness as discussed in Chapter 2. Figure 2

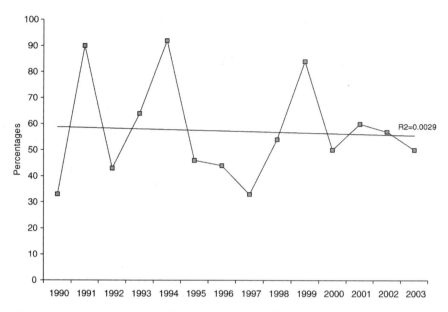

Fig. 2. Percentage of elections in Africa that were free and fair, 1990–2003

shows that the share of elections considered free and fair is also relatively constant after the annual fluctuations are collated.

As we can see, two dominant hypotheses about African politics—that there has been a general decline in the frequency of elections and a decline in their quality—have been refuted using exactly the same indicators and comparative method that produced the hypotheses. There are no indications of a general return to the neopatrimonial, politically closed pre-1990 politics in Africa.

THE DEMOCRATIC QUALITIES, ON AVERAGE

Although the frequency with which elections were held in Africa and the number of countries involved did not decrease, as was formerly believed, the issue of the three democratic qualities of the 232 elections that took place remains. Many researchers have stated that both participation and competition of elections in Africa is relatively poor and getting worse (e.g., Bratton 1997, 1998; Bratton and Posner 1999; Bratton and van de Walle 1997, 203 ff.), but their analyses do not include control for freedom and fairness of elections. This theoretically implies that whether elections are flawed or not has no significant effects on the other indicators. This implication is easy to test, and the results, based on the universe of cases in the present data set, are presented in Table 4. On average, more than half—129 out of 232—of the elections in Africa have been judged free and fair. That percentage agrees with earlier reports (e.g., Bratton 1997, 74), and it seems to me that if we are to take freedom and fairness seriously, this figure alone presents a difficult case for Afro-pessimists to argue against. At the very least, it represents a huge advance in democratic quality in comparison to the closed political climate prior to 1990. The second overall conclusion illustrated in Table 4 is that the difference between free and fair as compared with flawed elections is significant on all indicators except one (electoral regime survival). This important observation departs from much of the earlier findings on African elections, wherein the failure to control for freedom and fairness distorted the results.

Looking at the other indicators, the overall level of participation in these African elections is relatively impressive. Given the extremely low levels of education, high levels of poverty, poor infrastructure, and other mitigating factors, it is encouraging that on average 63 percent of voters cast their ballot in free and fair polls. Voters in Africa also seem to recognize a fake election, as evidenced by the noticeably lower turnout in elections judged to be flawed. Given, in addition to the deterring factors mentioned above, the high levels of violence and limited prospects for the opposition to win in many African countries, it is equally encouraging that opposition parties participated in over 90 percent of the fair elections. (These figures represent only those cases when *all* major opposition groups participated. Partial boycotts are treated as boycotts, in order to underestimate rather than overestimate the signs of positive developments.)

TABLE 4 *Democratic qualities of elections in Africa*

Dimension	Indicators	Free and Fair			Flawed			Significance	
		%	St. Dev.	N	%	St. Dev.	N	Value*	p
Participation	Voter turnout**	63	(17.8)	128	57	(16.7)	95	7.209	.008
	Opposition participation	92		119	43		44	.536	.000
	Autocrats gone	16		21	10		10	.230	.000
Competition	Winning candidate's								
	% of votes**	53	(17.3)	50	62	(20.2)	45	6.663	.011
	Largest party's % of seats**	60	(19.9)	79	61	(20.1)	52	6.963	.009
	2nd party's % of seats**	16	(11.8)	78	10	(13.0)	52	4.596	.034
	Turnover of power	30		38	5		5	.406	.000
Legitimacy	Losers accept outcome	57		73	1		1	.646	.000
	Peaceful process	33		43	9		9	.321	.000
	Regime survival	83		107	86		89	.048	.471
Total N				129			103		

*Spearman's Correlation, except for means where ANOVA F-values are used.
**These percentages are means. The other percentage figures refer to share of elections.

Some students of African politics (e.g., van de Walle 2002) and democratization (e.g., Schedler 2002b) have raised the specter of unfair boycotts, the dubious strategy in which parties that stand no chance of winning boycott fair elections in order to cast doubt on the legitimacy of the winner. This tactic has been used in Africa sometimes over the past 13 years, but not often. Partial boycotts of fair elections have occurred in nine instances, but a total boycott happened only once: Ghana's first parliamentary election on 29 December 1992. After the contested executive election on 3 November that year, the opposition parties decided to boycott the legislative elections. The incumbent Jerry J. Rawlings's ruling party, the NDC, and its close associates took all seats in a free and fair parliamentary election marked by a turnout of only 29 percent. So, while opposition parties participated in free and fair elections with only a few exceptions, they also participated in many obviously flawed elections. This might seem irrational, but participating in rather than boycotting flawed elections has been a successful strategy in the longer run. By providing experience, organizational strengthening, and campaign attention, as well as a parliamentary basis for oppositional politics, and furthering democratic procedural gains, contesting in elections has proved better than merely exiting in protest. Participation in flawed elections has tended to improve democratic qualities in future elections more than boycotts have.

The figures in Table 4 on the number of elections where the old autocratic guard is gone are also the most restrictive option, including only cases when neither previous authoritarian rulers nor their close associates participated in the contest. For example, cases in which a minister under the authoritarian regime vied for the presidency are not included. That the authoritarian rulers did compete for power in more than five out of six fair elections and in nine out of ten flawed elections is telling. This could be interpreted as a negative feature of political participation in Africa. Given that so many elections have authoritarians contesting and even winning, one wonders to what extent the continued irregularities, violence, and flaws are the responsibility of these lingering nondemocratic elites. On the other hand, one can also ask how many of these authoritarians are being forced by the incentive structures of institutions and international factors to behave more democratically. One possible interpretation is to perceive it as a positive trend if these old autocrats, in order to retain or regain power, are forced by the incentives of electoral regimes to behave increasingly democratically. We should then see that the democratic qualities of elections improve despite the continued presence of known antagonists to democracy.

The overall level of competition in African elections seems slightly less impressive than the extent of participation. Legislative majorities are generally overwhelming, achieving an average of 60 percent of the seats even in free and fair elections, while the main opposition party typically acquires only 16 percent of the seats. We also note that executive elections are on average much more competitive than legislative elections. A vast majority of the countries holding elections in this period—39 out of 44—operate presidential systems. The higher competition in the executive elections is encouraging, since in presidential systems much greater powers are vested in the executive office. The picture would seem gloomier if a higher level of competition occurred in the less power-bestowing legislative elections. Finally, for parliamentary elections a vast majority of countries operate majoritarian, mixed, or proportional representation electoral systems with small constituencies. These systems induce by design a relatively severe disproportionality between votes and seats in favor of a few larger parties. Hence, in comparison to executive elections it is not surprising that a lower degree of competition is recorded in the indicator for legislative elections. For these reasons, presidential elections provide a more valid measure of political competition in Africa.

The fourth indicator of competition in Table 4 is alternations in power, referring to electoral turnover of the chief political executive in presidential elections and a changed legislative majority in parliamentary elections. In systems with proportional representation and shifting coalition partners, a turnover is sometimes "half," in the sense that one or more parties leave the majority coalition and new parties replace them. Such cases are not included in the figures in Table 4 or in any of the other following tables. The rationale is to err in the direction of being too strict in accepting positive signs rather than risk positing questionable results. Therefore, only unambiguous cases of turnovers are taken as signs of increasing competition. Alternation in power is a reasonably recurrent phenomenon in Africa's free and fair elections, a third of which resulted in turnovers. The comparison with flawed elections is stark: only in 5 percent of cases did the opposition manage to gain power under conditions of electoral fraud and mismanagement.

Yet, these few instances highlight something discussed already in Chapter 2. The existence of political rights is not merely a "procedural" condition but a distribution of political power and opportunities and a springboard for exercising other political rights. This is illustrated by Madagascar's fifth executive election, held in December 2001. The former authoritarian ruler, Ratsiraka, had been reinstalled by the ballot in the 1996–1997 elections,[6] after a period of opposition rule. President Ratsiraka then engineered an extensive constitutional reform that greatly enhanced the power of the president and which was confirmed in a referendum on 15 March 1998 with 51 percent of the votes. In December 2001 when President Ratsiraka was losing the fifth presidential election to new opposition challenger Marc Ravalomanana, Ratsiraka instigated a series of irregular procedures, first during the polling, then in the collation and announcement of results, and lastly in the procedures for adjudication of electoral disputes—the High Constitutional Court—but in each instance these efforts ultimately failed. The irregularities during the polling and counting of votes were reported by local and international observers, and parallel counts contradicted official tallies. The official results were contested also by representatives of the bureaucracy, and the Supreme Court invalidated the president's attempts to manipulate the abjurations. Finally, when the rightful winner, Ravalomanana, and his supporters took to the streets, the military refused to exceed their constitutional authority and left the protesters and Ravalomanana not only to protest but also to assume office against the will of the outgoing Ratsiraka. The power of the institutions and the people's habituation, the learning and expectations they acted on, was too strong for that old authoritarian ruler to fight.[7] Even if the whole idea of cheating is to win, doing it successfully is another. While opposition parties have also attempted to tip the balance in their favor by cheating (for examples, see Hartlyn 2004), so far fraud has tended to reinstall incumbents. This fact enhances the significance of efforts by domestic civil societies and the international community to make elections increasingly free and fair and more in accordance with international standards.

The indicators of legitimacy in Table 4 seem mildly supportive of the Afropessimist view. Even among free and fair elections, the losing parties immediately accepted the results in only 57 percent of cases. Looser acceptance in this study is established first when none of the major players challenges the results in court or makes other serious charges following the polls. This is a stricter application than Bratton (1998) used, since even cases where the opposition initially protested but then later recanted, accepting parliamentary seats, are not included in the positive results here. Again, the concern is to avoid inducing excessively optimistic findings on shaky grounds. Nevertheless, 43 percent nonacceptance of results is a large percentage in free and fair elections. One of the more famous cases of nonacceptance was Angola's election in 1992. With international support and certification, a voter turnout of 91 percent, and 12 candidates for the office of the president, there was no doubt that the results reflected the will of the people, even if there were certainly some minor irregularities. Yet, UNITA, the main opposition party, refused to accept the results and went back to warfare, which continued until their leader, Jonas M. Savimbi, was killed in 2002. Niger's first elections, in 1993, which took place after massive international pressure on incumbent president Tandja, were also judged free and fair. Opposition candidate Mahamane Ousmane won in the second round, but the losing parties refused to accept the results and the new government eventually was overthrown, in January 1996, by a military coup that made it obvious that key elites had not accepted the legitimacy of the electoral regime. Playing according to the democratic rules of the game requires acceptance of defeat when you lose a fair combat, and the behavior of the losing parties in Africa's elections is far from satisfactory in this respect. More comforting, perhaps, is that in only one instance —Chad's second parliamentary election, on 21 April 2002—have the opposition parties immediately accepted a flawed result.

Only about 20 percent of all election processes during the study period qualify as "peaceful." Again, however, the criteria are very strict. Even cases with only a few reports of nonsystematic election-related violence were not coded as peaceful but rather placed in the intermediate category of low-intensity violence. Finally, an interesting observation is that incidences of complete breakdown of the electoral process (about 15 percent of all cases) are totally unrelated to the freedom and fairness of elections. One would perhaps have expected that breakdowns should more often follow fraudulent elections that inspired frustration, with parties reconsidering violent overthrows, and that contrarily free and fair elections would pave the way for stability. This does not seem necessarily to be the case, and there are obviously other factors at play.

In sum, the hypotheses of declines over time in the frequency and quality of elections in Africa can be refuted and the general outlook for African politics seems to support a moderate optimism about the democratic qualities of elections in Africa, rather than the pessimism that other studies produced. The findings of other studies based on these hypotheses can now also be challenged. Mozaffar, Scarritt, and Galaich's (2003) analysis of ethnicity, electoral rules, and voting, for example, is invalidated by thei mixing of free and fair elections with an almost equal number of flawed ones. It has been shown (Lindberg 2004b) that Yoon's (2001) analysis of women's legislative representation in Africa suffers from the same problem. Also, that the survival rate of newly elected regimes is completely unrelated to the flawlessness of elections seems to defy the standard recommendations. Insisting that elections be perfect and clean from the very beginning if they are to create and uphold credibility for democratic elections and thereby preempt backlashes has been the creed of the last decade, but it now appears that prescription may be misguided. It may be that survival is a highly context-dependent phenomenon, but it is also possible that there is something else to be said once the analysis is taken further. At this point, therefore, the case is rested with the reflection in mind that free and fair elections do not mitigate breakdowns and flawed elections do not spell breakdown.

DEMOCRATIC QUALITIES OF ELECTIONS OVER TIME

We now turn to another set of hypotheses in the literature on African elections and politics. Bratton and van de Walle (1997, 202) and Bratton (1997, 74) found about half of the early elections to be free and fair. Bratton (1998) reported that later elections in general, and second elections in particular, were of lower democratic quality. He also concluded that among second elections, the "late" ones, from 1995 onwards, were worse than earlier ones. With regards to alternations in power as one of the key indicators of how democratic a system is, Bratton reported that the later in time the election, the poorer the quality and the lower the likelihood that an incumbent would be ousted. A similar result was reported by Diamond and Plattner (1999) and echoed later in the recent influential comparative work of Cowen and Laakso (2002, 14). The last work builds on a limited set of cases, yet the claims are stated in general terms. The empirical analysis below challenges these accounts.

The following detailed analysis of participation, competition, and legitimacy in Africa from 1990 to June 2003 is subdivided into three periods. Other writers (e.g., Bratton and van de Walle 1997, Sandbrook 1996, Wiseman 1992) have referred to elections in the "early" period of transitions, after 1989, usually said to have lasted until 1992 or 1993. Elections and transitions taking place from 1994 or 1995 have been labeled "late" (e.g., Bratton 1998; Joseph 1998). The later period ended for these observers in 1997, more out of publication constraints than theoretical rationales. I have used a periodization that conforms as much as possible to that of earlier studies in order to enhance comparability, but timelines have been adjusted slightly to achieve uniformity of length and number of cases. My choice of data end-point, June 2003, was as much a matter of practicality as it was for other researchers.

An addition in the present analysis is that elections in countries holding *de jure* participatory and competitive elections before 1990 are also included, as a separate category with which to compare the more recent elections. The numbers of free and fair elections held in the three periods is shown in Table 5. Twenty-six elections in the sample were held in the period predating 1990 in the "old" democracies in Africa that are usually excluded from the analysis of contemporary democratization in Africa. Another 59 elections were held in the 4-year period from 1990 to 1993; these are considered the "early" or "first" transitional elections after the events in 1989. In the next period, from 1994 through 1998, came the "late" or "second" period of elections, containing 74 elections. The story of large-N comparative work on the quality of elections in Africa stops there. Only a little further research has been published since then.[8] The succeeding four and a half years, from 1999 to 30 June 2003, is re-

TABLE 5 *Percentage of free and fair elections in four chronological periods*

Indicator	−1989*	1990–1993	1994–1998	1999–2003	All	Significance**
Free and fair elections	42%	58%	51%	63%	56%	.094
N	11	34	38	46	129	(.154)
Total elections	26	59	74	73	232	
Countries holding free and fair elections	57%	64%	59%	70%	82%	—
N	4	20	24	28	36	
Total countries	7	31	41	40	44	—

*A few countries had held multiparty elections before 1990. Their first, second, and later elections are included in the "−1989" category as a point of comparison.
**Spearman's Correlation and significance.

ferred to as the "third" period in this data set and saw 73 elections. This periodization seems to fit well with that of earlier studies; hence, results should be comparable. In addition, this periodization divides the total number of years into relatively equal subperiods displaying roughly equal sample sizes that enhance the prospects for a sound statistical analysis.

The data presented in Table 5 show that Bratton and colleagues were both right and wrong. Elections in the second period, 1994–1998, were indeed slightly worse than in the first period; more of them were flawed. On the other hand, free and fair elections were rare in the pre-1990 period and the freedom and fairness picks up again in the latest period, hitting a record of 63 percent. Looking at this particular aspect from a chronological perspective, we see an S-shaped curve with a slight average improvement over time. The changes are not dramatic, and the real situation may be one of stability rather than a positive or negative change. Although the differences are not significant, they point—if anything—towards a slight improvement rather than backlash.

The figures in Tables 6, 7, and 8 also depict relatively stable levels of participation, competition, and legitimacy during these subperiods, making the most striking feature they describe continuity over time, even while more and more countries started holding elections. There are two separate trends behind these figures (which will be addressed in greater detail in the next chapter). On the one hand, as Bratton (1998) noted, more repressive regimes started to hold multiparty elections in the second period. Chad, Liberia, Sierra Leone, Sudan, among other countries, held first elections later than 1995, decreasing the general level of democratic qualities. At the same time, the early birds, who formed the dawn of political liberalization in the early 1990s, had moved on, improving the democratic qualities of their elections and gaining experience in how to operate within the new rules of the game. Benin,

Ghana, Sao Tome, and Namibia are examples of this positive trend. Presenting evidence for such a trend requires the type of analysis pursued in Chapter 4, but first we need to discuss some details of the comparison over time.

A Mixed Record of Participation

Voter turnout figures in Table 6 are a little puzzling in one regard; they show a higher level on average in the elections preceding 1990 and more or less stable levels since. Why this pattern when the tide of democratization reached Africa in the early 1990s? Perhaps we can find a partial answer in the type of countries these data relate to. As mentioned, more previously repressive regimes held multiparty elections in the 1990s than in the earlier period, when countries like Botswana, Mauritius, and Senegal were the only ones to hold such elections. The average voter had a reason to feel more reluctant about participation in elections in the 1990s, fearing that such behavior might be punished if the tide turned again.

A second reason that turnout seems to have declined is that greater international involvement in electoral administration made it harder for incumbents to manipulate turnout figures. Practices like inflating the voter registry and then having supporters of the incumbent regime vote twice or more and simply stuffing ballot boxes seem to have decreased in the 1990s (Schedler 2002b, van de Walle 2002). I believe this to be a large part of the explanation for the apparent decline in turnout. In Kenya, Ghana, Senegal, and Cape Verde, for example, this seems to have been the case.

Opposition participation in free and fair elections over the subperiods was relatively constant. There was a slight decrease in participation from 1990 to 1998, but almost complete participation is restored in the following period and these differences are not statistically significant. Table 6 also shows an increase during the 1990s in flawed elections in which opposition parties chose to participate. At this point, the reasons for this can only be speculated upon. It might be suggested that opposition parties are slowly learning that in many instances they have more to gain by participating than by boycotting. Ghana is one example where I know from my own interviews (Lindberg 2003) that the former opposition party, the NPP, regretted their decision to boycott the first parliamentary elections, held in 1992, for this very reason. The stories of Mali, Guinea, Senegal, and others present the same evidence. (More on this in Chapter 4.)

That autocratic rulers or their close associates, running as presidential candidates, usually retained power is indicated by the data in Table 6 and is noteworthy. There was only a slight increase of elections held in absence of an autocratic guard, from 12 percent to 17 percent, even among free and fair elections, and that is not a statis-

TABLE 6 *Electoral participation in four chronological periods*

Indicator	Type of Election	−1989	1990–1993	1994–1998	1999–2003	All	Significance* Period	Significance* Free & Fair
Voter turnout	Free & fair	66%	58%	68%	63%	63%	1.483	7.209
	St. dev.	(20.1)	(20.9)	(16.2)	(15.9)	(17.8)	(.223)	(.008)
	N	11	34	38	45	128		
	Flawed	68%	51%	54%	61%	57%	3.105	
	St. dev.	(12.9)	(15.7)	(18.6)	(14.4)	(16.7)	(.030)	
	N	13	22	35	25	95		
Full opposition participation	Free & fair	100%	91%	84%	98%	92%	.060	.536
	N	11	31	32	45	119	(.501)	(.000)
	Flawed	67%	32%	39%	44%	43%	−.070	
	N	10	8	14	12	44	(.482)	
Autocrats gone	Free & fair	45%	12%	12%	17%	16%	.166	.230
	N	5	4	4	8	21	(.060)	(.000)
	Flawed	0%	8%	14%	11%	10%	.051	
	N	—	2	5	3	10	(.611)	
Total Ns	Free & fair	11	34	38	46	129		
	Countries	4	20	24	28	36		
	Flawed	15	25	36	27	103		
	Countries	4	17	21	17	29		
	Elections	26	59	74	73	232		
	Countries	7	31	41	40	44		

*For ordinal variables, Spearman's Correlation values and significance; for the means analyses, ANOVA F-values and significance.

tically significant change. The old authoritarian leaders have proven to be antidemocratic and willing to govern by force and in violation of fundamental human rights. Even in Ghana, the much-cherished new president, John A. Kufour, who defeated former authoritarian ruler Jerry J. Rawlings's chosen successor, Dr. John Atta-Mills, in the December 2000 elections, was once a minister in Rawlings's military-cum-civilian regime. In Kenya, the situation is similar; the new president, Emilio M. Kibaki, who heads the National Rainbow Coalition of parties, used to be vice-president under Daniel Arap Moi's single-party autocratic regime. In Nigeria, a former military ruler, General Olusegun Obasanjo, is now president. He was reelected in the 2003 executive elections, in which two other old military rulers were his main competitors. It might be that Nigerians do not perceive Obasanjo as primarily an authoritarian ruler, but he is a military man who first came into power by armed force.

There are examples of oppressive regimes regardless of elections, such as in Togo, where President Etienne Eyadema continued his harsh rule until his death, which occurred in February 2005, during the completion of this book. But such cases are in the minority while the list of authoritarian elites recycled as democrats is long. It takes time for a new generation of leaders to emerge, and while the presence of authoritarian-minded individuals in political leadership perhaps remains troublesome in some parts of Africa, overall it does not appear to be a stumbling stone for democracy. There are only a few countries where the old guard is completely gone. In many cases it seems that former authoritarian leaders are learning to play by democratic rules of the game—at least to some extent. We should also be open to the possibility that some of these leaders, like President Kufour in Ghana, never were authoritarian-minded although they took part in authoritarian rule. I personally know several individuals from the inner circles of both Jerry J. Rawlings's PNDC in Ghana and Joachim Chissano's FRELIMO in Mozambique who were never keen on authoritarian ways but participated in the rule because they believed it had to be tolerated for a period of time and that they could do something good for their country. When proven autocrats and dictators cling to power via elections, it is an indication that the "democraticness" of those elections needs improvement. At the same time, it may also indicate that the institutions of democracy can make nondemocrats further electoral democracy.

Stable Competition at Acceptable Levels

As Table 7 shows, the level of competition in Africa's free and fair elections has been relatively stable from 1989 to 2003. Flawed executive elections have been less competitive and more volatile than the free and fair ones, as measured by the indicator for winner's share of the votes. Partly, this is an effect of opposition boycotts, since winning shares increase when one or several major opposition parties boycott the poll; yet, legislative majorities were overwhelmingly stable over the period.

The ultimate test of competitiveness—alternation in power—varied greatly during the study period, from a mere one in five elections leading to a turnover before 1990 to almost *half* of all free and fair elections during the first years in the 1990s. The level dropped in the mid-1990s but regained momentum in the later years. Many of the polls in the early 1990s were first elections, and voters were eager to change to new leaders after years of authoritarian rule. In the following years, many of these countries moved on to second elections. The electorates then, more often than not, decided to retain incumbent leaders. Then, with many third and later elections in 1999 to 2003, things started to normalize, producing a turnover rate of around 30 percent. While there is some variation, there is no evidence of a declining trend, as previously thought. If anything, we see encouraging signs in the data analyzed here.

TABLE 7 *Electoral competition in four chronological periods*

Indicator	Type of Election	−1989	1990–1993	1994–1998	1999–2003	All	Significance* Period	Free & Fair
Winning candidate's % of votes	Free & fair	—	54%	52%	53%	53%	.064	6.663
	St. dev.		(17.6)	(20.9)	(14.4)	(17.3)	(.939)	(.011)
	N	—	17	15	18	50		
	Flawed	73%	53%	68%	59%	62%	1.271	
	St. dev.	(10.5)	(24.2)	(19.8)	(19.9)	(20.2)	(.297)	
	N	6	10	16	13	45		
Largest party's % of seats	Free & fair	74%	58%	59%	57%	60%	1.582	6.963
	St. dev.	(13.8)	(24.2)	(20.1)	(18.7)	(19.9)	(.201)	(.009)
	N	11	17	23	28	79		
	Flawed	80%	61%	70%	70%	69%	.823	
	St. dev.	(13.8)	(24.9)	(19.0)	(21.2)	(20.5)	(.488)	
	N	8	13	17	14	52		
2nd party's % of seats	Free & fair	13%	14%	15%	17%	15%	.869	4.596
	St. dev.	(10.9)	(10.1)	(11.2)	(13.4)	(11.8)	(.461)	(.034)
	N	11	17	22	28	78		
	Flawed	11%	8%	9%	11%	10%	.558	
	St. dev.	(11.4)	(13.6)	(10.7)	(16.0)	(13.0)	(.645)	
	N	8	13	17	14	52		
Turnover of power	Free & fair	18%	47%	18%	28%	30%	−.067	.406
	N	2	16	7	13	38	(.449)	(.000)
	Flawed	0%	4%	0%	15%	5%	.131	
	N	—	1	—	4	5	(.187)	
Total Ns	Free & Fair	11	34	38	46	129		
	Countries	4	20	24	28	36		
	Flawed	15	25	36	27	103		
	Countries	4	17	21	17	29		
	Elections	26	59	74	73	232		
	Countries	7	31	41	40	44		

*For ordinal variables, Spearman's Correlation values and significance; for the means analyses, ANOVA F-values and significance.

Improved Legitimacy

Table 8 shows that although there was a slight improvement in the peacefulness of campaign periods and the process of postelection settlements, there was not a significant change. Losers' acceptance of the election results remained essentially unchanged on average across the periods. Interestingly, the increasing rate of survival of the electoral regimes after free and fair elections is the only indicator with a statistically significant relationship to the periodization. Starting at a rate of 68 percent in the early 1990s, it reaches almost 100 percent in the early twenty-first century.

Once more, this may have to do with the increasing number of countries that moved on to second, third, or later elections. As Chapter 4 discusses, the breakdown of an electoral regime is a phenomenon belonging almost exclusively to the time just after a first election has been held.

In the late 1990s and early twenty-first century, only three elections have been followed by a complete breakdown of the electoral process. In the Central African Republic (CAR), President Felix Patassé was reelected with 51.6 percent of the votes, against 19.3 percent for the former authoritarian ruler and general André-Dieudonné Kolingba, in what appears to have been an acceptably fair election, although only barely so. This did not prevent Kolingba from attempting two coups d'état in 2001, which President Patassé survived with the help of Libyan troops sent from Tripoli in trade for mineral concessions in the CAR. An insurgency then developed. The Libyan forces that had protected Patassé left in December 2002, and by 15 March 2003 the rebels had seized the capital. The constitution was suspended, the parliament dissolved, and General François Bozize installed himself as ruler, while President Patassé took refuge in Cameroon.

The second case is Ivory Coast, which held "second" first elections in 2000 after

TABLE 8 *Electoral legitimacy in four chronological periods*

Indicator	Type of Election	−1989	1990–1993	1994–1998	1999–2003	All	Significance* Period	Significance* Free & Fair
Losers accept	Free & fair	91%	56%	53%	52%	57%	−.087	.646
	N	10	19	20	24	73	(.325)	(.000)
	Flawed	0%	0%	0%	4%	1%	.147	(.142)
	N	—	—	—	1	1	(.142)	
Peaceful process	Free & fair	45%	18%	40%	37%	33%	.130	.321
	N	5	6	15	17	43	(.143)	(.000)
	Flawed	15%	0%	8%	15%	9%	.027	
	N	2	—	3	4	9	(.786)	
Regime survival	Free & fair	100%	68%	74%	98%	83%	.212	−.048
	N	11	23	28	45	107	(.016)	(.471)
	Flawed	100%	76%	83%	93%	86%	.029	
	N	15	19	30	25	89	(.773)	
Total Ns	Free & fair	11	34	38	46	129		
	Countries	4	20	24	28	36		
	Flawed	15	25	36	27	103		
	Countries	4	17	21	17	29		
	Elections	26	59	74	73	232		
	Countries	7	31	41	40	44		

*Spearman's Correlation values and significance.

the breakdown in 1999. The conflict that had caused the breakdown escalated, and in 2002 a real civil war broke out and the new electoral regime broke down.

The final case was the elections in the notoriously unstable federal island-state Comoros, which for the third time after a coup tried to hold elections. The regime broke down in 2003 before it really got started. All of the other first—or later—elections in this latest period have led to so far surviving regimes, indicating that the players have agreed to play by the basic rules at least in acknowledging the legitimacy of democratic elections.

CONCLUSIONS

Based on analysis of a longer period and more cases than earlier research studied, we can now say that there has been no decline in the number or frequency of elections in Africa. The common wisdom of the field was derived from that data available at the time, but it is no longer a correct depiction of reality. The frequency and number of elections held annually does vary, but at a more or less regular interval, and averaged out over time shows, if any change, a slight increase. The same goes for the number of countries conducting *de jure* participatory and competitive elections.

More than half of all elections in Africa during the study period were free and fair, and the overall trend is stability or even slightly positive, contrary to what has been believed based on earlier studies. There are significant differences between free and fair elections and flawed elections by all but one indicator. That earlier studies did not analyze these differences also limits the usefulness of their results. The one indicator for which there is no difference between fair and flawed elections is regime breakdowns. There appears to be no relationship between the quality of elections and the survival of electoral regimes in Africa over the period studied here. Granted, the continent is still in an early phase of what will surely be a long democratization process.

The currently available data indicate that the democratic qualities of the 232 elections did not vary substantially over different periods. There are some marked differences between pre-1990 elections and recent ones, but from 1990 until 2003 the lens of time portrays a picture of remarkable continuity. Regarding the individual democratic qualities, participation has been more than one might have expected, while the level of competition leaves room for substantial improvement, especially in legislative elections. Legitimacy is the only dimension showing a statistically significant improvement over time, but it is still fairly constant and lags far behind indicating a general acceptance of the rules of the game.

Time has been used in this chapter as a chronological frame of reference and carries no analytical meaning. In other studies, there is often an assumption of progression with time: Diamond (1997) assumes that with time democratization in Africa will take a stronger hold and deepen; part of Carothers's criticism of the "transition paradigm" (2002a, 2002b) is based on the teleology inherent in viewing history as necessary and one-directional. Indeed, lots of the study of democratization in Africa has assumed that any move away from dictatorial rule is a move towards democratization. Methodologically, Carothers is right. Our measurements should always allow for alternative analytical outcomes. Potentially much more damaging for results is that chronological order can mix phenomena of different kinds in the same basket simply because they occurred in the same period. For example, Botswana's sixth successive election, on 15 October 1994, in this analysis was placed in the same category of events as Malawi's third election, on 17 May 1994, and Guinea-Bissau's first election, on 7 August of the same year. These are arguably rather different kinds of events, which casts doubt on the usefulness of the approach. The next chapter presents a methodologically more valid analysis of the elections, based on their characteristic as the first, second, third, or later election.

CHAPTER FOUR

The Self-Reinforcing Power
of Elections

This chapter tests established hypotheses about the development of democratic qualities of elections in Africa after so-called "founding" elections and develops a new hypothesis, about the self-reinforcing power of elections. Do the democratic qualities of African elections indeed improve with the experience accumulated over several electoral cycles? This analysis suggests that they do, in two important ways: once regimes hold their second elections, they tend to survive; and when regime breakdown occurs, it is almost always after first elections.

It will be demonstrated that the electoral cycle creates a positive spiral of self-reinforcement leading to increasingly democratic elections. Third elections mark a cut-off point at which the democratic qualities tend to improve radically. It seems that playing within the rules of the electoral game feeds on itself, because the constitutive and regulatory distribution of power inherent in institutionalized electoral procedures serve as incentives for upholding the rules. Political actors either adapt to or learn about both the rules and the incentive structure. The implications of these findings are important, for it appears that regardless of the qualities of first and even second elections, chances are good things will improve. This translates into increasingly democratic elections in Africa, helping to prevent the coups and civil wars that are associated with breakdowns. Even the power of elected incumbent autocrats to sustain domination behind a façade of democracy seems to be outweighed by this self-reinforcing power of elections.

Our conceptualization of elections and democracy often, if not always, includes a time component. While the last chapter discussed chronology-based hypotheses, this chapter uses sequence as a defining attribute of the objects of study: first, second, third, fourth, and subsequent elections. Sequence of events is also a key aspect in studies of the various pathways of transitions to democracy, which are generally thought to start with liberalization of civil rights, followed by free and fair elections in due time as a result of mounting pressure for democratization. If elections are held first and political rights are not issued until after the elections, it is considered a pseudotransition at best. Transitions have often been seen as being short processes and requiring careful political timing, while consolidation takes a longer time, happens less often, and its tempo is erratic. Cycles of elections have been used as indicators of consolidation (e.g., Schmitter and Santiso 1998, 83–84), yet, as we shall find out in the next chapter, there are few theories of democratization that suggest that elections have a causal role in the progression towards democracy. Similarly, Linz (1994; 1998, 21–24) argues that differences in the sequence and duration of structures of democracy (for example, electoral cycles, deadlines for proposing new laws and regulations, presidential term limits, and parliamentary governments' maximum length in office) have effects on political outcomes.

GOING FROM BAD TO WORSE

Many studies of politics in contemporary Africa relegate discussion of elections to background information or use them as a means of chronologically ordering events. Although they take elections seriously, Bratton's and Bratton and van de Walle's seminal 1997 volumes report on only so-called "founding" elections. Bratton's often-cited 1998 article concludes that second elections were of significantly worse quality in comparison to first elections: only 30 percent of second elections were free and fair and participation was poorer, with an average of a 56 percent turnout compared to 64 percent for first elections, according to his figures. Opposition boycotts increased from 25 percent to over 30 percent, and competition decreased with second elections, turnovers were almost absent, and winning candidates' and parties' shares of votes and seats increased. Overall, while second elections helped some regimes to survive, the quality of elections in Africa was declining, Bratton concluded. In his judgment, Africa was returning to "an institutional legacy of 'big man' rule, and the electoral alternation of leaders [was] again becoming abnormal" by all indications (Bratton 1998, 64–65).

Bratton's argument was based on the available data at the time, and it is echoed by other scholars, like Diamond and Plattner (1999, 19, 32, 169) who argue that second elections were merely "transitions without change." Cowen and Laakso concluded that ruling parties' domination made it difficult for opposition parties to win second and successive elections and that the "massive voter apathy" spreading across the continent is undermining the meaningfulness and legitimacy of elections in Africa (2002, 14–15, 23). These more recent publications stand in contrast to Bratton and van de Walle's (1997, 187) conclusion that the higher the number of elections before 1990—no matter how uncompetitive—the greater the likelihood of a transition in the 1990s, ending with fair elections, the results of which are accepted even by the losing parties. Their theory is that historical institutional legacies played a major part in shaping subsequent outcomes. In other words, the more elections in the past, the higher the quality of subsequent elections. It seems to me that there is no theoretical reason why holding elections in the 1990s should be less conducive to present-day democratization than holding elections in the 1960s, '70s, and '80s. This is also the main hypothesis the rest of this book focuses on.

The results of the empirical analysis displayed in Figure 3 and Tables 9 through 12 are based on an analysis of elections over a longer period than has previously been examined, increasing the number of cases significantly. The conclusions run contrary to earlier findings in several important respects, as democratic qualities of elections are shown to improve significantly after first elections, in particular with third and fourth elections. In free and fair third or fourth elections, the aspects of participation are almost fulfilled, competition is fiercer, and the legitimacy of self-government is increasingly espoused. Second, controlling for different categories of countries—panel groups—the final analysis shows this indeed to be the general trend across the continent and not only regarding a few countries, as previously thought.

On a methodological point, this chapter shows that using years and periods as the means of identifying the unit of analysis can be highly misleading. It is not time as "one damn thing after another"—chronological time—that matters in institutionalization, as Diamond (1997, 5) posits for Africa. Rather, successive electoral cycles allow actors to gain experience and become habituated to electoral institutions, probably in terms of both learning and adaptation. Even flawed elections generate important experiential lessons (van de Walle 2002, 75), and it seems clear from the analysis below that this development is not dependent on all actors' being democrats. Finally, rather than the arrival of a democratic regime being indicated by a "founding" election, the transitional period typically appears to involve holding several elections; even free and fair elections often need to recur, as part and parcel of protracted transitions (Barkan 2000, 235). It appears that even autocratic regimes will get better if the cycle of *de jure* participatory and competitive elections continues. Whether this in turn leads to improvement of democratic qualities in the society or not is discussed and analyzed in Chapters 5 and 6.

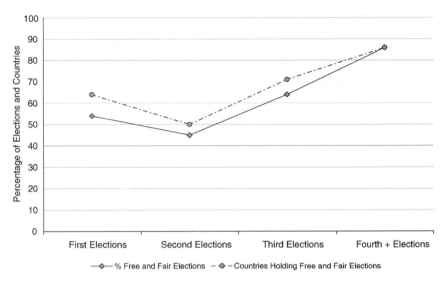

Fig. 3. Freedom and fairness over first, second, third, and later elections

FIRST, SECOND, THIRD, FOURTH, AND LATER ELECTIONS

Of sub-Saharan Africa's 48 states, 44 have conducted so-called "founding" elections, out of which 38 moved on to second elections and as many as 21 countries had completed three uninterrupted electoral cycles as of June 2003. Seven countries have managed at least four polls in a row (see Table 2, in Chapter 1). There are indeed some democratically dismal cases among these many electoral regimes: Chad, with two elections, has been under President Idriss Déby since 1990 and barely keeps an electoral façade; and in Togo, with three elections, Etienne Eyadema, until his death in 2005 the longest-serving African head of state, in power since 1967, ran a brutal authoritarian regime. Eyadema's reign survived almost a dozen coup attempts. One-party elections have been held in Togo since 1972, and the shift to multipartyism that was spurred by heavy international pressure during the early 1990s yielded little democratic advancement. However, in April 2005, after the death of President Eyadema, fresh elections were held and a longstanding and very popular opposition leader, in exile since 1992, returned. Togo might well take one of those routes to dramatic improvement after third elections, but only time will tell.

In Africa's largest country, Sudan, then Brigadier Omar Hassan al-Bashir seized power in a bloodless coup in 1989 from Prime Minister Sadiq al-Mahdi, who had been prime minister since 1986, when his Umma Party won a plurality of 99 seats in the legislature. Sadiq had won partly because polling was canceled in 27 out of the

68 constituencies due to the civil war in the south, and although hopes were initially high for a resolution of the war it soon picked up again. Bashir took over after a deadlock between the government and the army over the failing efforts to end the war. He promised democracy at the outset but his rule has not delivered on that promise. Flawed executive elections were held in both 1996 and 2001 and flawed legislative elections in 1997 and 2002. He has suppressed the opposition and curtailed several political and civil rights.

Notwithstanding the importance of these exceptions, a qualified majority of countries in Africa have been governed by civilian regimes over the 13-year period of this study; that in itself represents an important watershed in the political history of Africa.

Freedom and Fairness of Elections

Looking first at frequency of free and fair elections only, the picture, displayed in Figure 3, is somewhat encouraging. With repetition, the share of elections that were free increased, from roughly half of all first and second elections to 64 percent in third elections and 86 percent in fourth or later elections. The figure for the last group would have been higher had it not been for Zimbabwe's degeneration into near-total political collapse since the early 1990s. The number of countries holding free and fair elections is also encouraging: the more countries holding at least one free and fair election, the more that the people, opposition parties, media, and political elites are exposed to the process. The percentage of countries holding free and fair elections is generally higher than the share of free and fair elections. This simply means that several countries have experienced both fair and flawed elections.

Increasing Participation

The new data on a greater number of cases reveal no sign of a general trend of declining participation in second elections. To the contrary, Table 9 shows that participation is generally improving. Voter turnout seems to have slightly decreased after second elections, but the difference is not statistically significant. In free and fair elections, opposition party participation increased from an average of 88 percent in first elections to between 94 and 100 percent in the following elections.

Interestingly, opposition parties increasingly chose to participate in even flawed elections. Why? They likely made a rational calculation in response to learning and adaptation to the new dispensation of competition; by participating rather than boycotting, the opposition not only builds good will and organizational strength but also plays within the rules of the game as they wait their turn. The experience of countries with records of a series of bad elections, like Kenya, attests to this pattern; the opposition groups have been forced to sharpen their organizational and political skills and to give up particularistic tendencies and form coalitions. Even in repressive regimes, like Zimbabwe's, where there has been repeated intimidation of opposition parties in flawed elections, the opposition still chooses to contest rather than boycott. The mere fact of holding uninterrupted, repetitive elections creates incentives for the political elites to participate even when it is obvious that they cannot win a particular election. It seems that their calculation says they are better off in the long run participating than not competing.

Since elections tend to become free and fair with third and later elections, this calculation by the opposition is a potentially profitable strategy. Previous experiences give them the advantage of an established platform, practice with campaigning in urban as well as rural settings, existing organizational set-ups, and whatever past media coverage campaigning might have yielded. If they have also combined forces in umbrella parties or electoral coalitions, they have not only adapted and acquired skills of the electoral game but also learned the logic and pitfalls of collective action, preparing them better to handle future pressures. In all, they probably stand a better chance of winning than if they had boycotted previous electoral races.

Table 9 also shows that the old authoritarian guard starts to disappear from the political stage with second and later elections. This trend is the same for all elections, even though it is more pronounced in flawed elections. The individual cases show a process of slowly phasing out the old rulers, leaving room for a new generation to grow and mature to leaders, as for example in Kenya, Ghana, Guinea, and Madagascar. Benin is perhaps the best-known example. There, Nicéphore Soglo ousted incumbent Mathieu Kérèkou in the first presidential elections, held in March 1991. Soglo was no freshman on the scene, however. He was the nephew of General Christophe Soglo, who was president in 1963 and 1964 and again from 1965 to 1967. Nicéphore Soglo had been the prime minister in Kérèkou's military government, which lasted until 1990. While the political development in Benin has produced more democracy than in most other countries in Africa so far, one would be hard pressed to argue that multiparty politics in Benin has delivered a new top leadership of proven democrats.

There are other cases, however, where the old guard was thrown out almost immediately, with first elections. The first African president to be voted out of office in recent times was Cape Verde's authoritarian ruler, Aristides Pereira, leader of Partido Africano da Independencia de Cabo Verde (PAICV), who lost to opposition candidate Antonio M. Monteiro in the February elections of 1991. In Zambia, a return

TABLE 9 *Participation in first, second, third, and later elections*

Indicator	Type of Election	First	Second	Third	Fourth+	All	Number of Poll	Free & Fair
							Significance*	
Voter turnout	Free & fair	64%	66%	61%	60%	63%	.453	7.209
	St. dev.	(19.4)	(18.0)	(12.6)	(17.6)	(17.9)	(.715)	(.008)
	Flawed	56%	59%	57%	55%	57%		
	St. dev.	(18.2)	(16.4)	(14.6)	(04.7)	(16.7)		
Full opposition participation	Free & fair	88%	94%	100%	94%	92%	.206	.536
	N	51	30	21	17	119	(.002)	(.000)
	Flawed	31%	54%	50%	67%	39%		
	N	15	21	6	2	44		
Autocrats gone	Free & fair	7%	16%	14%	50%	16%	.375	.230
	N	4	5	3	9	21	(.000)	(.000)
	Flawed	2%	8%	33%	67%	9%		
	N	1	3	4	2	10		
Total Ns	Free & fair	58	32	21	18	129		
	Flawed	49	39	12	3	103		
	Elections	107	71	33	21	232		
	Countries	44	38	21	7	44		

*Spearman's Correlation values and significance for ordinal variables, and ANOVA F-values and significance for the interval variable.

to multiparty politics made all the difference. Zambia was a constitutional multiparty democracy from independence in 1964 until 1972, when it became officially a one-party state ruled by President Kenneth Kaunda and his United National Independence Party (UNIP). Meanwhile, Fredrick Chiluba, chairman of the national Zambia Congress of Trade Unions (ZCTU), was leading strikes, which erupted into riots after the expulsion of union leaders, including Chiluba himself, from the UNIP. Chiluba was detained several times. More strikes and riots followed, from 1983 to 1985 and again in 1987 and 1989. All this time, President Kaunda's ruling regime refused to give in to demands for political liberalization, declaring that it would bring a return of interparty rivalry and "stone age politics." Nevertheless, multipartyism was reintroduced with the first elections, in 1991. Chiluba, by then a seasoned political fighter with a huge and well-organized support base that was relatively independent of the old autocratic guard, won by a landslide, collecting three-quarters of all votes. Kaunda, the old independence leader, quietly left the political leadership of UNIP and never returned to politics.

These are examples of the trend we find depicted by changes in the first of our three indicators: an increase in the levels of democratic participation irrespective of the freedom and fairness of elections.

Growing Competition

The second dimension in the democratic quality of elections, competition, improved significantly in some respects with third elections. Table 10 shows the distribution of votes, seats, and frequency of regime turnover. The differences between results from free and fair elections compared with flawed elections are statistically significant and in the expected direction: irregular elections reduce competition. Competition was reduced to close to nothing in flawed elections—which is the objective of cheating, from the view of incumbents. After flawed elections, legislative majorities were often well beyond the two-thirds majority that in many African countries is enough to make constitutional changes without consulting the opposition. In flawed elections the main opposition party regularly acquired less than 10 percent of the legislative seats and alternations in power almost never occurred.

Four out of the five turnovers that occurred after flawed elections happened with first elections, during which the attempted manipulation by incumbents was not enough to prevent the opposition from taking power, examples of which are Ivory Coast, Madagascar, and Nigeria. The smaller margins of victory in flawed executive elections probably reflects what Schedler (2002a) posits are the effects of international attention, which has made it harder to cheat openly and very much. Credibility is also better if you win with 51 percent than by a margin of 20 percent or 30 percent. The higher level of competitiveness of executive elections is partly an effect of measuring the first round in two-round executive elections. Incumbents bent on winning typically allow more fairness in the first round than in the second, yet using figures from second rounds would distort the picture of competition since only two candidates remain and the winning candidate's share of votes would be inflated. For these reasons, only figures from free and fair elections are taken as reliable. In free and fair elections during the studied period, the winning presidential candidate's share of votes changed from an average of 51 percent in first elections to 62 percent in second, 48 percent in third, and 44 percent in the fourth and subsequent elections. These changes are highly statistically significant and indicate the increasingly fierce nature of political competition in Africa's executive elections.

The corresponding measures for legislative elections do not show a similar trend of increased competition. The wide discrepancy between winning presidential candidate's share of votes and winning party's share of seats is partly because many of the countries operate various forms of majoritarian electoral codes. The extension of the law-like consequences of electoral systems first developed by Duverger (1954) and

TABLE 10 *Competition in first, second, third, and later elections*

Indicator	Type of Election	First	Second	Third	Fourth+	All	Significance* Number of Poll	Significance* Free & Fair
Winning candidate's % of votes	Free & fair	51%	62%	48%	44%	53%	4.675	6.663
	St. dev.	(18.9)	(15.7)	(10.9)	(11.1)	(17.3)	(.004)	(.011)
	N	26	14	7	3	50		
	Flawed	59%	72%	50%	52%	62%		
	St. dev.	(21.1)	(17.9)	(16.5)	(—)	(20.2)		
	N	22	17	5	1	45		
Largest party's % of seats	Free & fair	57%	61%	59%	65%	60%	1.398	6.963
	St. dev.	(20.1)	(21.5)	(19.8)	(18.8)	(19.9)	(.247)	(.009)
	N	32	18	14	15	79		
	Flawed	62%	74%	79%	77%	69%		
	St. dev.	(21.6)	(19.3)	(15.5)	(26.2)	(20.5)		
	N	23	20	7	2	52		
2nd party's % of seats	Free & fair	16%	14%	14%	14%	15%	.454	4.596
	St. dev.	(10.0)	(13.6)	(15.6)	(9.4)	(11.8)	(.715)	(.034)
	N	31	18	14	15	78		
	Flawed	12%	8%	8%	9%	10%		
	St. dev.	(14.1)	(11.6)	(9.8)	(25.5)	(13.0)		
	N	23	20	7	2	52		
Turnover of power	Free & fair	41%	9%	33%	22%	29%	−.062	.406
	N	24	3	7	4	38	(.346)	(.000)
	Flawed	8%	0%	0%	33%	4%		
	N	4	—	—	1	5		
Total Ns	Free & fair	58	32	21	18	129		
	Flawed	49	39	12	3	103		
	Elections	107	71	33	21	232		
	Countries	44	38	21	7	44		

*Spearman's Correlation except for means where ANOVA F-values are used.

Downs (1957) has been evinced by the work of other scholars, including Bogdanor and Butler (1983), Lijphart (1984, 1994, 1999), Lijphart and Waisman (1996), Mair (1990), Nohlen (1996, 44), Powell (1982, 2000), Rae (1971), Reynolds and Sisk (1998), and Sartori (1968, 1986, 2001). The imperative of the majoritarian vision is the creation of stable legislative majorities through highly disproportional translation of votes to seats, typically in winner-takes-all single-member constituencies. Thus, it typically has a strong reductive effect on both the number of parties competing for legislative seats and the number of parties in parliament. This system therefore often manufactures large winning majorities in parliament, which are reflected in the figures of Table 10. In short, competition in legislative elections is probably more pronounced than the figures seem to say. Yet, Sandbrook's (1996) assertion that institutionalization of parties in Africa will entail institutionalization of dominant party systems, remains a real possibility. A preliminary analysis by Bogaards (2004) points in that direction.

However, it is also true that the opposition remains split in many countries, as the relatively low average seat share for the second party implies. Generally, only when the opposition is able to unite in electoral or postelectoral coalitions can they manage to assume power. Kenya is perhaps the archetypical example of this. The international community's pressure on President Daniel Moi to hold first elections bore fruit in 1992. Moi used various tactics, including intimidation and irregular election practices to win these first elections, and the second, which followed in 1997, but a unified opposition would have prevented both victories. The official tally for all the disunited opposition candidates in the presidential race amounted to 60 percent of the votes in the first election. The scenario was repeated in 1997, when both local and international election observers complained about poor organization, widespread violence, and fraud, yet Moi and his ruling party collected only 40 percent of the votes in the executive poll. However, in preparation for Kenya's third general election, on 27 December 2002, almost all the opposition parties united in the National Rainbow Coalition (NARC) and put forward Emilio Kibaki as their presidential candidate. He collected 62 percent of the votes and NARC got close to 60 percent of the seats in parliament. While President Moi had to step down, by constitutional requirement, I believe that is not a significant part of the explanation for the success of the opposition, because their share of the votes remained relatively constant from the first and second to the third elections; and the main change in 2002 was their united front in face of centripetal forces of ethnicity, clientelism, political competition, diverging policy stances, and hopes of free riding.

The difficulty of uniting opposition forces in Africa points to a collective action problem. It took ten years of experiential learning and adaptation by the opposition to come to the rational calculation that led them to unite in fighting Moi's KANU party. The smaller parties played out the dilemma of the individual versus collective optimal outcomes (March and Olsen 1989). If the individual opposition groups chose to join in a grand coalition, the collective good of winning might be achieved. The cost would be losing visibility and possibly even risking their continued existence as small parties. The temptation of free riding is strong for smaller parties in such a situation, as it might provide the small party with an optimal payoff. Should a major opposition coalition win the presidency but not the majority in parliament, independent small parties can get the best of both worlds. They can enjoy an opposition takeover and leverage it to trade votes for constituency benefits, as did the small People's National Convention Party, holding three seats, and the even smaller Convention People's Party, holding only one, in Ghana's Third Parliament from 2000 to 2004. The ruling National Patriotic Party held exactly 100 of the 200 seats, and with MPs frequently absent on ministerial, constituency, or private business and no system for canceling out absenteeism, these small parties were left with a certain amount of leverage. The tactic backfired in the Kenyan elections of 1997, when too many parties sought the free-riding advantage, causing opposition fragmentation and continued KANU rule. Learning is an essential ingredient in reaching collectively optimal outcomes that satisfy individual goals. The behavior of opposition parties in many African countries in the 1990s exemplifies such problems, but examples such as the third elections in Kenya also suggest that these hurdles can be overcome.

The developments in Senegal illustrate the force of the incentives that electoral politics induce in democracies, in new ones even more vividly. As former President Abdou Diouf, after taking over in 1981 from the legendary Leopold Senghor, progressed with the liberalization instigated by his predecessor, the opposition parties struggled to unite. The elections, in February of 1983 and 1988, were decidedly not free and fair; and the leading opposition candidate, Abdoulaye Wade, claimed victory only to find himself imprisoned, then freed, then given a ministerial appointment. Through all this, the opposition parties remained disunited. This situation prevailed in Senegal for most of the 1990s, fueled by the extensive clientelist networks involving the strategically placed marabouts, local Muslim leaders. But repetition of elections in Senegal improved their democratic quality and facilitated strategic learning among opposition parties, eventually leading them to solve their coordination problems and form an alliance in March 1999, in preparation for the 2000 elections.[1] When none of the main contenders won a majority in the first round, all opposition groups coalesced around Wade, who beat Diouf with 58.5 percent of the popular vote against 41.5 percent for the incumbent.

Turnovers are rare in second elections in Africa, as Bratton (1998) observed. Table 10 shows that while over 40 percent of the first free and fair elections led to alternations in power, 9 percent of second elections had the same effect. The frequency of turnovers picks up again in third elections, however, to 33 percent. Neither Bratton and van de Walle (1997) nor Bratton (1998) addresses third and later elections, and those works' conclusions were justifiable by the available data. In total, 43 of the 232 elections studied here resulted in alternations in executive or legislative power — almost one in three of all free and fair election. Hence, Clapham's (1998) gloomy but influential conclusion that few states in Africa offered prospects of turnovers as a result of reasonably free and fair elections has been proven wrong by subsequent developments.

My conclusion about turnovers is not affected by electoral term limits, since the measure of turnovers accounts for that (see Chapter 2). The data seem to reflect two main developments that converged with the holding of third elections: In countries where the opposition gained power in the first elections, as in Cape Verde, Malawi, Mali, and Sao Tome, voters tended to give the ruling party a second term, perhaps afraid to let go of the new beginning. This also in part explains the higher shares of votes by winning presidential candidates in second as compared to first elections, although the new ruling parties in many countries, such as Namibia and South Africa, are just very strong and becoming increasingly popular. In the other main development, incumbent authoritarian rulers managed to stay in power in the new democratic environment. With time, a more experienced opposition, and more international pressure, many of these rulers have been forced to accept a more level electoral playing field, and this has led the way to an opposition takeover in the third race.

The third election is also often when the incumbent ruler is constitutionally obliged to relinquish power, and the designated successors tend to lack the charisma and force of the old "big man." This phenomenon has indeed played a role in a few countries. Ghana's charismatic and still popular former president Jerry J. Rawlings is one example. When he seized power in his second coup, in 1981, the country was a shambles. His regime, the Provincial National Defense Committee (PNDC), was originally socialist and tried to associate with the regimes in the Eastern Bloc, but those countries made it clear that they had no financial support to offer. This put Rawlings and the PNDC in a bind, because they honestly cared about the fate of their country (unlike some other African autocratic regimes). Before long, liberals like former Supreme Court judge and later Speaker of Parliament J. D. F. Annan were enlisted to lead the regime, and economic realities forced Ghana to seek support from the World Bank and International Monetary Fund. Over almost a decade, then, Chairman Rawlings's PNDC accomplished significant improvements for Ghana. He therefore probably did not need to employ irregularities during the first two general elections, in 1992 and 1996, to stay in power.[2] When he was required to step down after serving his maximum term, his party lost to the opposition National Patriotic Party in the third elections. Rawlings and his PNDC party immediately accepted the defeat; they handed over power on 7 January 2001 in a historic ceremony at Independence Square in the capital, Accra. To accept competition is only the first step. Accepting the consequences of competition is quite another. Gracefully bearing the burden of defeat may become a new trend in African politics.

Turnovers of government in Africa have always been tricky and often have brought periods of violent transition. In 20 countries, elections led to opposition triumphs and complete turnovers. In another five countries the alternations in power were incomplete in the sense that either the new president had been serving in the authoritarian regime, as in the Central African Republic, Djibouti, Kenya, and Malawi, or the new parliamentary majority coalition consisted in part of partners with the old ruling coalition, which has happened four times so far in Mauritius. Almost half of the turnovers have not had happy conclusions. Alternations in power quickly translated into a breakdown of the political process in Burundi, Comoros, Sierra Leone, and the Republic of Congo. In Zambia, the new regime adopted autocratic habits, leading to significant erosion of the infant democracy, although it has since improved. By June 2003, only one country had clearly passed Huntington's (in)famous "two-turnovers-of-the-executive test": Madagascar had a third turnover with the last, and controversial, executive election on 16 December 2001, which led to a political stalemate and in 2002 a serious political crisis. This crisis was quickly resolved and Madagascar is back on track again (Marcus 2002).

Some students of African elections would point out that Cape Verde also experienced two alternations in power, but the first one occurred with the first election, which according to Huntington's criteria does not count. In Benin there were also two alternations in power, following the executive elections of 1991 and 1996, respectively. The first alternation came with first elections, and Nicéphore Soglo, who took over, had, as noted above, been the prime minister in the incumbent authoritarian government. The 1996 alternation in power, the first real one, was from President Soglo back to the old autocrat, Mathieu Kérèkou. Such semiturnovers are not exactly what Huntington had in mind.[3] Malawi and Sao Tome had similar experiences. Mauritius is something of a special case in that its parliamentary system has produced several ruling coalitions over the years but there has never been any clearcut alternation in power, yet few would question that the country has long been a consolidated democracy.

In sum, there are few signs of a decreasing trend in the democratic quality of competition in African elections over sequences of elections. Contrary to dominant assumptions, the level of competition has increased as measured by the two most important indicators: the winner's share of the voters in executive elections and alternations in power. As pointed out in Chapter 2, there is such a thing as too much competition, but the time when that situation might occur in these countries seems far off. However, the level of competition has increased as countries have held third and fourth elections, in particular if these were free and fair.

Rising Legitimacy

As Table 11 demonstrates, the legitimacy of elections in Africa is on the rise. It seems that again third and fourth elections represent the crucial break with the past.

The average legitimacy of elections increases substantially at this point, with losers accepting defeat in 76 percent of these elections. Even though incidence of violence did not decline at a commensurate rate, the share of peaceful elections still grew from 17 to 50 percent. The overall argument of this chapter—that the democratic qualities tend to improve with repetition of *de jure* participatory, competitive, and legitimate electoral cycles—is reinforced by these measures of legitimacy.

The rate of regime survival substantiates the trend further. New electoral regimes are at greatest risk of regime breakdown between first and second elections. Electoral regimes survived after 107 free and fair elections and 89 flawed elections. Hence, breakdown of the electoral cycle followed a total of 36 elections, and out of these, 72 percent (26) occurred after first elections. In most cases, those states in which the first elections were followed by a breakdown tried again with a "second first" election. Five countries in sub-Saharan Africa experienced more than one coup or the outbreak of a civil war after two attempts at first elections during the studied period: Central African Republic, Comoros, Ivory Coast, Nigeria, and Niger. The last holds the unflattering record with three first elections during the 1990s, but it seems to have stabilized after that. Lesotho had two breakdowns in August 1994 and in September 1998, but they were not caused by violent overthrows, although a lot of unrest unfolded in and around these events and eventually South Africa and Botswana intervened with military forces and restored peace during the September 1998 crisis. For the "third first" Lesotho elections, in May 2002, a new electoral system was adopted, because the first-past-the-post system had been blamed for much of the chaos after the May 1998 election. The legislature now combines 80 seats elected in single-member constituencies by absolute majority, with 40 deputies elected by proportional representation and national party lists. In my data set, the crisis in 1998 is classified as a breakdown because of the extent of the violence, which brought an eruption in the political development and elicited military involvement by other countries, but this categorization may be too strict. It could be argued that the same electoral regime and the same leaders continued after the crisis and that the elections in 2002 were therefore second elections. In that interpretation, Lesotho would add one case to countries clearly supporting the thesis of this book, but I decided to err on the side of being too restrictive rather than the reverse.

Only eight cases of breakdown of the electoral regime (22 percent) in six countries occurred after second elections had been held. Out of these eight, three came after premature elections. Comoros's premature second elections, on 26 December 1993, were followed by a coup in September 1995. The country has since experienced two coups d'état and one serious coup attempt, the last in December 2001. In a similar scenario, first elections were held on 21 July 1992 in the Republic of Congo and

TABLE 11 *Legitimacy of first, second, third, and later elections*

Indicator	Type of Election	First	Second	Third	Fourth+	All	Significance* Number of Poll	Significance* Free and Fair
Losers accept	Free & fair	52%	44%	76%	72%	57%	.200	.646
	N	30	14	16	13	73	(.002)	(.000)
	Flawed	0%	3%	0%	0%	1%		
	N	—	1	—	—	1		
Peaceful process	Free & fair	17%	47%	43%	50%	33%	.229	.321
	N	10	15	9	9	43	(.000)	(.000)
	Flawed	6%	10%	17%	0%	8%		
	N	3	4	2	—	9		
Regime survival	Free & fair	72%	88%	91%	100%	83%	.239	.048
	N	42	28	19	18	107	(.000)	(.471)
	Flawed	80%	90%	100%	100%	86%		
	N	39	35	12	3	89		
Total Ns	Free & fair	58	32	21	18	129		
	Flawed	49	39	12	3	103		
	Elections	107	71	33	21	232		
	Countries	44	38	21	7	44		

*Spearman's Correlation.

premature second elections held on 6 October 1993 after President Pascal Lissouba lost a vote of censure, which was followed by the dissolution of Parliament. Civil war resumed, then ended with a victory by the former authoritarian ruler, President Denis Sassou-Nguesso, in 1997. Five years later, President Sassou-Nguesso staged a façade "second founding" election in RoC. In Niger, before the regime was terminated by a coup, they managed to squeeze in a second legislative election after the premature dissolution of Parliament in 1995. Thus, there are only five cases of breakdowns after the genuine conclusion of a full first electoral cycle with ensuing full-term second elections. These regime failures represent a mere 7 percent of all 71 electoral regimes by second elections, and they occurred in only 8 percent of the countries. In conclusion, complete breakdowns are rare after one full electoral cycle has been completed—no matter what the quality of elections.

The few regimes that have not survived after one full electoral cycle broke down before 1995. Only in the Central African Republic was a second election after 1995 followed by a breakdown. All the remaining second elections held after 1995 survived, even if a couple are rather discouraging cases. Equatorial Guinea's second legislative elections, held on 7 March 1999 amidst widespread violence and intimidation of the opposition, were neither free nor fair, but they did not result in a turnover.

The incumbent authoritarian ruler, President Teodoro O. Nguema, and his once-single party, the Democratic Party of Equatorial Guinea (PDGE), are still in power and continue to play the game in much the same way as before the introduction of multiparty elections. Likewise, the authoritarian incumbent in Guinea, President Lasana Conté, who came to power in a coup in 1984, won both the first and second executive elections—the latter on 14 December 1998—under very controversial circumstances. The second legislative elections, originally scheduled for 2000, have been postponed three times. These are clearly cases of "electoral authoritarianism" (Schedler 2002b).

Gambia is the only country where a coup unseated a civilian government after third elections. The July 1994 elections sparked protests within the rank and file of the military over back pay for service in the peacekeeping operations in Liberia, and this unrest led Lt. Yaya Jammeh to power. President Jammeh has since won two successive elections. In the controversial 1996 first-again elections, no parties were allowed to campaign but three opposition candidates stood against President Jammeh. The second-again presidential elections, in November 2001, were of a less dubious quality; and although violence tainted the campaign, the Commonwealth observation mission declared the elections satisfactorily conducted. The electoral process has gradually resumed in another 10 of the 14 countries where the process had broken down: Angola, CAR, Guinea-Bissau, Ivory Coast, Lesotho, Niger, Nigeria, RoC, Sao Tome, and Sierra Leone. In sum, violent breakdowns are most likely by far after first elections. Since 1995, only one second election has been followed by a breakdown. All other countries that have managed to muddle through third elections have stayed on track.

Valid Conclusions?

Overall, it seems from the empirical analysis of developments over several cycles of elections in Africa that a learning-by-doing process is taking place shaped by incentives provided by the electoral institutions themselves, among others. The democratic qualities of elections tend to improve steadily with practice. Third elections represent a point of separation with the past, as the average quality of the elections increases significantly then. Many more of third, fourth, and later elections were free and fair than were first and second elections, electoral participation and competition increased significantly, and the authoritarian rulers left the scene in increasing numbers, all while slowly but noticeably the signs of democratic legitimacy gained ground. Can proponents of democracy start to relax after third elections, then? Unfortunately, the answer is no.

The case that most dampens such hopes, the black sheep of fourth-plus elections, is Zimbabwe. Its fifth parliamentary election, in June 2000, was marked by irregularities, violence, and opposition outcry at the results. The campaign before the third executive elections, held in March 2002, turned into a sham, littered with censure, violence, intimidation, presumed vote rigging, and refusal to accept international observers. The country is a deviant case, however.

More common are countries such as Ghana and Mauritania. Ghana's 1992 first executive and parliamentary elections were partly flawed and hotly disputed. All opposition parties boycotted the legislative election and refused to accept the results, and turnout was only 29 percent. Second elections, in 1996, had deficiencies but not to the extent of affecting the outcome. All parties participated in them, bringing the turnout up to 77 percent, and all major actors eventually accepted the outcome. The third consecutive elections, held in 2000, took place under an interparty agreement that placed party agents at each polling station. The elections were essentially free and fair, monitored primarily by 15,000 domestic election observers, and all parties accepted the outcome immediately. The authoritarian ruler President Jerry J. Rawlings, who had stepped down from the highest office after two complete terms, immediately conceded that his party's candidate, Dr. John A. Mills, had been defeated by the opposition, who had united behind NPP's John A. Kufour.

In Mauritania Colonel O. S. M. Taya, who had assumed power in a bloodless coup in 1984, agreed to hold first multiparty elections in 1992. As in Ghana, the incumbent ruler won the first elections by using some unfair means. Opposition parties boycotted the parliamentary poll, voter turnout was only 38 percent, and none of the opposition groups accepted the results. Unlike in Ghana, though, Mauritania's second legislative elections of 1996 and second presidential poll in 1997 were plagued by political violence, arbitrary arrests, and frequent irregularities. The third parliamentary election, held in 2001, was significantly different, however. All parties contested in this election and the irregularities that occurred did not seem to alter the outcome. Although the incumbent dominant party in parliament reclaimed a majority of the seats, all the other contesting parties immediately accepted the results and assumed the role of a peaceful opposition.

These examples illustrate what seems to be happening increasingly in Africa today: countries are starting to hold multiparty elections, even if sometimes of miserable quality initially, and once the electoral cycle has been repeated it develops into a force that changes actors' behavior, which in turn reinforces and improves the democratic qualities of subsequent elections. Thus, it is not necessary that elections be perfect from the beginning; rather, electoral maturity comes with practice.

However, we need to test the robustness of these findings. There is a potentially significant selection bias in the way the sample has been analyzed so far. The set of first elections includes virtually all of the sub-Saharan countries. The analysis of subsequent sets of elections reflects a "natural" selection of cases, by virtue of those countries' having succeeded in conducting such elections. Countries that have held only first and second elections, for example, are not recorded in the categories of third elections. Can we generalize about all countries on the basis of elections held in fewer countries—those that have had the time and stamina to conclude three or four electoral cycles? On the one hand, there are advantages to analyzing all elections together. We do not have to select among the universe of cases, opening up the possibility of other kinds of selection bias; we get higher numbers, which often result in more reliable conclusions; and so on. Yet, we run the risk of a "natural" selection bias. Therefore, the analysis will proceed with a time-series panel-group comparison.

A PANEL-GROUP COMPARISON

The analysis of all elections *ensemble* above suggested that there is a trend of positive socialization, or perhaps habituation, taking place across Africa. A panel-group, time-series analysis offers a way to assess the validity of such a cross-continental claim, since it allows us to compare the developments of subsets of countries with each other to determine if the overall results are driven by one particular group, or not. The single most important methodological choice for this analysis is the differentiating criterion of the panels, since that determines how countries will be grouped. For the present purposes, it seems natural to use the number of successive elections as the defining criterion for each panel group. The rationale is simple. The argument above resonates of something like the proverbial "practice makes perfect": the more experience a country acquires by holding more elections, the more and better the democratic qualities their elections display. We can be relatively sure that this is true for the most experienced countries. It is these countries' elections we find in the category of fourth-plus elections. From the analysis in the previous sections we already know that on average these elections had better democratic qualities than first and second elections. How do countries with only two or three subsequent elections compare? Is the general trend described above a result of selection bias and thus invalid, or not?

In other words, we need to control for country type. This is done by presenting three panels of countries. The first panel group (results for which appear in the first group of columns in Table 12) consists of the most experienced countries, those which have held four or more successive elections without a breakdown. It includes the few longstanding electoral regimes in Africa: Botswana (since 1969), Madagascar (since 1982), Mauritius (since 1976), Senegal (since 1978), and Zimbabwe (since 1980). But we also find two newcomers that have now qualified as "experienced" electoral regimes: Benin and Mali.

The second panel group consists of countries having successfully held three multiparty elections in an unbroken series (results in the middle section of Table 12). Many of these countries illustrate the positive trend: Burkina Faso, Cape Verde, Djibouti, Ghana, Kenya, Mauritania, Namibia, Sao Tome and Principe, Seychelles, and Zambia. But this group includes a few bad apples, countries with little if any democratic development: Cameroon, Gabon, and Togo. The third panel group consists of countries that as of June 2003 had concluded only two successive elections but have scheduled third elections (last three columns of Table 12). Many of the countries in this third panel group are the relatively problematic latecomers or countries that have experienced breakdowns: Central African Republic, Chad, Equatorial Guinea, Ethiopia, Gambia, Guinea, Malawi, Nigeria, Sudan, and Swaziland. A few are beginners, yet to become more experienced, such as South Africa, Mozambique, Tanzania, and Uganda. Comparisons within each panel group provide generalizations about each group. Comparisons between groups tell us if and how the groups resemble or differ from each other and therefore if the analysis presented so far is valid for all countries or not.

Looking at the results in Table 12, two striking general observations can be made. First, the group with the longest record of elections has always had the better quality of elections. On average, their first three elections show a higher degree of democratic qualities than the two less experienced groups' corresponding elections. In rank, the middle group of countries in number of elections also occupies the middle position in terms of electoral democratic qualities, while the least experienced group's elections have the least frequent democratic qualities. This first overall observation seems to suggest that a selection bias indeed has played a part in the results discovered so far. However, the second observation corrects that: There is a trend towards a steady improvement that is similar for all three panels. While the groups started off differently—latecomers being less benign—the self-reinforcing power of elections seems to be a general phenomenon. When we compare the changes recorded from first to second to third elections among these three panel groups, both the direction of change and the magnitude of the changes are analogous across panels on almost all of the indicators.

Looking first at the bottom of Table 12, the frequency of free and fair elections among the latecomers—the last panel group—is generally lower than in the two other groups, but it improves according to the same pattern. Among the first and most experienced group, 58 percent of the first elections were free and fair, while

TABLE 12 *A panel-group, time-series comparison of elections in Africa*

		Countries with a Record of											
		4+ Elections					3 Elections				2 Elections		
Dimension	Indicator	First	Second	Third	Fourth+	All	First	Second	Third	All	First	Second	All
Participation	Voter turnout	52%	52%	55%	59%	55%	58%	62%	62%	61%	66%	72%	68%
	St. dev.	(22.7)	(24.6)	(16.6)	(16.5)	(19.3)	(19.4)	(12.8)	(11.3)	(15.2)	(15.0)	(13.9)	(14.6)
	N	10	12	12	21	55	28	27	18	73	29	25	56
	Full opposition participation	50%	75%	75%	91%	75%	68%	67%	84%	72%	52%	78%	65%
	N	6	9	9	19	43	19	18	16	53	16	21	39
	Autocrats gone	33%	33%	33%	52%	40%	0%	15%	16%	10%	3%	0%	2%
	N	4	4	4	11	23	–	4	3	7	1	–	1
Competition	Winner's % of votes	61%	67%	48%	46%	55%	62%	69%	48%	62%	58%	63%	60%
	St. dev.	(21.9)	(23.5)	(16.2)	(9.6)	(20.2)	(19.7)	(16.7)	(12.0)	(18.6)	(16.7)	(15.2)	(15.5)
	N	5	5	5	4	19	14	13	6	33	12	12	25
	Largest party's % of seats	56%	68%	65%	66%	64%	67%	72%	65%	68%	59%	68%	63%
	St. dev.	(23.3)	(25.9)	(27.1)	(19.1)	(22.0)	(18.2)	(18.3)	(17.6)	(17.8)	(16.3)	(21.2)	(18.9)
	N	7	6	7	17	37	14	14	13	41	15	14	30
	2nd party's % of seats	14%	8%	9%	13%	12%	13%	9%	14%	12%	18%	13%	15%
	St. dev.	(11.6)	(7.6)	(9.5)	(10.9)	(10.3)	(13.6)	(13.2)	(16.3)	(14.3)	(12.5)	(15.1)	(13.6)
	N	7	6	7	17	37	14	14	13	41	14	14	29
	Turnover of power	25%	0%	25%	24%	19%	21%	7%	21%	16%	10%	0%	5%
	N	3	–	3	5	11	6	2	4	12	3	–	3
Legitimacy	Losers accept	60%	17%	42%	62%	47%	36%	37%	47%	39%	13%	11%	15%
	N	6	2	5	13	26	10	10	9	29	4	3	9
	Peaceful process	25%	25%	25%	43%	33%	18%	37%	42%	31%	7%	22%	13%
	N	3	3	3	9	18	5	10	8	23	2	6	8
	Regime survival	100%	100%	100%	100%	100%	96%	96%	100%	97%	87%	93%	87%
	N	12	12	12	21	57	27	26	19	72	27	25	52
	Free and fair	58%	50%	50%	86%	65%	50%	48%	68%	54%	36%	44%	42%
	N	7	6	6	18	37	14	13	13	40	11	12	25
	Total elections	12	12	12	21	57	28	27	19	74	31	27	60

the corresponding figure for the middle panel was 50 percent and was only 36 percent for the last panel. However, over second and third and fourth elections, all
groups improved, and signs are that the latecomers will continue to follow that trend
and eventually catch up with the others. The N is lower than in all the previous
analyses, so care should be taken in judging the magnitude of these differences, but
the direction of the trajectory is suggestive.

With regard to participation, the two most important of our three indicators, voter
turnout and opposition participation, show very similar trends over the three panel
groups. Turnout levels were actually noticeably higher in first elections among the
latecomers (66 percent) than in the other two, more experienced groups (58 and 52
percent respectively). Over subsequent elections, popular participation improved
significantly in each panel group. Opposition participation is similar across the three
panel groups as well, reaching full participation in 67 to 78 percent of all elections
already by the second electoral cycle. We also note that, even though the last panel
group started elections with a much lower participation figure than the middle panel
group, the figure is practically the same as the most proven group's corresponding
figure. With second elections, the last panel's opposition participation improved
faster than the middle groups' and apace with the most advanced group. Only the
deposition of authoritarians in leading positions seems to improve less between first
and second elections in the last panel group, but, as mentioned earlier, this ambiguous measure may not necessarily indicate a democratic quality, which makes
the reported figures less of a concern.

The four indicators of the second democratic quality of elections, competition,
also show a similar pattern across the three panel groups. The winner's share of votes
in executive elections hovered around 60 percent in the first elections, climbed on
average five to seven percentage points in second elections, but decreased by almost
20 percentage points in third elections, meaning that these elections were highly
competitive affairs. It seems that the two trends of incumbents staying for two terms
and voters being patient with new leaders, discussed above, were indeed general developments across different groups of countries in Africa. Largest parliamentary parties' shares of seats follow the same pattern, although—for the reasons discussed in
the foregoing analysis—the share of seats tends to indicate less competition in the
legislative elections. The second largest party's relative weakness is also general
across the panels. The main opposition party tends to gain significantly less than 20
percent of seats in parliament. The African voter does not like losers, perhaps, and
the electoral system in many countries allocates seats highly disproportionately.
These three indicators show a wavelike pattern: the competitiveness of first elections

is reasonable, decreasing with second elections, only to improve appreciably with third elections.

A worrying sign about the latecomers in the last panel group is the rate of turnovers. Alternations in power happened in only 10 percent of their first elections, while the corresponding figures for the other two groups were 21 and 25 percent. A decrease in turnovers with the second election is common to all, however, as is a rebound of turnovers in third elections in the two groups that held them. If we can assume that the latecomers will follow the same pattern on this indicator as with the others, rates will pick up in their cases too, and the democratic quality of elections will improve in this respect also.

On legitimacy, we find the only really significant deviation of the last panel group. Losing parties' and candidates' acceptance of first election results is on average much lower than in the other two panel groups and the acceptance figure does not rise in second elections. Looking more closely at the figures for the other two panels, we might not expect an increase until third or fourth elections, however. In the second panel group, the figures for first and second elections display almost exactly the same level of losers' acceptance, at 36 and 37 percent, respectively. For the first panel group, with the supposedly good cases, the average rate of acceptance was 60 percent in first elections, a mere 17 percent in second elections, and slowly climbed up again, with 47 percent in third and 62 percent in fourth and later elections. Apparently, on this indicator there is no general trend among countries in Africa. Losers' acceptance is a contentious issue, with significant ramifications, and one we should continue to follow.

The peacefulness of the electoral process and the survival rates of the electoral regimes show highly similar levels and trends across the panels. It is regrettable that even by third and fourth elections not even half of the elections are entirely peaceful, but slowly, at great pains, elections are becoming more and more peaceful in Africa. This is still an area where much work will have to be done, though, in order to realize the quality of electoral legitimacy. Regime survival rates are better and seem to indicate, as discussed at some length above, that already after second elections, the survival of the electoral regime is relatively safe.

Zambia's political development over the 1990s illustrates how hard it is to stop the forces of pluralism and prodemocratic incentives once they have arrived in a country. After the first elections, in 1991, which overturned the incumbent, Kenneth Kaunda, opposition leader Fredrick Chiluba took over and tried to turn Zambian politics back to a kind of electoral authoritarianism. By 1993, there was a mass exodus from Chiluba's Movement for Multiparty Democracy (MMD) party, as leaders,

MPs, and ministers who now had a stake in appearing to be democrats left. If Chiluba had been allowed to recreate authoritarian rule, these individuals' power and careers would have been at the mercy of an autocrat. In the more democratic arrangement, they had their own power bases. A struggle ensued between the major political actors about the rules of the game, and the 1996 elections were widely discredited. In 2001, Chiluba's successor in the MMD, Levy Mwanawasa, managed to win the elections by a small margin only after making many concessions to other actors. To respect and reinforce the rules of the game was suddenly in the interest of the powerful actors, who were building their future political careers on an electoral foundation. They put strong pressures on President Mwanawasa. Meanwhile, Chiluba was charged with corruption and misuse of power, and under heavy pressure from many sources with prodemocratic incentives Zambia has regained much of its lost democratic qualities.

This exemplifies how *de jure* participatory, competitive, and legitimate elections provide an arena for political struggles that gives even dubious actors incentives to act for rather than against further democratization. They also create new actors and remold old configurations that can serve to strengthen, deepen, and broaden a democratization process. Even within old authoritarian parties, individuals who achieve strong electoral support assert their own new power base. Such individuals are important to the process, because they reduce the incumbent party's need to engage in potentially costly fraudulent practices. Even nondemocratic MPs develop vested interests in the continuation of electoral cycles as long as they stand a chance of winning. In the best of circumstances, such efforts produce spirals of mutual checks, forcing nondemocrats to produce more democracy in the battle to keep their own position. If others cheat and by doing so decrease your chances of winning parliamentary seats, you would naturally try to unravel their efforts, to eliminate competition. All actors will be likely to act similarly and to realize that others are doing so, increasing the cost of indulging in fraud, since the risk of being detected grows. When these power-seeking individuals are within incumbent and authoritarian parties, they promote democratic rules of the game versus an intrusive executive, because that increases their own political leverage and furthers their personal ambitions. Thus, by annexing and reworking old rules, these actors become the forces of change and transformation as they adapt to democratic institutions.

The less experienced countries in the last panel group, queued to hold third elections next, seem likely to follow in the footsteps of the more experienced countries towards more democratic elections. Although Jammeh in Gambia came to power with the power of the gun, he seems to be willing to step down when the time comes.

In Mozambique, Malawi, and Uganda the prospects of peaceful and legitimate alternations in power via the ballot box in upcoming third elections are also good. In Namibia, South Africa, and Tanzania, it seems unlikely that the opposition can win, but it seems equally unlikely that the democratic qualities of elections there should deteriorate, although that could happen on the island of Zanzibar. More than half—seven out of thirteen—of the countries in this panel group seem to have relatively good prospects of succeeding in third elections.

Guinea and Ethiopia are less encouraging cases in this group. While Guinea raised hopes among observers, being one of the earliest countries to hold a referendum on a new constitution, its referendum, in 1990, led to a transitional authority—the Transitional Committee of National Recovery—which decided on a rapid return to multiparty politics, in 1992. Subsequent developments have been disappointing, however. The first presidential elections, held in December 1993, were not free and fair; the second ones, in December 1998, were marked by increasing violence, arrests of opposition leaders, abolition of the electoral commission, and widespread fraud. The second legislative elections, held in June 2002, were two years late and essentially meaningless.

Ethiopia's record of accomplishments is hardly much better, although it looked not too bad at the beginning. After the Tigre-based insurgents forced government forces loyal to President Mengistu's regime to surrender and Mengistu fled to Zimbabwe on 21 May 1991, another period of less-than-democratic rule began. The new president, Meles Zenawi, first headed the temporary administration set up after the Ethiopian People's Revolutionary Democratic Front's (EPRDF) victory. The administration organized a conference to form a transitional government and held local elections a year after the military victory, on 21 June 1992. Although international observers noted significant problems in the vast and mostly rural country, the elections were seen as a satisfactory beginning. A constitution-drafting committee was set up in March 1993 and Eritrea seceded and became independent shortly thereafter, on 24 May 1993. Somewhat better elections, even if boycotted by some opposition groups, were held on 5 June 1994 for a constituent assembly, who approved the new constitution in December of the same year. So far, things had developed reasonably well, albeit gradually. But the first "real" elections, to the Yehizbtewekayoch Mekir Bet—Council of People's Representatives, the lower house of parliament—on 7 May 1995, were boycotted by nearly all the opposition parties, who rejected the outcome. The EPRDF collected 88 percent of the seats; their allies added another 10.5 percent. The second elections, in May 2000, were not much different, even though some of the real opposition parties participated. International observers were not allowed to monitor the elections, and there was plenty of evidence of intimidation, violence, and vote rigging. In the end, the opposition groups managed to secure 15 percent of the 540 seats, but there is not much to suggest that holding elections has improved the state of democracy in Ethiopia.

With enough pressure from South Africa, Swaziland may leave the power of King Mswati III behind. Chad, Equatorial Guinea, and Sudan look like they will be the hardest nuts for democracy to crack. Chad's president, Idriss Déby, has shown little patience with calls for further liberalization that would allow for *de facto* competitive elections. Equatorial Guinea is still ruled by President Teodoro Nguema's harsh regime based on an economy of coffee, timber, and cocoa. Elections there have been mockeries of the democratic process, and even mild criticism of the president and his rule is not allowed. These contradictory cases notwithstanding, the majority of countries that continue the process of holding regular elections have exemplified the self-reinforcing, self-improving power of these institutions.

Finally, a few words are appropriate about the countries that were excluded from the panel-group comparison because they had not yet held first or second elections. In some of them, the situation is not promising. The island nation Comoros, during recent years a federal state, has been plagued by conflicts among the heads of the various "national" governments of the three units of the federation. In the past, Comoros experienced several coups in which mercenaries were involved, and its distant location and relative unimportance to the international community reduce the external pressure to change. Similarly, the Republic of Congo is devoid of clearly prodemocratic leaders and has been haunted by mercenaries, guerillas, and factions within the so-called national army. In 2002, President Denis Sassou-Nguesso manufactured second first elections, in an attempt to give his authoritarian rule legitimacy. As for Burundi, at the time of writing it remains doubtful that the many political actors there will stick to the recent peace and reconciliation accord and go through with a return to multiparty politics, but if they do and the international community lives up to its promises of support, the situation might well improve quickly.

In Guinea-Bissau, a second first election, in November 1999, brought Kumba Yalla into power after General Mane had ousted the winner of the 1994 first election, President Joao B. Vieira. President Yalla was in turn overthrown, in September 2003. More encouraging for democracy are conditions in Angola after the death of guerilla and opposition leader Jonas Savimbi. Liberia experienced another civil war, in which the longtime authoritarian ruler Charles Taylor was defeated and departed to Nigeria, and it has since been relatively stable. In Sierra Leone, the process of holding elections is back on track, heavily supported by the United Nations and bi-lateral donors, and many efforts have been made at transferring best practices from other countries, such as South Africa's on reconciliation and Ghana's on election management. So far, these efforts have paid off. Niger's third first election, held in October 1999 after the coup in April of that year, ushered into power Mamadou Tandja of the National Movement for a Developing Society (MNSD). Niger is try-ing a new semipresidential system, employing a revised proportional representation formula that reduces the number of parties in parliament to five (from what would have been nine if the electoral system had not been revised). Hence, it appears from current evidence that at least half of the countries excluded from the panel-group comparison have reasonable prospects of mounting increasingly democratic elec-tions.

CONCLUSIONS

Taken together, the two types of analysis pursued in this chapter corroborate the hypothesis about the self-reinforcing power of repetitive elections, and at the same time qualify it. In one way, there is obviously no singular African experience with re-gards to elections and democratization. If one wished to emphasize the distinguish-ing features of various countries, those would not be hard to find. There is a world of difference between Botswana's unbroken adherence to democratic elections and its unity since 1969 compared to neighbors such as Swaziland, with its few and fraud-ulent electoral experiments under monarchical rule or Mozambique's emergence from a long and malicious civil war to hold managed but relatively peaceful elec-tions or Zimbabwe's degeneration into chaos, unabashed despotic rule, and defiance towards its many friends turned staunch critics. Similarly, one may ask what Ghana's successful transition over three electoral cycles has in common with its fellow West African countries: the continuation of severely constrained electoral authoritarian-ism in Togo, the repetitive military coups in Niger, and the civil war and failing at-tempts at first elections in Sierra Leone.

While acknowledging the disparities of these and other unique experiences, this study shows that across the many cases a similar development is nevertheless taking place in a large majority of countries whereby the democratic qualities of elections are improving with experience and with increasing institutionalization. Even very early in African electoral regimes, an uninterrupted series of *de jure* participatory and competitive elections has led to identifiably higher levels of democratic qualities. Since elections constitute a core characteristic of modern representative democracy, democratization is apparently being both reinforced and improved simply by the holding of a series of elections.

The evidence of this self-reinforcing power of elections is not trivial, particularly given the prevalence of Afro-pessimistic arguments that tend to degrade the value of elections. Such arguments typically build on a belief that authoritarian rulers who orchestrate fake competitive elections successfully subvert the drive towards democracy by making outside donors and intellectuals mistake them for real democracies. This has undoubtedly been true in a few cases but it is much more common that such rulers fail in these aims, if indeed they have them. It also remains to be shown that the international community is actually being bamboozled by such charades, something I find hard to believe. The typical scenario is that the repetition of electoral cycles more often than not leads to a further deterioration of authoritarian traits. According to the evidence, rather than an enduring autocratic guard perverting the electoral institutions, the incentives and pressures of the new political processes take on their own power, forcing the autocrats to behave increasingly democratically.

It is impossible for us to get inside the heads of the leaders in Africa, new and old, who have previously served in authoritarian regimes; we know little of what the Kufours, Kibakis, Soglos, Muluzis, and so on would have wanted to do if there had been no restrictions on their behavior. We do know that Fredrick Chiluba, after being democratically elected, did what he could to make Zambia's political arena suit his own personal interests and those of his entourage but that he had little success at it. We know that in many other cases the "new" rulers have sought to alter term limits to allow for renewed neopatrimonial rule in democratic disguise.

The rules of the electoral game are tested, strained, and sometimes broken. By testing the rules, and even by breaking them, actors learn about these rules and decide whether to agree and play by them or not. In this sense, the findings described in this chapter also corroborate Rustow's (1970, 345) hypothesis that establishing institutions of democracy can foster democrats. It might even be possible to trick, lure, or cajole nondemocrats into democratic behavior. The outcomes of these processes are recorded—incompletely, for sure—in the data presented here. The implication is that elites do not necessarily have to be convinced democrats at the beginning of a democratization process, that institutions can create prodemocratic behavior, which in time may turn into democratic beliefs. If indeed elections lead to better performance of essential democratic institutions as well as better performance of elites, it would seem that elections, in and of themselves, are a worthwhile exercise.

On the other hand, there are obvious differences among the African countries. The panel-group comparison confirms that the generation of "latecomer" electoral regimes in Africa started off from a much less promising position. First elections in this group were generally less democratic than such elections among the earlier generations. Even if the recent beginners replicate the trend towards better quality, the trend is so far less pronounced and has yet to produce the same degree of improvements in democratic qualities. But regardless of the starting point, the trend is towards elections that are more democratic. The teleology in this conclusion is not theoretical or methodological, but only empirical.

CHAPTER FIVE

The Causal Effects of Elections

Chapters 3 and 4 reaffirmed Dahl's (1989) assertion that electoral rights cannot be reduced to "mere procedures" and argued that the repetitive exercise of the formal procedures and practices of electoral cycles fosters the realization of political rights: increased political participation, more intense competition, and deepening legitimacy of the idea of self-government. The analysis of elections as a partial regime in the previous two chapters largely ignored democracy in its broader sense. The approach was appropriate, given the research objectives, the existing hypotheses in the field, and the democratic qualities of elections as an important, legitimate, and interesting subject in itself. Do elections spur democratic gains outside of the electoral context? Do repetitive elections facilitate, or even generate, democratic qualities in society, or are they at best reflections of democracy, as the bulk of the literature on democratic transitions would have it? This chapter evaluates the effects of elections in society, probing the ability of elections to institute, broaden, and deepen democracy beyond the political arena and the political system as such. The overall hypothesis tested here is that the longer an uninterrupted series of elections a country has, the more its society will become imbued with democratic qualities. It is also hypothesized that increases in democratic qualities are the effects of holding elections. As a general idea to be précised in this chapter, we will assume that societal democratic qualities are evidenced when people behave democratically towards their fellow citizens, expect such behavior from them and from social actors and institutions, and there is a general respect for democratic behavior.

The chapter is divided into three main sections. The first is concerned with defining and operationalizing the dependent variable, the level of democratic qualities in society; the second revisits the scant literature on democratization, drawing links in terms of the causal effects of elections on the level of democracy; and the third deductively develops a framework of seven causal links detailing how the holding and repetition of elections can cause increased democratic qualities in society. While the links drawn cannot be tested one by one because of a lack of data and inadequate model precision, five contradicting hypotheses are formulated. Testing these is a relatively efficient way to find out if the essence of the causal links is corroborated. The actual testing, by way of five alternative appraisals, is carried out in Chapter 6.

DEMOCRATIC QUALITIES IN SOCIETY

An analysis of the impact of elections on societal democratization calls for the construction of a reasonably valid measure of degrees of democracy as, first, an attribute of society and, second, as sufficiently independent of electoral procedures to avoid meaningless tautology. Since democracy as discussed in Chapter 2 is more than just elections, democratization can be conceptualized as also consisting partly of an increase in democratic qualities beyond the political system. In Chapter 2 I argued that equality of political participation was based on a legally equal distribution of sovereign freedoms for citizens, translated into voting rights and freedom to form political parties and the ability to contest elections and to compete for power. To ensure and facilitate citizens' active participation in self-government outside of electoral processes, there must be freedom of assembly and demonstration, open public discussion, and the right to form and join civic organizations including trade unions and professional organizations, in short, civil liberties. The more these civil liberties are realized, the greater the democratic quality of participation in the society.

In Chapter 2 I also argued the importance of the right to choose among alternatives in a competitive electoral arena. For free competition to be realized in the social sphere, there must be personal autonomy and economic rights that provide the foundations for independent alternatives. Freedom from indoctrination and from excessive dependence on the state are necessary to guarantee the autonomy of the social sphere, protection of private property rights, the autonomy of organizations and individuals, legal gender equality, and educational and professional opportunities to make competition and alternatives available and fairer. In addition, basic institutions of the rule of law are needed, to ensure personal autonomy and economic rights, an independent judiciary, equality under the law, and protection of the citizenry from terror and torture. The legitimacy of self-government is manifested within society by actual intrasocietal acceptance in associational life, through genuine free public and private dialogues, peaceful alternation as dominant advocates, and the absence of insurgencies. The indicators of democratic qualities in society used in this analysis may be summarized as:

- participation—rights of assembly, to form and join civil society organizations, and of open public discussion;
- competition—personal autonomy and economic rights, freedom from excessive dependence, and gender, educational, and professional equality; and
- legitimacy—intrasocial acceptance and peaceful coexistence of organizations, and absence of insurgencies.

Analyses of the political sphere often deemphasize these aspects of civil liberties and democratic qualities, because the social sphere is relatively independent of electoral procedures and formal political rights. We can capitalize on that independence, however, in evaluating the relationship we are interested in. Although there are no perfect indicators of democracy in the social sphere, Freedom House has been ranking levels of civil liberties globally since 1972 in its civil liberties (CL) index. Preferred by most researchers, Freedom House's classification system is based on 15 criteria,[1] including all the civil liberties mentioned above, as dimensions of democratic qualities in society. The Freedom House index is also suitable for the current purpose because it measures the realization of liberties "on the ground" rather than just their legal existence and because it is the best available measure of democratic aspects distinct from elections. It is regregable that Freedom House does not provide the score for each indicator but only a composite measure with just one value. One would have liked more independent indicators; one for each democratic quality. This lack has restricted the sophistication of the assessment of the main hypothesis and the causal links that is performed in the next chapter. Freedom House's methodology also makes determining how the 15 indicators combine into the single values difficult. We are provided an aggregation of scores for each country that translates into the 1-to-7 scale on which (counterintuitively) 7 represents the worst state of affairs and 1 the best. Their use of panels of experts to rate different countries introduces the risk of subjectivity, and assessment of this risk is impossible because checklist responses are not available. Also not made available are the scores on distinct indicators, how these are weighted, and by which rule they are aggregated. With regard to whether cases from all over the world have been treated equally in the process, we can be almost certain that there are variations due to differences in information, distortion, and personality of the involved researchers, and we would have welcomed the opportunity to test for such biases. The nonavailability of the raw data from Freedom House and our ignorance of both formal coding and aggregation rules are the most severe liabilities of the index (cf. McHenry 2000, Munck and Verkuilen

2002). Yet, among the alternatives, this is the index most widely accepted as matching empirical realities. It is also the only index with annual scores over the period studied that relatively independently measures the sphere outside of electoral practices. Even though there are several measures of democracy used in the literature, for our purposes Freedom House's CL measure does the best job of capturing a dimension of democracy distinct from election-related phenomena. (For more information on the Freedom House index, see Appendix 3.)

The alternatives indexes also have methodological limitations. The Polity IV index of democracy (Marshall and Jaggers 2001) builds on four indicators, measuring only aspects of political competition and constraints on the chief executive.[2] This index does not provide information on distinctly nonelection-related aspects; even if it did, it is meant for long-term major shifts in the nature of polities around the world and cannot be used for finer gradations of democracy and it lacks a measure of participation. The Polity IV index provides dimensional data but does not present data on the empirical bases for the values assigned to the dimensions (cf. McHenry 2000, 169; Munck and Verkuilen 2002). Much the same criticism applies to Vanhanen's (1997) composite measure based on two indicators: voter turnout and the smaller parties' shares of the votes, which is too narrow to provide a good reflection of the empirical differentiation in the field (cf. Moore 1995) and is more suitable for identifying the "big picture" over the long period (1850–1993) that it surveys. Vanhanen does not provide a theoretical justification for the inferences he makes from the objective measures. The scale he constructs is built entirely of election data, rendering it inappropriate for use in this case. Several other measures provide data only for a year (e.g., Arat 1988, Bollen 1979, Coppedge and Reinicke 1990, Hadenius 1992). All of these measures focus on political democracy understood as one version or the other of polyarchy and are in effect too closely tied to electoral procedures, their character, and results to be suitable for the present purpose; the distinction between independent and dependent variables would collapse.[3] Having a measure for only one year precludes the necessary time-series analysis that assesses the causal direction and effect over several electoral cycles.

The Freedom House CL index provides the only cross-national and time-series measure of democratic liberties outside of the political system. It will therefore be used as the indicator of the dependent variable: the level of democratic qualities in society. Freedom House also produces a political rights (PR) score, and some readers will probably object that it and the CL score are closely related and that there is a tendency for one set of rankings to pull the other in the same direction. True also in Africa, the two indices are empirically closely related such that their correlations typically hover around .850 (Pearson's correlation coefficient). One must remember,

however, that merely holding an election does not boost the PR scores and if an election of poor quality is held it will, to the contrary, result in a lower rating on the PR
scale. Perhaps particularly in Africa there are numerous examples of elections associated with no change in the PR scores or even a lowering of the PR ranking. As specified below, elections are investigated here as a causal factor regardless of their quality; hence, the effect should be independent of the PR scale and its possible spillover
effects.

A MISSING FACTOR OF DEMOCRATIZATION

Hypothesizing a relationship between independent and dependent factors ought
to be framed by a theory of causal links,[4] to avoid unabashed empiricism. While it
is impossible to conceive of representative democracy without elections (Clark 2000,
Zakaria 1997), Karatnycky (1999, 116) notes that "the emergence of electoral democracies has been the best indicator of subsequent progress in the areas of civil liberties and human rights." This is exactly the kind of thinking the analysis in Chapter
4 provoked and the issue we are interested in here. The overall relationship discussed
here is displayed in Figure 4.

Revisiting the central tenets of some of the most influential democratization theories, we find that elections as a causal factor, in the way displayed in Figure 4, are
largely ignored in the third wave of democratization literature. O'Donnell and

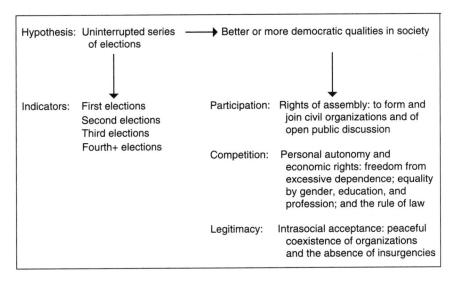

Fig. 4. Main hypothesis of overall relationship between elections and democratization

Schmitter's (1986) *Transitions from Authoritarian Rule* quickly became the most referenced work on transitions to democracy. Defined by the Latin American experience, their approach was for long the orthodoxy, positing "founding" elections as the hallmark of a successfully completed process of deposing an authoritarian regime and installing a democratic dispensation.

In the ensuing theoretical and empirical work, aspects like number of elections, voter turnout, competitiveness, and turnovers have been used in analyzing the degree or process of democratization (e.g., Barkan 2000, Herbst 2001, van de Walle 2001), the level or quality of democracy (e.g., Altman and Pérez-Linán 2002; Foweraker and Landmann 2002; Vanhanen 1997), and the consolidation of democracy (e.g., Fomunyoh 2001; Diamond 1999; Huntington 1991). Elections viewed in these ways have little to do with transition processes except as an indicator of its successful completion. This kind of approach was also adopted in works, for example, by Diamond (1993, 1996), Diamond and Plattner (1999), Günther, Diamandouros, and Puhle (1995), and Valenzuela (1992). The influential volume by Linz and Stepan (1996) even uses the date of the first election as the day when the transition process ended. Bratton and van de Walle (1997, 195) imported this use of "founding" elections to their analysis of African politics. The "democratic experiments" in Africa were deemed successful once a new regime was installed through free and fair elections in which the opposition participated and accepted the results. Even though these criteria make theoretical sense, they focus exclusively on first, or so-called founding, elections and make no argument about causal effects of elections.

Assuming, then, that a democratic regime had been installed, scholars proceeded to the issue of regime survival or consolidation of these fragile new regimes. With this came the subdiscipline of "consolidology" and the upsurge of democratic consolidation concepts in comparative politics (see Munck 2001b). Consolidation was originally identified by O'Donnell (1992) as an insulation against erosion or slow death of democracy that eventually leads to a *democradura*. These analyses were largely accepted as providing answers to the vital question of when new democracies can be said to have survived the threats of democratic breakdown.[5] Or, as Di Palma (1990, 141) put it, "at what point . . . can democrats relax?" In Linz's (1990) classic formulation, consolidation is generally depicted with the "only game in town" metaphor focusing on attitudes and behavior. Yet, arguments about the effects of electoral cycles on these processes are conspicuously absent, and with its increased popularity, little care was taken to conserve the integrity of the concept of consolidation. The original analytical meaning of regime stabilization was stretched and redefined to cover a panoply of problems found throughout young democracies in the "third wave." Schedler (1998, 96–101) argues that conceptual confusion can be avoided by clarifying different usages of the same term, yet in none of the five uses of *consolidation* that he identifies in the literature do elections play a part other than to signify the genesis or completion of consolidation.[6]

A recurrent methodological problem with consolidation studies is the presumption that factors generating democratic stability are also causal in reproducing it. But this notion of constant and linear causal effects cannot be taken for granted. A second problem is that making predictive inferences necessitates a set of rules—the causal assumptions—that enables extrapolation from the past and present to the future (King, Keohane, and Verba 1994; Munck and Verkuilen 2002; Schedler 2001a). The strategy in consolidation studies is typically to define consolidation as expected regime endurance, then deductively introduce assumptions about which factors cause and sustain democratic stability. Citizens' attitudes and beliefs and/or an active civil society are typically presented as the main causal factor(s). However, since consolidation as an argument based on prospective reasoning cannot be measured directly, high values on the posited causal factors are often used as indicators of consolidation.[7] Rather than debate the soundness of these approaches, we note that consolidation studies have not modeled elections as a factor endowed with causal or even facilitating qualities. At best, they have treated elections as indicators of consolidation, as in Huntington's (1991) use of two alternations in power after successful completion of first elections—the "two-turnover test."

Nevertheless, an important contribution of consolidation studies is the blurring of boundaries between transition and the supposed consolidation and the awareness that a transition to democracy is not necessarily over with the "founding" election (e.g., Schedler 2001b). Among Africanists, Bratton (1998), for example, observed that transition processes in Africa were often not over even with second elections. Young (1999) and van de Walle (2002) have also contributed in this regard. This qualification has unfortunately led some theorists (e.g., Herbst 2000a, 253ff.) to assert that elections have no role in democratization and are of no use as indicators of a country's process of democratization.

A few contributors should be noted. Schedler's (2002b) work on electoral routes to democracy is concerned with "nested two-level games" involving the strategic dilemmas of actors in contexts of structural ambivalence during transitions. His is an ambitious agenda leading into a complex, multidimensional, and interactive causal nexus. The strategy here is slightly different, with a focus on the ability of repetitive elections to cause an increase in the level of democracy in society. This is a hypothesis about a one-directional relationship, and it will be theorized as such, even though we suspect reality to be much messier than that. The whole point is to find out just how much influence the power of elections has.

One of the few analyses specifying a causal association between elections and de-mocratization is Seligson and Booth's (1995, 269–271) study of six nations in Central America. Their inductive inquiry posits that more elections promoted democracy in a couple of ways. By opening up the political space for citizens, elections enabled people to mobilize and pursue their interests, petition government and local au-thorities, obtain and exchange information, and in effect have expanded civil liber-ties. In addition, over a few electoral cycles, the initial mistrust between actors di-minished among elites in the six countries. While the first is clearly relevant and will be used to inform the framework below, Seligson and Booth's latter causal mecha-nism of an intra-elite argument does not suggest a direct causal effect on the demo-cratic qualities in society. Similarly, Eisenstadt's (2004) detailed study of the pro-tracted Mexican transition over its 27-year period provides an argument about indirect, rather than direct effects of repetitive elections. Nevertheless, the implica-tion of one of the main findings is crucial for the present study. In the incremental Mexican transition under an electoral authoritarian regime, election periods pro-vided the main locus for further democratization. The repetition of elections made further gains possible by inspiring actors to use electoral processes as the main plat-form for challenging the ruling regime, and actors from both political and civil so-ciety worked to increase civil liberties in Mexican society. This causal link may have a more general application, and that is developed further in the next section.

Bratton and van de Walle (1997, 222–224) use the significance of holding elections in the past to explain developments in the early 1990s in Africa. Their focus on dem-ocratic traditions in terms of previous experiences opens the discussion up for the possibility of elections' playing a role during the transition period. But, they did not develop a hypothesis that current elections are playing such a role, only that expo-sure to electoral institutions in the past predisposed countries to a more democratic trajectory in the 1990s. The authors envisaged elections both as a proxy for political participation (1997, 140) and as a cause of it, in terms of more frequent popular protests (1997, 143–144), particularly in one-party regimes. Bratton and van de Walle suggest something similar to what is developed below—expressed here in my words, not theirs—that the institutional framework that bestowed rights (even if strictly lim-ited) of participation and the practice of participatory and to some extent competi-tive political processes empowered ordinary citizens by experiential learning to de-mand more democracy when the time was ripe. The issue of historical legacies is a related subject but distinct from investigating if and how societal democratization is furthered directly by holding elections in the present. Yet, I bring along the acknowl-edgment of the reasoning by Bratton and van de Walle.

Another long-time student of African politics has noted that current elections can contribute to democratization. Barkan (1998, 39) suggests that Kenya's second elections, in 1997, reinvigorated civil society there as a result of the struggle for constitutional reform. A coalition of churches and human rights nongovernmental organizations, together with opposition parties, assumed a "decisive role in advancing democratization during, and especially following, the elections" (Barkan 1998, 41). Nevertheless, it is also obvious from the Kenyan case that the preelection period can be used by incumbents to clamp down on opposition, the media, and civil society, thereby reducing the levels and degree of democracy in society. Yet, looking at six African nations, Barkan (2000) concluded that the preparations for and holding of elections often gave rise to increased room to maneuver for actors, even when the elections were flawed. The space for civil society and the media thus increases, and a gain made in the political arena is often used to increase more freedom in the social sphere. This is certainly one possible linkage meriting further elaboration. This analysis also contradicts the old thinking that democracy has to await a certain level of development or societal modernization, a contradiction suggested also by Hadenius (2001, 83–87) in his conclusion that it is usually better to initiate pluralistic politics sooner. His is another version of the socialization and learning argument detailed below, that institutions of multipartyism even if not perfect independently stimulate development of peaceful conflict-solution skills and organizational capacity among political groups, thus furthering democratic citizenship.

In conclusion, neither the dominant theories of democratization nor those depicting consolidation of democracy have promoted elections as a causal factor in the democratization process. Although the importance of elections in furthering democratization seems to have a powerful grip on the international community, there are only a few theoretical suggestions to that effect in the literature to build on. This makes theory building more difficult, because the terrain is relatively unknown, but it is therefore also less demanding in terms of sophistication.

HYPOTHESES AND CAUSAL LINKS

From our point of departure — that it is the unbroken series of elections that seems to matter the most — it is not far to the idea that reiteration under a stable set of rules prompts actors to make different rational calculations than they would make for a one-shot occasion. Repetitive elections in newly democratizing countries may be similar to the classic "prisoners' dilemma" game, in which actors have incentives to engage in noncooperative behavior for short-term gains but adopt cooperative strategies when the game is likely to be repeated or prolonged indefinitely. The literature on game theory highlights the rationale for tit-for-tat cooperative strategies as the best possible norm of behavior (Axelrod 1984, Taylor 1987, Tsebelis 1990), the point being that the logic of action changes when the game is repeated. Recurring elections can perhaps be interpreted in this light. Actors learn the rules through experience, and their calculations change once they realize that the process is continuous. Stability of the rules of the game—whether it be perceived or real—causes the behavior of the actors to change because their rational calculations are based on different circumstances than they would be if it were a one-shot game, just as the incumbent MPs and candidates in electoral races force more democratic behavior upon each other in pursuit of their rational self-interest to get reelected.

To really investigate the applicability of such models to what is happening in contemporary Africa, one would need to closely inspect such processes and collect a wealth of data on individuals' responses and reasoning to changing conditions of politics, a very difficult but not impossible task. While case study–based process tracing cannot be pursued here, we can still take the reiterated game as a point of departure. Such a view of democratic transitions comes with seeing that the transition period involves several elections and constitutes a theoretical departure from the dominant theories of democratization (e.g., Collier and Adcock 1999, Diamond 1999, Linz and Stepan 1996, O'Donnell and Schmitter 1986, cf. Munck 2001b, 126). Following this approach, constitutive rules are crucial for the outcome because they condition the vested interests of those involved.[8] In chess, the constitutive rules defining the board and the roles of the chessmen cannot be changed, or it is no longer chess. If players reach a mutual understanding, certain rules can be altered; this is done in teaching new players, for whom rules are relaxed, while experienced players often add constraints, like time limits. In the end, frequent playing of the game makes chess players bent on winning the contest rather than questioning and testing the rules. This could perhaps explain the metamorphosis of many previous African autocrats into proponents of democratic elections. Creating electoral institutions reconstitutes actors and some of their basic preferences. For example, when party leaders in an autocratic regime become elected members of parliament in competitive elections, they gain new interests and stakes. Power distribution within a party or ruling group is typically based on new kinds of resources. In the new institutional setting of elections—even if they are not free and fair—an MP with a strong electoral base builds his or her own higher standing within the party. Strong electoral support decreases the incumbent party's need to subvert electoral processes to stay in power, and for the incumbent MP, the incentives are now to retain the electoral game.

Similarly, when independent electoral commissions are initiated, the staff gradually find that their careers and status are becoming linked intrinsically to preserving and upholding the rules of the game. To the extent that such bodies do in fact have some autonomy, it induces prodemocratic behavior. The same could be said about supreme court members, who have to adjudicate electoral disputes. These are plausible examples, but the analysis pursued in this book can only be indicative of such processes. More suitable evidence acquired by process-tracing techniques will be required in future research. Yet, this suggests that we can use an institutionalist framework in making the argument about causal links between elections and increased democratic qualities in society. Elections and electoral practices are, after all, political institutions in the traditional sense, defined succinctly by Levi (1990, 405) as "formal arrangements for aggregating individuals and regulating their behavior through use of explicit rules and decision processes enforced by an actor or a set of actors formally recognized as possessing such power." The contemporary institutionalism in comparative politics, underpinned by a rational-actor perspective, traces back to a few seminal works. Arrow's (1951) and Downs's (1957) early studies contributed by explicating how collective assumptions structured individual choice in ways that can be thought of in terms of institutions and provoked a critique that spurred further work on the importance of the institutional context. Olsen's (1965) influential study on the problems of collective action in face of a constant tendency for individuals to become free riders directly pointed to the need for institutions. With the right incentives provided by rules and regulations that shape expectations among individuals with regard to others' behavior, preferred collective outcomes can be achieved.

More recently, understanding the outcome of games or processes given a certain set of institutions has been developed by scholars such as Neumann and Morgenstern (1994), North (1990), and March and Olsen (1989) (cf. Munck 2001c). From deductive models and games, such as the famous "prisoners' dilemma" (Axelrod 1984), to empirical process tracing and historical analyses, it has been shown how institutions in important ways constrain actors' capabilities and choices (e.g., Bates 1989, Moe 1990). While actors can be thought of as self-reflexive individuals in a social context with abilities to discern and decide on their own preferred actions, choice is always conditioned, and institutional theory has revolved around the ways and means by which a set of formal or informal rules structures such choices.

There is a long tradition in comparative politics of studying the origin and shape of institutions, such as electoral systems, constitutional design, and agenda control.[9] One strain has focused on the role of institutions in aggregating preferences. Another approach has been to study the role of institutions in coordinating behavior that in turn generates patterns of political behavior that are self-reinforcing (Carey 2000, 736–739). This structuring of choice is done both by defining the actors (e.g., as MPs, voters, or independent news media) and by providing incentives for some actions rather than others (e.g., to contest elections rather than to pick up an AK-47); these examples illustrate the constitutive and regulatory aspects of institutions. Cox's (1997) book on strategic electoral behavior and party system realignments as tipping equilibria, Ordershook's (1992) and Weingast's (1997) work on constitutions as expectations among political actors, and Vanberg's (1998) study of how constitutional courts constitute and coordinate citizens' beliefs exemplify how institutions are self-reinforcing while having multiple equilibria and bumpy roads (Carey 2000, 745–746). These and other studies in the genre also show how key political institutions contribute both to constituting actors and to structuring their incentives, beliefs, and expectations.

For the study of the effects of electoral processes on increasing democratic qualities in society, it seems particularly relevant to focus on both constraining incentives and enabling incentives. It seems plausible that institutionalized uncertainty tends to constrain ruling elites, enabling actors in civil society to more effectively demand and use their civil liberties. This is not to suggest a return to crude functionalism in the sense of Ridley's (1975) suggestion that the design of a house will determine who will inhabit that house and what they will do in there. But, there is certainly a lot of suggestive evidence in the institutionalist literature that the initial conditions of constitutive and regulative rules envisaged by institutions constrain and enable the choice of behavior among particular individuals, while the strategies of individuals become mutually dependent on expectations of how other individuals will behave in ways that lead to self-fulfilling expectations. When the number of individuals is large and relations are impersonal, institutions play an even greater role in structuring and making such expectations plausible. Elections are such institutions *par excellence*, structuring expectations and choices for entire nations of citizens. It is not unlikely that such structuring can also affect the existence and improvement of civil liberties.

These expectations and the learning and adaptation that occur over time and with multiple elections place particular demands on the perception of political time. Both the elites' and the people's thinking about political time and time components in the regime (like duration in office, respect for necessary time boundaries in democratic procedures) must change during the course of democratic transition and consolidation. This might be one of the most essential parts of what is said to constitute democratic consolidation. Scholars like Goffman (1969), Hägerstrand (1973), and Zerubavel (1981) have elaborated on different perceptions of time, showing how those factor into the social organization of modern, as well as premodern, life[10] (cf. Giddens 1993, 105–110). Social perception of time is different from the use of time both as chronological reference, as discussed in Chapter 3, and from time as a sequential attribute of the unit of analysis, as in Chapter 4. In the present study of elections in Africa, the concept of increasing experience rests on this understanding of time. Actors come to accept, adapt to, and reproduce certain conceptions of time rules and by doing so institutionalize electoral cycles and procedures. This is one way we made sense of the effects of electoral institutions and their relative democratic qualities in Chapter 4. Changing social constructions of time is also a concurrent theme in several of the causal links suggested here that will be evaluated in the next chapter. With increased exposure and experience, actors adopt new conceptions of electoral time rules and regulations, causing them to become social entities whereby the actors modify their behavior.

A Framework of Seven Causal Links

How then can such causal links be visualized? The theoretical framework below outlines seven broad categories of possible causal linkages. Within each of these assemblages, there are variants of specific causal chains with distinct empirical implications. Naturally, it is not possible in the present work to investigate and test all of these possible linkages. Some of them demand their own kind of data collection about such factors as the views and reasons, calculations and preferences of individual actors in concerted action, mass attitudinal data, and so on. All of the suggested causal links are, however, related to the level of civil liberties in society in ways spelled out below, making it reasonable for the CL rankings to either corroborate or disprove the relevance of the causal links.

Consider first the voter as citizen. The fundamental features of equal sovereignty in elections as manifested in one man–one vote, the right to choose between candidates and parties, freedom of opinion and voice, and the right to form and belong to associations are all rules of the electoral regime that also constitute the citizen as such. These are rights and freedoms that the citizen is likely to encounter first as a voter in a transitional first election. Many citizens are likely to be targeted by voter education campaigns and messages conveyed by officials, activists, radio, newspapers, and, in urban areas at least, television. These activities are part of constituting the citizen as an equal sovereign (although the distribution of sovereignty will never be perfect) endowed with rights to participate and choose between alternatives under legitimate procedures. Once the election is over, the citizen does not necessarily lose the recognition and understanding acquired during the election, since the cognitive and experiential steps taken cannot be undone. Some citizens will become agents who carry political participation into civil activities, making more people, for example, willing to insist on gender equality, using their right to demonstrate to protest violence against women. Similarly, trade unions and other professional and civil organizations are likely to watch developments during election campaigns and copy the behavior of political parties in using the freed space for advocacy and spreading information and opinions created by the electoral processes, pushing for liberties such as professional equality and personal autonomy.

Those individuals and groups who learn to identify with the values inherent in democratic electoral practices provide a second area of linkages. Once self-perceived as promoters of democratic participation, competition, and legitimate governing, and recognized as such by friends, family, and perhaps even enemies, these individuals are vested with—locked into—an interest in voicing their concerns in the social sphere. Such lock-in mechanisms may even be active in individuals who are not committed democrats but whose social status, role, or influence has become associated with a perceived active prodemocratic stance. Such expectations create a particular incentive structure. It seems plausible that, as electoral cycles are repeated, a growing number of citizens will insist on the recognition by authorities and other groups of rights and freedoms in the social sphere. In dealing with local and state authorities; school, civic, football, and local development associations; and formal and informal political institutions such as village, town, and ward assemblies, some citizens who have been empowered by electoral socialization will expect adaptation from other actors and institutions on freedom from excessive dependence and principles of the rule of law.

The empirical implications of such linkages can be formulated in terms of specific hypotheses. For example, a citizen subjected to unjustified imprisonment is more likely to have the case brought to the public by family and friends or civic organizations in an electoral regime with such incentive effects at work than a citizen in a nonelectoral regime is. The same seems probable for citizens affected by gender discrimination, denial of a fair trial, violation of personal autonomy, infringement of religious or associational rights, and so on. In short, citizens in electoral regimes are empowered with formal electoral rights that, when exercised, also become weapons in the fight for expanded democratic qualities in society. As citizens do take up the fight and when they meet resistance, some are also likely to assert themselves by organizing local development or pressure groups for women, traders, youth, communities, or other interest groups. Alternatively, they may choose to use existing village groups or other associations to champion their cause. Therefore, the formal and real empowerment of the citizen as a voter is one potential source of diffusion to the empowerment of the citizen *writ large*. With growing pressures for participation, increased associational participation, growing competition, and demands for legitimate governing of social affairs, civil liberties are likely to expand and improve. With more civically active groups in society, the scope of alternatives and thus the competition increases.

A third set of linkages has to do with the role of self-fulfilling expectations, sometimes referred to as "discounts of the future." At a certain point, prodemocratic behavior is likely to come for more than political entrepreneurs, altruistic believers, and those with vested interests because of their organizational or other affiliation. When a critical mass of individual citizens have reason to believe that other citizens and the most important elites expect democratic rules to stay in place in the foreseeable future and expect electoral politics to prevail, this is likely to work as a self-fulfilling expectation. In a fashion similar to that described by Coleman (1990) and Elster (1982) for other social phenomena, elections spread democratic qualities to society in what we may call a self-fulfilling diffusion process when citizens have reason to believe that crucial elites—be they military or political leaders—and a majority of citizens will accept and play by the new rules. At some point, even risk-averse and perhaps even nondemocratic citizens are likely to climb on the bandwagon and demand or enact democratic principles in society. The optimistic tone in this possible causal link should not be confused with an unqualified idealism of assuming equality among citizens. Even with an increased spread and deepening of democratic participation and competition, a newly democratizing society will most certainly still be unequal. Individuals who are better equipped—in terms of education, financial resources, power, status ambitions, and social capabilities and positions—are more likely to take advantage of the new possibilities, thus creating new elites. The point is not that democratization in society leads to *perfect* equality but rather that it contributes to *greater* freedom in self-government for citizens.

A fourth possible causal link is provided by associations already in existence or those spawned by the coming of elections, that play an active role in the electoral activities. Civil society actors participating as election observers, for example, or working in voter education campaigns learn about electoral rules and procedures, issues of transparency, eligibility criteria, how to detect and mitigate fraud, political rights and civil liberties, procedures for complaint and adjudication, and so on. It seems plausible that individuals in such organizations learn about and build civic capacities and organizational experience during the massive mobilization and excitement that typically surround elections in transitional regimes. As organizations engage in activism, an aura of prodemocratism adheres to them, by which future engagements are likely to be judged. Electoral activities may thus create lock-in effects in terms of expectations and vested interests for organizations as well as for individuals, in particular on intersocial acceptance and peaceful coexistence of organizations. The future status and recognition of the organizations become conditioned on being prodemocratic. If donor contributions are involved, the financial rewards related to prodemocratic activities of civil society organizations will probably further strengthen constraints on the behavior and agendas of these organizations. It is also true that organizations typically seek an outlet for putting new capacities to use in a competitive organizational environment. At the same time, individuals working in the organizations are able not only to acquire new skills and capabilities but may direct their careers towards advancing rights of participation in social affairs, competition of ideas and agendas in society, and legitimate procedures for governing.

Fifth, individuals engaged, even temporarily, by these civil organizations may be either enticed or disillusioned by electoral campaigns, but they are likely to find new causes and actions to be involved in once the elections are over, probably bringing to them new capacities and an expanded awareness. When the elections are over and these individuals return to their normal lives, possibly including activism on non-election issues, these newly acquired skills are transferred into other areas of the society. It seems likely that some of these people will become norm entrepreneurs, transferring their new skills and attitudes to others in the social sphere. Then local authorities, village and ward community leaders, and media representatives will register a new pressure for implementation of democratic qualities in the local society on issues such as the right to open public discussion. This is another type of linkages with distinct empirical implications that should be investigated in more detail in future research.

The sixth area of possible linkage is the judicial system. With the coming of electoral rules and regulations, law adjudication and enforcement authorities are given a formal role in the protection of political rights. It becomes possible for members of the court system, as well as military, police, and security agencies, to advance their status, individual careers, and prominence on prodemocratic actions.[11] There then develops a payoff structure, with costs and benefits, whereby being antidemocratic is no longer necessarily the default option. Allowing and defending the democratic rights of the people to participate in political processes by other means than voting, such as demonstrating, petitioning authorities, filing complaints, and calling on the police for protection during electoral practices, is likely to spill over into other social affairs. The defense of the competition of ideas and organizations and property rights, as well as legitimate procedures for hearing and adjudication of them in the social sphere, are possible avenues for asserting a new standard. Once these democratic qualities are instituted, it seems plausible that the protection of the same rights is likely to be furthered. Even though these factors cannot be estimated on an individual basis here, improvements in them are likely to be reflected also in CL rankings.

The media provide a seventh set of potential causal links. The freedoms of expression, information, and association constitute the media as an independent actor
in society, to the extent that they are realized in practice. Elections are one time
when media entrepreneurs may test, stretch, and redefine the boundaries of both political and civil liberties and by doing so advance the democratic qualities by being
the public forum for society. The media form one of the main channels of pressure
on elected politicians and candidates to improve the rights and liberties of the people. The more media actors serve as transmitters for the prodemocratic calls and
complaints of individuals, organizations, think tanks, state actors, and other bodies,
the more they enhance democratic participation and the competition of ideas about
the governing of society, by ensuring open public discussion. However, if an autocratic ruler retains a tight grip on the financial sustenance of media actors and suc-
ceeds in exercising a great degree of centralized authority, the media can be used to
control information and tighten the monitoring of participation rather than to be a
means of spreading democratic qualities. Yet, with the institutionalization of political rights that comes with repetitive elections, such a manipulation is less likely to
be successful.

These are the suggested areas of causal links between electoral practices and the
positive effects of democratic qualities in society created by the exercise and repetition of de jure participatory, contested, and legitimate elections. The list of areas and
empirical implications is not exhaustive, and these hypothesized effects are severely
simplified. It is a first attempt at a comprehensive theoretical framework in this field,
to be evaluated empirically in a large-N study. The linkages discussed above are also
deficient in that on their own they do not explain why the effects of electoral practices tend to occur in conjunction with elections, as suggested by the main hypothesis, and not at just any time. The key to this lies in elections being a struggle for political power: It is during election campaigns and their immediate aftermath that
individual and organizational political and civil activism peaks, and consequently
this is when pressures for change are highest. Being the largest peacetime mobilization of political activism, elections provide a time for change and challenges. For example, in Ghana, it was during the first and second elections that pressure increased
on the incumbent regime to improve civil liberties. Civil organizations and political think tanks such as the Center for Democratic Development, the Institute of
Economic Affairs, independent journalists, and privately owned newspapers surveyed the operations of the armed forces and spoke out on issues of gender inequality, the rights of the "girl child," criminal libel laws, and freedom of the press, to mention a few. Constituted by procedural regulations and armed with rights and liberties
necessitated by the holding of elections, these actors encouraged debates addressing

further realization of associational, civil, and religious freedom. All of these actors took advantage of election times in much the same way as described by Eisenstadt (2004) for Mexico and Barkan (2000) for Kenya. The civil liberties ranking for Ghana increased from a low of 6 in the preelection period to a good standing of 3 by the third elections.

Second, the competition for executive and legislative power that occurs in and around elections provides opportunities and means for citizens and organizations to demand and exact concessions from politicians and state authorities. These conditions seldom exist in nonelection times. To the extent that there is some degree of competitiveness in the election race, the concept of "throwing the rascals out" also inspires responsiveness by incumbents. The promise of improved democratic liberties in society provides an obvious opportunity for opposition parties. Such circumstances can lead to a competition over who can improve the democratic qualities and freedom in society. Finally, election time is typically when scrutiny of a newly democratizing regime by the international community and international news media will give more attention to the country. Watchdog organizations such as Election Watch, Amnesty International, and Human Rights Watch capitalize on these occasions to apply pressures for reforms and improvements in civil liberties. And, I argue, the link between elections and democratic qualities in society is not dependent on the freedom and fairness of elections. Disappointments during a bad experience with electoral practices—inflated voter registries, political violence during the campaign and polling day, outright fraudulent voting and collation of votes, and intimidation of voters and political opponents—may stimulate activism in society even more than free and fair elections do.

Causal Model and Doing the Possible

As suggested, the possible causal links between elections and increased democratic qualities in society are multiple, but they are not necessarily additive and independent of each other. They are probably interactive and may add, multiply, and divide according to a complex set of formulas, making it very difficult even to think in terms of a formal model of combined linked effects to be estimated. There is also an information problem in that we do not have the comparative data necessary for large-N analysis on all the empirical implications of the causal links described above. Also, some of the implied effects do not lend themselves to statistical analysis but would require the closer inspection of qualitative techniques that can capture elements such as the perceptions and reasoning of individuals in civil society organizations. Partly because of the complexity of the modeling problem and partly because of the somewhat rudimentary status of existing theory and available data, the following testing is based on the direct relationship between the holding of repetitive elections and the status of democratic qualities in the society as indicated by the CL index.

Taking this crude but applicable approach, we can now proceed to investigate if improvements of democratic qualities in society are an effect of electoral activities. It should be noted that the hypothesized relationship is unidirectional. This is not to say that in reality there are no feedback mechanisms or interactive relationships, only that this inquiry is limited to one direction. Yet, the causal model is not linear nor does it assume a constant effect; and the effect is not necessarily proportional, so the change from zero elections to one may produce great effects. First elections may, for example, have greater effects on democratic qualities than do second or third elections. The assessment of this hypothesis is best done in three steps and the empirical analysis in the next chapter is structured accordingly. First, we test for correlation between the two variables: Is there a general association between first, second, and subsequent elections and an increase in democratic qualities in society, as measured by the Freedom House index of civil liberties (CL)? If the skeptics of the transition paradigm and the importance of elections are right, we should see no relationship—the null hypothesis. The main hypothesis, that democratic qualities in society improve with subsequent elections, is evidenced if the average CL ranking after second elections is better than after first elections. In the same way we expect the average ranking after third elections to be better than after second elections, and so on. The evaluation is addressed by comparing Freedom House CL rankings at the year of each election over first, second, and subsequent elections. We can strengthen the robustness of the results if the same relationship is found when we use countries instead of elections as the unit of analysis.

This leads to the second part of the assessment: that improvement in democratic qualities in society tends to occur not only in conjunction with but as a causal effect of electoral activities. This unidirectional relationship is one possibility. Another possibility is that an increase in democratic qualities in society heightens the likelihood of successive elections. A third possibility is that both of these relationships exist and that they are mutually reinforcing. Finally, increases in democratic qualities in society as indicated by CL may be caused by another set of factors, such as elites' behavior and decision, class, or ethnic struggles; therefore the third part ventures into a multiple regression analysis. The following empirical analysis has to be designed to evaluate these contradicting possibilities. In a simplified manner, the possibilities are displayed in Figure 5.

If the main hypothesized causal relationship (H_1) exists, we expect to see im-

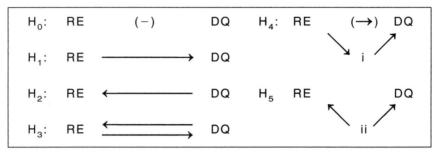

Note: RE = repetitive elections, DQ = democratic qualities, i = intervening variable, ii = other independent variables.

Fig. 5. Alternative hypotheses of relationship between elections and democratization

provements in CL rankings to occur in conjunction with elections while periods before and between elections are associated with no or even negative changes. H_4 and H_5 can, in theory, give rise to a similar outcome but are less likely to. Moreover, intervening and spurious relationship is controlled for in the multiple regression analysis even if there is always a risk of omitted variable bias in the estimation. Hence, if H_1 gets support from the empirical analysis, we need to go further and control for other known causal factors, to eliminate H_4 and H_5. If instead it is one of the other hypotheses that is right, improvements in CL rankings will occur (a) preceding and in between elections, in particular if the causality runs the opposite direction, as in H_2; or (b) in all phases, for example if the causal relationship is reciprocal and non-recursive, as in H_3; or (c) unrelated to electoral cycles, as in H_0. Many scholars, emphasizing civil society or the rule of law, for example, argue that civil liberties are the cause of the improvements of elections and the stability of electoral regimes. In that case, improvements in civil liberties should precede elections. Other students of democratization, emphasizing the role of elites or class struggles or the like, argue that civil liberty improvements are a product of a set of other factors. In this case, improvements of civil liberties rankings should prove unrelated to electoral cycles. In sum, there are mutually exclusive hypotheses with distinct empirical implications in both of these parts of the general hypothesis that elections cause democratization. These are subjected to empirical evaluation in the next chapter.

CHAPTER SIX

Democratization by Elections?

This chapter presents an analysis based on five alternative tests, the empirical results of which indicate that repetitive elections are a causal factor in democratization rather than, as often assumed, merely a reflection of democracy. Controlling for some of the standard factors in democratization, the analysis below also suggests that the democratizing power of elections is authentic, refuting parts of Carothers's (2002a) negative assessment of the transition paradigm and showing that the international community's focus on elections is neither misguided nor overemphasized.

The main hypothesis formulated in Chapter 5 suggests a relationship between independent and dependent variables over a sequence of elections. Table 13, using the same grouping of countries by duration of electoral regime used in Table 2, presents the state of democratic qualities in societies in Africa as of June 2003 as measured by the Freedom House civil liberties index (CL). Countries that have held more elections tend to have a better CL rating. Obviously, the holding of first elections cannot be credited to the power of elections within that same country, but first elections can have ripple effects on electoral processes in neighboring or other strategic countries. It might also be that political transitions are a direct result of external pressure from the international donor and financial community to hold elections (see, e.g., Lindberg 2002, Pridham 1991, Whitehead 1996). With the inception of elections, however, it seems possible that even first elections start to create and affect institutions, actors, and processes of change.

Table 13 does not provide a real test, however. The hypothesis and the precise direction of causality can only be tested on countries that have had an uninterrupted sequence of elections. Hence, the following analysis builds on the set of countries

TABLE 13   *Civil liberties ratings as of 1 July 2003, by electoral history*

Broken Down Still	CL Rating	1st Elections	CL Rating	2nd Elections	CL Rating	3rd Elections	CL Rating	4th or More	CL Rating
Angola*	5	Comoros*	4	Chad	5	Burkina Faso	4	Benin	2
Burundi*	5	RoC*	4	Eql. Guinea	6	Cameroon	6	Botswana	2
CAR*	6	Guinea-Bissau*	5	Ethiopia	5	Cape Verde	2	Madagascar	4
Ivory Coast*	5	Lesotho*	3	Gambia*	4	Djibouti	5	Mali	3
Liberia*	6	Niger*	4	Guinea	5	Gabon	4	Mauritius	2
		Sierra Leone*	4	Malawi	4	Ghana	3	Senegal	3
				Mozambique	4	Kenya	4	Zimbabwe	6
				Nigeria*	5	Mauritania	5		
				South Africa	2	Namibia	3		
				Sudan	7	Sao Tome and			
				Swaziland	5	Principe*	2		
				Tanzania	3	Seychelles*	3		
				Uganda	4	Togo	5		
						Zambia	4		
Mean rating	5.4		4.0		4.5		3.8		3.1

Note: The CL rating is on a scale of 7 to 1 on which 7 indicates the worst conditions and 1 the best. The measure, compiled and tabulated by Freedom House, has been taken since 1972.
   *Indicates that a coup, civil war, or similar event interrupted the electoral process at some point during the period studied.

and elections that were used for the panel-group analysis in Chapter 4: those current regimes that as of June 2003 had completed at least two elections in a row. That reduces the sample to 184 elections in 33 countries, in effect the countries in the last three columns to the right in Table 13.

ELECTIONS ARE ASSOCIATED WITH CIVIL LIBERTIES

Addressing first the question of a possible correlation between increasing number of elections and increasing civil liberties—as spelled out in the preceding chapter, Table 14 shows the average CL ranking after first, second, third, and fourth and later elections. It also presents differences between free and fair elections and flawed elections. The relationship between increasing numbers of elections and higher levels of democratic qualities in society is substantial and highly significant ($p = .002$). The enhancement of civil liberties with increased exposure to and experience with the core representative democratic institution supports the H_1 hypothesis (as displayed in Figure 5 in the previous chapter), although the effect is concentrated during the first three electoral cycles. The magnitude of the overall change, from an average of 4.3 to 3.3, might not seem dramatic, but the FH scale is not an interval measure and the distances between the ratings are not necessarily equal across the range of the scale. Freedom House and most analysts regard somewhere between four and three as the cut-off point between partly free, partly democratic societies

TABLE 14 *Civil liberties ratings at first, second, third, and later elections*

	Type of Election	First	Second	Third	Fourth+	All	Significance* Number of Poll	Significance* Free & Fair
Civil liberties	Free & fair	3.5	3.4	3.1	3.1	3.3	5.076	88.603
rating (mean)	Flawed	5.1	4.8	4.3	4.7	4.8	(.002)	(.000)
	All	4.3	4.2	3.6	3.3	4.0		
Total elections		71	61	31	21	184		

Note: The CL rating is on a scale of 7 to 1 on which 7 indicates the worst conditions and 1 the best. The measure, compiled and tabulated by Freedom House, has been taken since 1972.
*ANOVA F-values and significance.

and free, democratic ones,[1] and changes of this magnitude are considered substantial (e.g., Karatnycky 2001). The striking change is the 5.3 to 3.3 from before elections to after four or more, which will be seen in Table 15 later in this chapter.

The results also confirm the expectation that free and fair elections are associated with even better civil liberties at each point. Free and fair elections produce CL ratings that average 1.5 full points better than flawed elections, and the difference is highly significant ($p = .000$). However, over sequence of electoral cycles the *trend* is the same for the two categories, and it is interesting that these improvements are most pronounced in flawed elections. This might seem counterintuitive, since authoritarian regimes running flawed elections are not usually associated with improvements in the rule of law, religious and associational freedoms, and absence of economic exploitation and protection from unjustified imprisonment. Yet, as suggested by the discussion of causal links, even flawed electoral experiences involving manipulation, rigging, and violence can be efficient in provoking actors to work harder to increase civil liberties in society. Taken together, Tables 13 and 14 provide sufficient empirical basis, corroborating the ideas in the last chapter, to justify a more detailed examination of the relationship between elections and democratization.

Analyzing Effects over Electoral Periods

Although suggestive, the tables above do not qualify as tests of the main hypothesis and are therefore not submitted as evidence, since they say nothing about *when* the positive changes in civil liberties occur. The simple comparison of means in the tables above offers little insight into the direction of possible causal relationship between CL and electoral cycles. Similarly, a correlation analysis between the number of the election and the rating of CL at the beginning of an election year confirms a relationship and its statistical strength (Pearsons $-.292$, $p = .000$) but tells us nothing about cause and effect. The only thing these approaches establish is a positive relationship between number of elections held in an uninterrupted sequence and levels of civil liberties. What remains to be analyzed is the direction and dynamic of this positive relationship and the issue of when in changes civil liberties occur.

The following analysis does not differentiate between free and fair elections and flawed ones. We know from Table 14 that free and fair elections tend to be associated with higher levels of civil liberties, but we also established that the direction of change is similar regardless of the freedom and fairness of the elections. Since our concern here is relative changes in civil liberties over a series of electoral cycles and not the exact levels, there is no methodological reason to distinguish between the free and fair elections and flawed elections in the following analysis. There also is no theoretical requirement to disaggregate the analysis accordingly, because, to the contrary, the stated hypothesis assumes that all *de jure* participatory, competitive, and legitimate elections proceeding in a sequential and constitutional manner have similar effects on civil liberties. For these reasons, the following analysis can be based on all of the cases with a record of at least two elections.

First and "founding" elections are particularly interesting, by comparison, given the role ascribed to them in many theories of democratization. The rationale for labeling first elections as "founding" is built on the premise that a democratic regime is manifestly installed by the conclusion of first elections. The implication of that argument is that improvements in civil liberties have come independently and ahead of first elections. The implication of my hypothesis is to the contrary, that the immediate preparations for and holding of first—as well as subsequent—elections result in general improvements in democracy.

In order to evaluate these two mutually exclusive hypotheses, we need to analyze the relationship between the independent and dependent variables over time. First, electoral improvements are operationalized as increasing numbers of successive elections, moving from first to second and successive elections. Improvements in democratic qualities in society are measured as improvements in CL on the scale provided by Freedom House, in which rankings start at seven for worst cases and improve to a score of one for best cases. Second, a crucial point in establishing causality is tied to chronological time, since cause necessarily must precede effect. In assessing hypotheses H_0 through H_5, using chronological time may oversimplify the cause and effect relationship to an extent that undermines the analysis. If actors anticipate an event, they typically adjust their strategies and behavior accordingly, thus, an event may have effects before it actually occurs. Elections are typical in this regard, for, in anticipation of polling day, political parties and other actors educate voters, train domestic election observers and polling officials, debate issues and democratic procedures, disgrace opponents, and do other things in an effort to sway the vote. Civil society organizations may demand and adopt more freedom in their actions; the media may expand their openness and criticism ahead of polling day, all as part of the electoral process. Therefore, we expect that if elections have positive effects on civil liberties, these effects will start occurring before polling day.

It is reasonable to calculate that these effects may occur as much as a year in advance. At the same time, elections are not over until the votes are counted, collated, possibly transported, reported, and translated into winning candidates and legislative seats, and the victorious candidates have assumed office. Disputes may arise and need to be settled and the often-contentious issue of interpreting the meaning of the elections can take months to settle. Specifically election-related events are therefore likely to occur up to six months after polling day. When operationalizing the measure of effects of elections on civil liberties, this must be taken into consideration. Empirically, we look at the changes in civil liberties at points in time before, during, and after first, second, third, and fourth and later elections. In order to account for the period before the start of elections, we measure changes in CL rating before the first election from $t(-4)$ to $t(-2)$. This is the difference up till one full year before the election year t. That should be sufficient to insulate the recorded changes that might occur as a result of preparations for elections that typically take no more than one year. In cases of "second" first elections, after a coup or similar event, the year of the previous election is taken into account as well so that an election year is not part of the measure of the preelection period.

To gauge the change occurring as a result of an election, we measure changes in CL rating from $t_i(-2)$ to t_i, changes that occur during the year ahead of the election and during the election year. It seems reasonable that most changes effected by the procedures of elections, such as campaigning, voter registration and education, demonstrations, going to the polls, and the postpolling processes, will occur during the year ahead of the election and shortly after the election. This is to some extent moderated by the timing of the election during the election year. Some countries, like Kenya and Ghana, have their general elections in the last quarter of the election year. In those cases, the measure of eventual change in CL is adjusted so that a year less in advance of the elections is recorded. At the same time, the following year's score is taken into account on occasion. For other countries, such as Cape Verde and Senegal, that hold their elections early in the election year, only one full year ahead of the elections is recorded as change resulting from the elections, while nine or more months following the poll are recorded. This seems to be the most reasonable way to account for variations using the Freedom House score, which provides rankings for every annum but does not disaggregate or account for when significant changes occurred. This is simply the best we can do, and it seems that we do not lose too much information and do not introduce any serious bias in the sample by the procedure followed here.

After the first election, our measure must be modified slightly, in order (a) to capture changes in CL in the periods between elections while at the same time making this measure as independent of changes in conjunction with elections as possible, and (b) to make the measurements as similar as possible in a context defined by a range of electoral cycles of different lengths, premature elections, and the like. First, we want to measure the change from after the first election, operationalized as $t_1(+1)$, to the second year ahead of the second election, or $t_2(-2)$. Second, this operationalization means that the length of the period measured varies with the length of the electoral cycle. A few countries have four-year electoral cycles, and in that case we measure changes from one year to the next. That period is a little short, but there seems to be little alternative, since the effects of elections are likely to start showing already at $t_i(-1)$. Other countries have five-year electoral cycles, and we measure their changes over two years. A few countries have six- or seven-year electoral cycles. In those cases, the period from $t_1(-1)$ to $t_2(-2)$ is longer. It is not a completely satisfactory situation, but reality seldom is fully cooperative with scientific methodology. We must work with the fact that the constitutions in some countries give more room for change between elections than others do.[2]

An alternative approach would be to measure changes over two years regardless of the length of electoral cycles, for example from $t_2(-4)$ to $t_2(-2)$. That would compromise validity in both the case of four-year electoral cycles and longer cycles, since several years of possible changes would then be left unregistered. An issue that complicates this measure a little more is that a few countries in Africa run presidential and parliamentary elections on different intervals. In Burkina Faso, for example, there are seven years between presidential elections but only five years between parliamentary elections. In these circumstances, the period of measurement has been adjusted to capture years unaffected by elections. However, the CL ranking was changed in only a few of these cases.[3] Finally, the analysis is constructed on a probabilistic conception of causal relationships, and a few deviating cases do not refute the theory but make an interesting observation. Once a general tendency is established, understanding and explaining the odd ones is an equally important exercise.

Positive Changes in Civil Liberties

Launching an independent variable in what might seem like a field crowded with existing alternatives is always difficult, and skeptics are likely to object. Therefore,

TABLE 15 *Civil liberties development over electoral periods*

	1st Period		2nd Period		3rd Period		4th+ Period	
	Pre-election	1st Election Effects	Non-election	2nd Election Effects	Non-election	3rd Election Effects	Non-election	4th+ Election Effects
Mean change	.19	.84	−.05	.21	.00	.13	.00	−.10
Mean ranking	5.3	4.3	4.3	4.2	3.7	3.6	3.2	3.3
Total elections	70	70	60	61	30	30	21	21

five tests are performed below with the idea to check the robustness of the evidence and maximize leverage on theory. By shifting not only measurements and alternative indicators of the independent variable but even switching unit of analysis, the following demonstrates that the main findings are not sensitive to choice of indicators and methods.

The first analysis, showing mean changes in CL from the period before first election to after the fourth and later elections, is presented in Table 15. The mean measures overall direction of changes associated with election activities and with periods between and independent of elections respectively. The differences between first, second, and third elections, and the adjacent nonelection periods are stark. The pre-first-election period is perhaps the most surprising. The theories of democratization building on small-N comparative and case studies have posited that a significant expansion of civil liberties precedes first elections, and the traditional view of "founding" elections as the end of a transitional period stems from that premise.

The data from Africa suggest that only small positive changes occur before first elections. The period preceding first elections displays a low level of civil liberties, at an average CL rating of 5.3 on the Freedom House scale. The average positive change of .19 units in CL ranking in the three to four years leading up to the elections does not signify a radical change in the democratic quality of these political systems. It should also be taken into consideration that the worse the CL ranking to begin with, the more room there is for improvement; once a country attains higher levels of democratic qualities the room for significant positive change is decreased. In this light, the modesty of improvement in civil democratic qualities ahead of first elections in Africa seems particularly disappointing, since most countries started from very bad scores.

The measure of positive changes as effects of the exercise of electoral activities is much more impressive. The .84 average change during the brief period of first elections stands in contrast to the relatively small changes in the preelection period. It

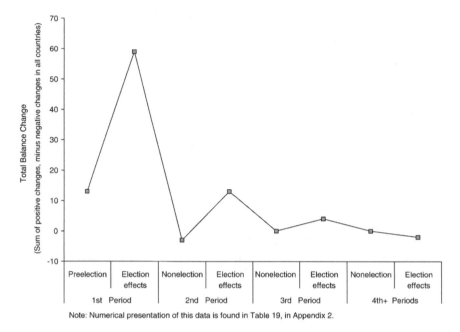

Note: Numerical presentation of this data is found in Table 19, in Appendix 2.

Fig. 6. Changes in civil liberties in Africa, by electoral period, using Freedom House civil liberties index

also corroborates the idea that improvements in democratic qualities beyond the narrow sphere of elections are an effect of holding elections. It appears that elections are not primarily facilitated by increased civil liberties but rather that repetitive elections have indirect or direct effects on democratic qualities in society. The argument is further strengthened by the data for the successive changes independent of elections as well as those occurring as effects of election periods. The difference between nonelection-period effects and election-related changes is continued over second and third elections, even though the recorded changes decrease in magnitude, which is in accordance with the reasoning above that when significant improvements have already been accomplished the room for additional positive changes decreases.

Comparing means does not show the total extent of changes. A graphic presentation of the total balance in unit changes provides an alternative test. In Figure 6, the total number of negative changes in CL has been totaled with the positive changes in CL at each interval period.[4] The result for each interval assesses the magnitude of total change in each period. Over time, these totals produce the wavelike line in Figure 6, further strengthening the results based on the means comparison.

The first wave of change shows that the magnitude increase in civil democratic qualities was almost six times greater after elections began than in the period immediately preceding them. In other words, first elections tend to be the cause of a huge improvement in civil liberties, not the effect of them. Benin and Malawi gained as many as four points in this first period and Nigeria went up by three CL points. These were the best performers; the majority of countries made gains of two points in CL, among them Zambia and Mali. Other countries made a modest gain of one point. After first elections and before second elections, in the period with no election-related activities taking place, the development stalled or even reverted, as indicated by balance of changes in CL, which fell below zero. In most countries, this was a period of relative stagnation. The results support the reasoning expounded in the last chapter, that both supply of momentum and political openness are likely to decrease in this nonelection period, as well as the willingness of political leaders and higher staff of key institutions to accept and support the expansion and deepening of civil liberties. The period after the first election was associated with clear reversal of gains already made in, for example, Mauritania, Zambia, Nigeria, and Uganda, while Chad declined one point on the CL ranking even though it had made no gains during the first election.

Another set of positive changes occurred as a result of second elections in some countries, among them Tanzania, Seychelles, Madagascar, Zambia, and even Ethiopia. Bratton (1998) noted that second elections in general, and late second elections in particular, were of lower democratic quality than first elections. Chapter 4 corroborated that finding, although the difference now appears less pronounced than has been believed. Yet, even when the democratic qualities of elections decreased, the elections still resulted in improved quality of civil liberties in the society! This is a very important finding and lends support to the parts of the reasoning about causal links positing that negative electoral experiences can spur increased efforts among individual and collective actors for improvements of civil liberties in society. It also speaks to the relative independence of the variable of democratic qualities of elections in the spreading and deepening of civil liberties. Elections do not have to be free and fair or fully democratic to have democratizing effects; regardless of their quality they tend to improve the democratic qualities in the societies where they are held. Following the electoral campaigning, voter education, political meetings, demonstrations, public debates, and the exercise of political rights and democratic procedures during second elections, civil liberties expand again in many countries.

Even though recorded changes in CL scores in Africa as effects of holding third elections were modest (again, the relatively lower magnitude of change is expected, given the significant gains resulting from the first and second elections), changes

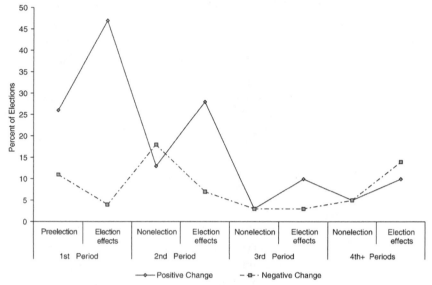

Note: Numerical presentation of this data is found in Table 20, in Appendix 2.

Fig. 7. Percentage of elections related to positive and negative changes in civil liberties, by electoral period

were still positive, unlike during the nonelection periods before and afterwards, which saw zero net change. For the sake of a comprehensive outlook and as a way to cross-check the robustness of these findings, a third alternative analysis is presented in Figure 7. Both the analysis of means and the calculating of unit balance scores can be skewed by extreme values in a smaller number of cases. Therefore, we change indicator completely for the third test and look at the number and share of elections associated with changes in civil liberties rather than the aggregated magnitude of such changes. Figure 7 presents the share of elections in each subperiod that led to positive and negative changes respectively.

The solid line represents the share of elections accompanied by gains in CL. Slightly more than 25 percent of all first elections were associated with changes in the preelection period. Thus, only about a quarter of all first elections in Africa followed expectations from the transitions literature and displayed a general liberalization preceding first elections that installed an elected regime. However, improvements of civil liberties occurred in almost half of all elections *as a consequence* of first elections. Expressed in a different way, no less than two-thirds of all positive changes in civil liberties in conjunction with the first electoral cycle occurred as effects of elections. The pattern is repeated with second and third elections.

In conclusion, the findings reported in Table 15 and Figures 6 and 7 appear robust. Three alternative assessments of the direction and magnitude of the causal relationship between elections and further democratization produce essentially the same conclusion. The emphasis in the transition literature on the liberalization during the pre-first-election period and the characterization of first elections as "founding" seem not to apply to Africa. Rather, the transition period has typically been extended, often over several electoral cycles, before enough gains were made in civil liberties for the electoral regime to become democratic. A few cases corroborate the hypothesis of the mainstream democratization literature, but most countries seem to have democratized through the power of elections rather than anything else. Among the hypotheses displayed in Figure 5 in the previous chapter, the tests favor the main hypothesis (H_1) while ruling out the null hypothesis (H_0), the reversed causation hypothesis (H_2), and the hypothesis about reciprocal, nonrecursive causation (H_3). The distinct waves of changes, with culminations of change associated with elections, point to the need for a reconceptualization of the role of elections in the democratization process. There is power in elections. That power propels democratization in the sense of improving the democratic qualities of participation, competition, and legitimacy in society outside of the electoral sphere.

ANALYZING BY COUNTRIES

The evidence above is based on elections as the unit of analysis, a method necessary both to assess the relevance of elections to democratization and to probe the direction and strength of the relationship. Continuing the exercise of trying to falsify the main hypothesis, the next step is to change the unit of analysis from elections to countries. Two crucial questions can thus be addressed that could not be analyzed using the approach above: (a) How many countries corroborate the hypothesis? (b) To what extent does the number of elections held in a country explain the level of civil liberties enjoyed there? The first question is critical in that the causal links suggested in Chapter 5 build on different kinds of experiential learning and adaptation effects. If these effects are indeed operating to the extent of influencing the outcome, as indicated so far, we should expect to see the main hypothesis fit a large share of the countries. The second question is necessary to measure more precisely the relative, if any, effect of holding elections versus other factors known to influence democratization.

To answer the first question—in a fourth test of the robustness of the main hypothesis—the individual countries' series of elections have been scrutinized, asking to how many of them the hypothesis applies. The answer is that no less than 64 percent of the countries fit the patterns: 21 out of the 33 countries that held at least two successive elections and had surviving electoral regimes as of June 2003. The details about each of these 21 countries' surviving regime are reported in Table 20 in Appendix 2. Among the countries that do not conform to the theory, Sao Tome and Principe presents a special case that many observers would expect would support the main hypothesis. First and second elections were held there in 1991 and 1994, followed by a brief breakdown in 1995 due to a coup that lasted only a few days. The elections that were held in 1996 are therefore coded as second-time first elections. Freedom House's score for Sao Tome and Principe did not record the brief coup, and at that point, Sao Tome had already made gains, scoring 2 in CL ranking. Hence, in my data set of surviving regimes Sao Tome and Principe register as a case without changes in CL and so not supportive of the theory. But even when the elections in 1991 and 1994 are factored in, Sao Tome and Principe does not support the hypothesis fully. The first elections in 1991 did produce an increase in civil liberties by 2 full points on the ranking scale, but so did the preelection period; and since then, scores have been unchanged. The case has therefore been considered ambiguous and included in the remaining one-third that have either inconclusive records of accomplishments, in the sense of providing evidence neither for or against the hypothesis, or a development that speaks against the hypothesis. The four countries in that group offering inconclusive evidence so far might well corroborate the hypothesis in the future.

This fourth test shows not only that overall mean changes in CL, unit balance scores, and the share of elections are associated with improvements but also that the development in at least two-thirds of all countries corroborates the main thesis of this book. There seem to be no distinct regional variations; northern, southern, eastern, and western parts of Africa are represented among the states that corroborate the hypothesis. Type of representative system also does not seem to matter, as parliamentary systems and many presidential systems are in both main groups, those that corroborate the thesis and those that do not. There are both island states, such as Cape Verde and the Seychelles, and landlocked ones, like Lesotho; and we find both countries still more authoritarian, such as Equatorial Guinea and Swaziland, and more democratized ones, like Ghana, Kenya, and Benin, among the two-thirds fitting this hypothesis. Unstable societies, like Nigeria, are mixed with countries that have enjoyed peace and stability for quite some time, including the two longest-surviving democracies on the continent, Botswana and Mauritius. Among the countries that fit the hypothesis are the richer nations, such as South Africa with an adjusted GDP per capita of US$10,492, as well as poorer nations, like Sierra Leone with a corresponding GDP per capita of US$556 (both figures from 2003), and also small states, like Gambia (10,000 km²), and huge ones, like Mali (1,220,000 km²). Religion may have a slight influence on the results. Democratization by elections has occurred in countries with Muslim shares of the total population ranging from negligible, as in Madagascar and Zambia, to almost the entire population, as in Mauritania and Gambia, but the average is higher in the group of countries not corroborating the hypothesis. Since almost two-thirds of the countries in Africa corroborate the hypothesis, we should not be surprised that such a wide variety exists among them, but this diversity suggests that the power of elections is a general phenomenon.

The 12 countries (about one-third of the total) that present us with either ambiguous or inconclusive track records or which directly contradict the thesis of the power of elections are not necessarily cases where democracy has failed. Mozambique, Namibia, Sao Tome, and Senegal have improved their democratic qualities significantly over the past 15 years, but these improvements do not seem decisively to be effects of the elections per se. These are, rather, countries that lend more support to the transitions thesis that civil liberties expand and deepen most radically before the holding of first elections. Burkina Faso and Tanzania indicate the same pattern but to a lesser extent, and in both countries future developments may involve further improvements that would lend support to the argument of this book. But there are certainly other cases that are less propitious. Guinea has had only two presidents since independence in 1958. The republic's first president, Sekou Touré, held power until his death, on 26 March 1984, from a heart attack while out of the country. Shortly thereafter, the current president, Colonel Lansana Conté, seized power in a coup d'état on 3 April. Sekou Touré's one-party state was ruled by decrees, and plots, arrests, detentions, secret trials, and executions of political opponents were rife; but Conté announced economic liberalization, structural reforms, and political rights at the outset of his reign, and he publicly declared plans for an introduction of two-party politics in 1988, before most other countries.

When the tide of reforms swept over Africa in the early 1990s, Guinea followed suit, legalizing political parties in April 1992 and holding the first multiparty presidential elections on 19 December 1993. These were not free and fair elections: while almost all opposition groups participated, none accepted the outcome; there was frequent violence, and international observers left in protest the day before polling day. According to official results, President Conté collected 51.7 percent of the votes and was reelected without a runoff. The first legislative elections were held on 11 June 1995 after having been postponed for almost two and a half years. Violence and irregularities were considerable, but international observers nevertheless proclaimed it satisfactory, given the conditions. The opposition parties cried foul and refused to take their seats in the new parliament at first, but they later accepted that President

Conté's Parti de l'Unité et du Progrès had won 71 out of the 114 seats, or 62 percent in total.

Second presidential elections were held in December 1998 after a period of high tensions and occasional violence from 1996 to 1998. The electoral commission was abolished and the Ministry of Interior took over its functions in a move by President Conté to strengthen his grip on power. Violence was frequent in the run-up to the elections; civil society organizations and groups were repressed and several opposition leaders and activists were detained two days after the election, among them the main opposition figurehead, Alpha Conde of the Rally of the Guinean People's Party, who was not released until two and a half years later, in May 2001. In 2000, regional upheavals started in the southeastern part of the country, leaving at least 400 people killed and providing President Conté with a pretext to postpone the second legislative elections. His political opponents then turned to armed struggle, along the borders with Sierra Leone and Liberia.

Conté's next step was to set up a referendum on a constitutional amendment to remove the two-term limit on the presidential office and prolong the term from five to seven years. The amendment would also turn theretofore elected local government officials into presidential appointees. According to official results, 98 percent of the voters approved the amendment in the November 2001 referendum; and when the time came for second legislative elections, on 30 June 2002, the general climate had changed to one of indifference and disillusionment. Only two opposition parties participated, and the European Union, among other outside organizations, refused to contribute any assistance or to send observers. The second elections were, if anything, worse than the first, and one can only hope that this will change with the third elections or the fourth elections, if they are held in the future. Improvements have arisen from similar situations in other countries, and with constant and increasing pressure from neighboring countries and from donors it might actually happen. In any case, Guinea in 2003 did not lend support to the hypothesis about a self-improving and democratizing power of elections.

Moving on to the fifth and final test, we must adjust our methodology further. While the preceding analysis carefully avoided assumptions of a linear causal model with symmetric and constant effect, those restrictions should now be relaxed, the rationale being that the tests above, displayed in Table 15 and Figures 6 and 7, measured the *extent* of changes in civil liberties and *when* the changes occurred. The latter was also what we tested for on a country basis in the fourth analysis. In these tests, assuming a symmetric linear relationship would not have been reasonable. Indeed, the main hypothesis actually proposes a constant but erratic causal effect, due to the cyclical nature of the independent variable. The analysis also showed that to a great extent changes in the democratic qualities in society as measured by civil liberties were associated with the repetition of elections and that the changes in civil liberties occurred as effects of holding those elections. Subjecting the data to a country-based longitudinal analysis strengthened the conclusion further by showing that it applies to at least two-thirds of all countries in Africa. The main hypothesis thus has been subjected to four different tests and so far has not been falsified.

Taking the next step, we inquire if and to what extent also the *level* of democratic qualities in society, again as measured by civil liberties, in any one country can be explained by the number of elections held. In other words, in our next attempt to falsify the hypothesis we ask if repetitive elections—still regardless of their qual-ity—can explain not only when positive changes occur but also how far the coun-tries experiencing them have come in their democratization. The simple bivariate relationship lends support with a Pearson's coefficient at $-.515$ ($p = .000$) (the neg-ative relationship again because of the counterintuitive Freedom House rankings), but to address the question of spurious relationships and/or intervening factors, as depicted in H_4 and H_5, we proceed with a multiple regression analysis. While the dependent variable continues to be the level of civil liberties, a rationale for the se-lection of independent variables and indicators is in place.

One obvious suspect for intervening variable or creator of spurious findings is in-ternational influences. In Africa, two international influences, of the various possi-bilities, seem especially likely and will be controlled for. The dependency argument (cf. Hadenius 1992), that higher rates of economic reliance on the more developed states in terms of trade and capital investments affects democratization negatively, was corroborated recently by Li and Reuveny (2003). If countries in Africa are af-fected by economic ties to a world economy dominated by countries insisting on both elections and expansion of civil liberties we could have been misled by a spu-rious relationship. To measure this aspect we use a rather uncontroversial proxy for relative involvement in the world economy, the net sum of exports and imports as share of GDP—from 1990, in order to ensure sufficient delay between the inde-pendent and dependent variables, and based on figures from the World Bank De-velopment Indicators (WBDI). Second, another of the usual suspects is that reliance on foreign aid, through political conditionalities, has been instrumental in pressur-ing authoritarian regimes into both holding elections and improving the level of democracy. This hypothesis has been the object of studies that found a zero rela-tionship (e.g., Bratton and van de Walle 1997) but also of ones (e.g., Lindberg 2002) demonstrating a positive relationship. Because of the contentious arguments and to avoid speculation that the results are driven by the choice of indicator, two different indicators are used to measure this aspect: (a) total overseas development assistance

(ODA) as share of GDP using data provided by the World Bank from 1989 that Bratton and van de Walle compiled but with values missing from their data replaced with corresponding figures from 1992 and 1993; and (b) Bratton and van de Walle's (1997) count of the number of structural adjustment programs (SAPs) signed by each country, which they argued was a better indicator of de facto donor influence.

A variation on influence of economic ties is the theory that the presence of easily accessible and concentrated natural resource wealth, typically minerals such as oil, copper, and gems, exerts a negative influence on the spread of democracy. The argument is that shadowy international involvement in the lucrative extraction and trade of these substances prevents a democratic development by fueling state failure or that abundance of concentrated wealth makes extensive spending of patronage possible, as in many of the Middle Eastern countries. In the African context, this subject has been the object of case and small-N comparisons by scholars, such as Reno (1998); but it has also been included in global cross-national analyses, some using as indicators, for example, the export value of minerals as fractions of GDP (e.g., Teorell and Hadenius 2004). The weakness of such indicators is that so much of the export of gems in particular but also precious metals occurs on the black market, for which we have little information. Estimates (e.g., Reno 1999) have concurred that up to 75 percent of markets in these substances and of foreign direct investments associated with the trade are unrecognized, so, including an indicator like the export value of minerals in the present analysis would stretch the demand for reliability too far. It seems less likely that oil and other fuel exports are susceptible to the same measurement problem; therefore, the importance of an oil-dominated economy was assessed by using the value of fuel exports as a percentage of merchandise exports using data from the WBDI. Values are from 1989 for as many countries as possible, but in order to ensure full coverage data from the closest adjacent year was used to replace missing values.

The modernization hypothesis, originally expressed by Lipset (1959) as the more well-to-do a nation the more democratic it is likely to be, must certainly also be included. Rowen (1996, 309), for example, observed that in 1990—near the time this study takes as its starting point—among the 28 countries with a per capita income over $8,000 per year, only Singapore was rated less than free by Freedom House. Many studies have corroborated the thesis (e.g., Burkhart and Lewis-Beck 1994, Londregan and Poole 1996, Gasiorowski and Power 1998) through measures of modernization based on economic indicators, while the earlier studies, including Lipset (1959) and Cutright (1963), used a range of social as well as economic indicators. Hadenius (1992) also found that literacy best predicted the level of democracy. An available composite is the Human Development Index (HDI) from the United

Nations Development Programme, consisting of GDP per capita adjusted for purchasing-power parities, average literacy, and life expectancy. To address uncertainty to some extent but avoid collinearity, I used both [log]GDP per capita, from 1989 adjusted for purchasing-power parities, and the HDI measure from 1992—in order to include as many cases as possible, since the HDI figures from earlier years are missing many values—in two separate models. Bratton and van de Walle's GDP per capita measure was not used, at the expense of reducing comparability of the results, because their measure did not adjust for purchasing-power parities, reducing its validity. Instead, I used data from the WBDI from 1989, but the models were also run using Bratton and van de Walle's measure and the GDP per capita without the logarithm, with no significant effect on the results.[5]

One of the most influential recent studies, Przeworski et al. (2000), however, claims that modernization theory has little if any explanatory power to offer (2000, 137). Instead, they claim, economic conditions that developed under nondemocracy cannot be used to predict the emergence of democracy but democracy is much more likely to survive under prosperity. Another set of related studies has focused on the impact of short-term economic trends on transitions from authoritarian rule (e.g., Remmer 1996) and progress of democratization (e.g., Gasiorowski 1995). In Africa, the outrageously poor economic performance of most of the economies in the 1980s has been suggested as a causal factor in bringing the authoritarian regimes down (e.g., Ake 1993, Bratton 1994, Westebbe 1994). In order to assess these possible confounding effects I included two additional indicators. First, the [log]GDP per capita adjusted for purchasing-power parities, following Przeworski et al., was used with data from 2003. Because of collinearity problems, this was assessed in a separate model from the assessment of modernization effects, using the same measure from 1989. Secondly, average annual growth from 1990 to 2000, also with data from the WBDI, was used to indicate regime performance. Although some of the studies mentioned above found it hard to demonstrate nonlinear relationships, it is assumed here that good economic performance furthers democratization by making people generally more satisfied with the regime and vice versa.

Another recurrent finding has been the consistently negative impact of Islam; this is found in Lipset's early (1959) article and in later ones, such as Ross (2001). To assess the importance of this variable relative to the holding of elections, the supposedly more or less constant share of the population that adheres to Islam was employed in the model; and in order to further facilitate comparability, data was drawn from Bratton and van de Walle's (1996) data set. Another and related issue recently prominent in the literature is ethnolinguistic factionalization, where the debate on the soundness of various measures has been heated (e.g., Chandra 2004; Mozaffar,

Scarritt, and Galaich 2003; Posner 2004; Scarritt and Mozaffar 1999). Regardless of that debate, however, a high level of factionalization has been thought to impede democratization by infusing the polity with too high stakes in fierce competition in more traditional societies. Bratton and van de Walle's (1996) data set includes a measure of the effective number of ethnic groups. Such a composite is known to have the problem that the same figure can refer to many different situations, just as when it is used to measure party system composition, as discussed in Chapter 2. For this reason it was not used here. Instead, the ethnic heterogeneity index from Ellingsen (2000) was used, which also has the distinct advantage of providing coverage of all cases.

Finally, Lipset, Seong, and Torres (1993), in the aftermath of the revolutionary changes in Eastern Europe and Africa after 1989, tested the influence of popular mobilization on democratization. In Africa, perhaps the most renowned finding from Bratton and van de Walle's (1997) study was that popular protests were one of the key driving forces in the introduction of democracy on the continent. This finding has been questioned, however (Lindberg 2002), using the original data set; but it is still influential in the literature and therefore merits closer scrutiny. I included it, using Bratton and van de Walle's own (1996) measure of the number of politically motivated protests between 1985 and 1994.

Descriptive statistics for the independent variables outlined above are listed in Table 16 (on facing page).

With this selection of independent variables it becomes necessary to run a minimum of four models, to avoid problems of collinearity. It should be noted that the analysis here does not attempt to develop a full model that can be used to explain the level of democratization but only to explore a range of variables' possible role as intervening factors or as sources of spurious relationship. As long as the control variables do not eradicate the significance of elections' statistical relationship to the level of civil liberties, the result is positive, indicating support for the argument of this book. The results are presented in Table 17 (p. 139), where all values reported are unstandardized beta coefficients. It was decided to drop Bratton and van de Walle's measure of the number of structural adjustment programs after running the first model, since it showed no significance whatsoever but had the liability of reducing the size of the sample significantly. Finally, in order to err on the side of presenting too much of the results rather than the reverse, a fifth model was added in which only the two statistically strongest predictors are included, to make sure that the inclusion of the other variables did not introduce noise that diminished the statistical significance of the second predictor: amount of aid as share of GDP.

One conclusion of this exercise is unavoidable: no matter what their quality, the

TABLE 16 *Descriptive statistics for independent variables*

Variable	Indicators	Min.	Max.	Mean	Std. Dev.	Number of Countries
Elections	Number of successive repetitive elections as of 2003	0	7	2.25	1.71	48
Oil export	Fuel export as share of merchandise exports (%)	0	96.6	10.642	24.448	48
International influence	Overseas development assistance share of GDP, 1989 (%)	1.1	124.4	17.94	21.62	46
	Number of structural adjustment programs	0	15	5.19	4.49	47
Modernization	Human Development Index for 1992	207	821	407.21	153.25	47
	GDP per capita/ppp*, 1989 (US$)	396	9,635	1780.27	1964.41	44
Regime performance	Average GDP growth, 1990–2000 (%)	−8.2	18.9	.484	3.87	45
	GDP per capita/ppp*, 2003 (US$)	550	16,944	3055.71	3876.95	48
Religion	Muslim share of population (%)	0	100	28.64	33.90	47
Ethnicity	Ethnic fractionalization index	0	93.0	65.8	23.04	47
Popular mobilization	Number of popular protests, 1985–1994	0	26	9.05	7.56	42

*ppp = purchasing-power parity.

longer the series of elections, the higher the level of democracy in a society. Controlling for some of the most well-established and thoroughly researched factors affecting democratization does not wipe out the effect of elections. Rather, in present-day Africa those standard factors seem to have a more marginal impact on the level of democracy in society. Although this is not the main point here, it is unavoidable to note that modernization, as observed by Przeworski et al. (2000) on a global level, does not contribute to an increase in the level of democracy, neither do regime performance, ethnic fractionalization, or even concentrated resource extraction as measured by fuel exports. The most surprising negative finding, perhaps, is that in Africa, as distinct from much of the rest of the world, a large Islamic presence does not negatively affect the level of democracy. This might be temporary, but if it is not, leaders of the free world should pay closer attention to Africa, because part of the answer of how to combine a religious orientation towards Islam with support for democracy might be found there and lessons learned that could perhaps be used to solve this pressing issue in today's world.

The only variable that seems to exert some influence at all independently of elections is the international influence brought to bear on governments through the provision of overseas development assistance (ODA). This is good news from the perspective of donors, since increasing shares of ODA are now tied to support of good governance and democratization. The indicator achieved statistical significance only at the weaker, .10, level; but it is the only one that does even that in these models. Regime performance as measured by average annual growth does indicate statistical significance but only in the first model, which excludes the largest number of cases, 10, and is therefore not considered a substantial finding.

It is a little surprising that the combination of these factors cannot produce much of an influence, showing an explained variance in the 15 to 20 percent range. The exception is the fifth model, which reaches well above 27 percent using only two indicators; and in that model the lion's share of the explanation is provided by the power of elections, while the ODA adds only 3.6 percent to the adjusted R-square value. While this provides food for thought and a rationale for further inquiries into what can explain the development of democracy in Africa and how it develops differently there than in other parts of the world and at other periods, the agenda here is limited to testing for confounding factors of the preceding analysis. In sum, the switch from elections to countries as the unit of analysis strengthens the main hypothesis of this book further. The number of elections held in any one country on its own and independently of the other factors explains almost one-quarter of the variance in level of civil liberties in Africa. The claim is that, independently of the structural characteristics of oil exports, modernization, regime performance, popular

TABLE 17 *The power of elections and possible confounding factors*

		Model Number				
Variable	Indicators	1	2	3	4	5
Elections	Number of successive repetitive elections as of 2003	−.644 .002***	−.411 .013**	−.399 .007***	−.431 .003**	−.425 .000***
Oil export	Fuel exports as share of merchandise exports, ca. 1990 (%)	−.006304 .467	−.003516 .677	−.004252 .576	−.003926 .637	
International influence	Overseas development assistance share of GDP 1989	−.02099 .159	−.02762 .070*	−.02305 .137	−.02726 .080*	−.01522 .070*
	Number of structural adjustment programs, 1980–1990	−.05169 .395	−.02243 .634	−.02043 .666	−.02410 .617	
Modernization	Human Development Index for 1992	.0005288 .807	−.0005772 .787			
	GDP per capita/ppp† 1989 [log]			.350 .660		
Regime performance	Average GDP growth 1990–2000	.102 .060*	.06499 .216	−.007329 .926	.07076 .256	
	GDP per capita/ppp† 2003 [log]				−.101 .905	
Religion	Muslim share of population, ca. 1985	.009644 .170	.005408 .428	.007425 .211	.006256 .292	
Ethnicity	Ethnic fractionalization index	.0151 .193	.005788 .601	.009506 .362	.00659 .550	
Popular mobilization	Number of popular protests, 1985–1994	.0273 .411				
	Constant	4.358 .002***	5.283 .000***	3.555 .210	5.354 .092*	
	Adjusted R^2	.195	.165	.159	.164	.278
	Significance	.078*	.071*	.082*	.072*	.000***
	N	38	43	42	43	46

Note: The top number in each cell is unstandardized beta coefficient and the bottom number is *p*-value. * *p* = .10, ** *p* = .05, *** *p* = .01.
Dependent variable: Freedom House ranking of civil liberties for 2003.
†ppp = purchasing-power parity.

forces, international influences, and culture often put forward as causal factors of democratization, the power of elections is still at work.

CONCLUSIONS

Over the past decade, the view on the importance of elections has become one of pervasive skepticism in many academic quarters. There is a growing attitude that elections at best are harmless, mere procedures of little value to democratization and to the quality of democracy. Recently, Carothers (2002a) declared that the dominant "transition paradigm" of democratization was built on five erroneous assumptions. Surprisingly, one of these is clearly misleading the way Carothers puts it when he argues that it has been assumed that elections will be "not just a foundation stone but a key generator over time of further democratic reforms" (2002a, 8). Even a cursory reading of the dominant literature of the transition paradigm shows this not to be the case. It might be a commonly held belief in advocacy and policy circles but not an assumption or hypothesis in scholarly work. Rather, dominant theories of democratization describe elections as functioning in one of three ways: "founding" elections as indications of the end of the transition period, electoral characteristics as indicators of democracy, or repeated alternations in power as indicators of consolidation of democracy. All the most frequently used indices of democracy build on electoral qualities such as competitiveness of the executive, voter turnout figures, liberty of political parties, and political campaign activities. While many students of democratization working comparatively or on case studies advocate qualitative evaluations far beyond electoral qualities, assuming elections to be irrelevant, large-N analysis relies heavily on electoral characteristics as reflective of democracy and none of the more influential democratization theories has explicitly modeled repetitive *de jure* participatory, competitive, and legitimate elections as a causal factor. By measuring positive and negative changes in democracy beyond elections—as indicated by CL rankings—as effects of elections and nonelection periods, this study provides a first step in this regard.

Elections seem to have a strong positive effect on the expansion of civil liberties. Positive developments in democratic qualities in a society typically come in waves related to election periods. During and shortly after elections, civil liberties expand and deepen, and when negative changes occur they tend to take place in periods before or between elections. Liberalization does not occur first, after which civil society and other actors use their new rights to press for elections. Rather, a decision to hold elections comes first and that causes further liberalization; for each successive electoral cycle the democratic rights and liberties tend to be strengthened. Finally, through a multiple regression analysis, it has been shown that the power of elections has an influence on the level of democracy in society independently of the most prevalent structural factors of democratization analyzed in the literature. In short, elections seem to have the power to expand and improve democracy writ large, but improvements in civil liberties have little effect on the prospects of holding more elections. In other words, the causal effect seems to go from elections to democracy and not the other way around.

CHAPTER SEVEN

Comparative Perspectives
and Reflections

This book analyzes elections as a core institution of representative democracy without presupposing that they actually work as an instrument of democracy. Sklar (1987) noted that most political systems combine both democratic and undemocratic features; Dahl (1971) argued that polyarchy was a matter of degree. In the same vein, this book is concerned with the comparative study of the "democraticness" of elections, in African regimes from clearly authoritarian Chad, Sudan, and Swaziland to hybrid regimes like Kenya before 2002, Benin, Mali, and Tanzania and the electoral and liberal democracies of Botswana, Mauritius, and Ghana after 2000. Focusing on elections has made it possible to include in a single study the complete universe of African cases with a potential to have or develop key democratic qualities. It is now time to reflect on what these overall results in Africa might mean for existing theories of democratization, directions of future research, and policy making.

While it is certainly not a difficult task to find evidence of political and economic stagnation in Africa, disentangling and weighting the setbacks and gains in the continent's recent political history is not easy. The Afro-pessimist view, fueled by the evidence of decay and disillusion that abounds in the numerous political and economic blunders of African states, has gained currency during the latter half of the 1990s and the first years of the twenty-first century and needs qualification. Even though the data presented here also illustrates the difficulties of political transformation and the variations in degree of determination with which democracy is being pursued, the detailed information shows commonalities, allowing generalizations across the continent and over time. Those generalizations convey a measured optimism. It might be that some African countries may never become full liberal democracies or even electoral democracies, but it is important to note that at the time of writing 47 out of the 48 sub-Saharan states are in one stage or another of planning or holding *de jure* participatory, competitive, and legitimate elections: all 48 sub-Saharan African states save Eritrea have either held elections or are preparing to do so. Moreover, even though there have been numerous regime breakdowns over the period studied, in every single case the new leaders have promised—and more often than not held—elections soon after assuming power. While some countries have completed six or seven electoral cycles and appear to be stable democracies, others, like Niger, have struggled through multiple military coup–plagued first elections, finally appearing to be on track, while some, like DRC and RoC, are back on square one. For some countries, the electoral experiences have—in contradiction to the main thesis of this book—resulted in a regression in democratic qualities, but two-thirds are slowly and steadily moving forward.

The main argument of this book is that elections not only signify democracy; they breed democracy, through the self-reinforcing, self-improving quality of repetitive elections. Though this might seem teleological, I suggest that it is the evidence and not the theoretical argument that is teleological. To put the essence of this book in a single proposition for new electoral regimes: the more successive elections, the more democratic the regime. This is not to say that elections are the only or even the main causal factor of democratization. Even the multivariate analysis in Chapter 6 was not meant to pursue any such line of argument. The only claim is that elections in new electoral regimes in Africa have shown a significant and positive causal effect and that this power of elections has so far been underestimated and understudied.

What might these region-specific findings mean for the field of comparative democratization in general? Allowing for a measure of speculation under the untested assumption that the findings of this book are generalizable outside of the continent, what does the bigger picture look like? What perspectives and further stimulation of new issues might these findings offer to the study of elections, democracy, regime transitions, and politics in other societies?

THE TRANSITION PARADIGM

Mainstream literature on the third wave of democratic transitions in the developing world is sometimes referred to as the "transition paradigm." The experience of democratization in Southern Europe and Latin America has been central in this genre, and studies from Eastern Europe and Africa remain peripheral to those who draw data from what has become the "heartland" of democratization. In addition, most of what we know about the factors that promote or hinder democratization stems from small-N comparisons (e.g., Diamond, Linz, and Lipset 1989; Linz and Stepan 1978; O'Donnell and Schmitter 1986). This study challenges one of the core assumptions in the field of democratization by showing that first elections are not necessarily "founding" but are more often just a step in the transition process, and this corroborates Carothers's (2002a) critique on the point. Bratton and van de Walle (1997, 277) argued that liberalization was a necessary prerequisite for free and fair elections. As in most of the transition literature, political liberalization was operationalized by Bratton and van de Walle as regularization of political associations. Since elections by definition are not free and fair if parties are not legal, the conclusion that transitions in Africa occurred first as liberalization then democratization is a tautology. The methodology here avoids that approach and allows for a correction of this mainstream proposition. Elections are not the outcome of liberalization and/ or indicators of democratization but seem to be a causal factor for both. While this study does not contribute to answering the puzzle of why first elections are embarked upon, it does show that liberalization generally does not precede such decisions but rather follows from them—at least this is how things developed in Africa during the period studied.

At the same time, the pervading pessimism built around concepts of hybrid or electoral authoritarian regimes since the mid-1990s is challenged by this study. Using relatively short periods of study, skeptics have posited hybrid regimes as evidence that many countries are not moving towards democracy although they are moving away from harsher authoritarian rule. The analysis in this book suggests that moving from authoritarian rule to a competitive electoral regime tends to lead to further democratization. No matter what the emerging regimes of Africa are to some academic observers—hybrid, electoral authoritarian, patrimonial, or *democraduras* (Diamond 2002, Karl 1995, Luckham 1995)—successive uninterrupted cycles of elections tend to promote greater "democraticness" of both the electoral regime and the society. This is certainly not a justification for building teleological frameworks. To the contrary, such empirical conclusions can only be drawn once the framework is open to alternative outcomes. Yet, the time frame of the present study is also limited, and this should caution against too determinate conclusions. On the other hand, the period used here is the longest so far available on African elections. We cannot know, based on this study, to what extent this is also a trend in other parts of the world.

Another recurrent theme, stemming from O'Donnell and Schmitter's (1986) original work, is that a harsh previous authoritarian regime benefits democratization because of its deterrent effect on the population. This hypothesis is also questioned by the African experience. The countries having experienced the longest continuous series of elections are certainly not those that previously had the harshest authoritarian regimes. Benin, Ghana, Madagascar, Mali, and Senegal are examples that speak to this, while the regimes in Togo, former Zaire, Gabon, and Ethiopia are examples of harsh previous regimes that have not led to noticeably better records.

Economic Development and Elites

Taking an even wider perspective, what are the possible implications for classical explanations of democracy, such as economic development and the agency of elites? After more than half a century of heated debate, few seem to contest the notion that economic development has a positive relationship to democracy. While the original formulations of Cutright (1963) and Lipset (1959), for example, have been reformulated (e.g., by Cheibub et al. 1996, Gasiorowski and Power 1998, Hadenius 1992, Londregan and Poole 1996), the central tenet remains. The analysis in this book adds a dimension to this debate. While economic development obviously affects democracy (Burkhart and Lewis-Beck 1994, Gasiorowski and Power 1998, Haggard and Kaufman 1997, Londregan and Poole 1996), or at least the survival of democracies (Przeworski et al. 2000), the effects of electoral institutions seem to be constant over a vast diversity of economic contexts in Africa. If, as traditionally thought, economic development makes for stability because the people are less likely to revolt and protest once their conditions of life improve, we would expect countries with relatively worse economic conditions and underdevelopment to be more prone to electoral regime breakdown. The analyses in Chapters 3 and 4 of this book show that regime survival in Africa has little relationship to the level or rate of economic development. If it did, poorer countries or countries with negative economic development would have had only short sequences of elections, first and maybe second elections, and the countries with longer series of elections would have been wealthier and with higher growth rates, which is not the case. Supporting this conclusion, the multiple regression analysis performed in Chapter 6 indicates that economic variables have little, if any, impact on the development of democratic qualities in society. This certainly provides a rationale for a further venture into these dynamics, especially since so much of the global literature has found this relationship powerful.

On the other hand, Fosu (2002) has shown that military coups d'état have adversely affected the transformation of economic growth into human development in Africa. By demonstrating that the self-reinforcing power of elections helps prevent such coups, this study suggests that repetitive elections indirectly further human development. In a recent study, Haan and Sturm (2003) present strong evidence that increases in political freedoms cause increases in economic freedom, not the other way around. This finding opens another line of inquiry into the significance of elections in Africa. Since elections seem to be important promoters of increases in freedom, they may also indirectly contribute to increases in economic freedom. The catch, in policy terms, is that finding ways to spur economic development has proven a hard nut to crack in most African countries. Elections, on the other hand, can easily be supported and influenced in the short term, and that might make it possible to further economic growth indirectly. Similarly, Dreher (2003) recently showed that countries with democratic elections are much less likely to thwart International Monetary Fund programs than those with elections of lesser quality. This finding seems to suggest that movement towards better quality of elections, particularly third and later elections, potentially has several positive economic effects. But the nature of these relationships must be investigated further, and it promises to be a fascinating research agenda.

There is close to a consensus in the comparative democratization field on the importance of elites (Bunce 2000). Political, economic, social, and cultural or traditional elites are seen as among the prime movers in transitions. This focus on elites perhaps reflects the predominance of case studies and small-N comparisons; the close inspection and detailed knowledge of persons and processes involved in such studies may make the actors take on a prominent position in explanations. Without questioning the importance of agency and elites' decisions, we need to ask why the elites in so many diverse countries have tended to act similarly. The contribution to an answer made by this study is that the repetition of the electoral processes affects the rational calculations of the political actors through adaptation and learning, creating similar outcomes in diverse countries. The framework of causal links suggests that elites of various kinds across Africa seem to adjust their behavior and strategies accordingly with increasing experience with elections. Seligson and Booth (1995, 269–271) suggest that elections furthered democratization in Central America through learning and adaptation processes along the same lines. Analogous processes arguably were pivotal in post–World War II Japan and Germany, where imposed democracy settled as elites adapted to the new rules and learned to explore the possibilities. This process seems now to be taking root in Africa, as fear and mistrust among political rivals in places like Mali, Kenya, South Africa, Mozambique, and Namibia is slowly replaced by more-peaceful coexistence, acceptance, and competition.

A related hypothesis in the literature is that protracted transitions are more likely to be successful than short ones, because incremental processes favor accommodation and adaptation by political elites (e.g., Huntington 1991, chaps. 4, 5). Learning and adaptation by definition do not occur overnight or by flux but are slow, dynamic, and multifaceted processes partly governed by incentives. Many transitional processes in Africa have been protracted, and even free and fair elections transitions stretched out over many years (cf. Barkan 2000, 235; Lindberg 2004a). It seems to me that Africanists have sometimes tended to exaggerate the rates at which change is taking place, thus concurring with Bratton and van de Walle (1997), who argued that the transitions in Africa were short in a comparative perspective but that short is good and that the rapid transformations have been more successful than the protracted ones. The evidence presented in this book suggests that a majority of these processes have been protracted courses. Madagascar, which started its current track of competitive elections with the elections in 1982, is a case in point.[1] Twenty years and five successive presidential and parliamentary elections later, Madagascar testifies to the reality that transitions may take time if they are ever to become full-fledged electoral democracies. Many African countries' transition processes are still incomplete; many aspects, like accountability and responsiveness, still need to be established or strengthened. A fair number of regimes are still electoral authoritarian, while a few, such as Equatorial Guinea, Cameroon, and Sudan, are only patchy façades of electoral regimes. Yet, the power of elections in Africa to spread democracy has proven to be significantly stronger than most academic observers had believed it could be.

There are many hurdles to be taken and many options for exit that might be taken by political elites in these countries faced with multiethnicity, poverty, authoritarian pasts, low levels of education, and countless other problems. Things like the contentious relationships between Muslims and Christians in Nigeria and between northern and southern Sudanese have created difficulties, casting doubts on the viability of electoral politics. Yet, in countries with longer electoral histories such divides have tended to become less politicized over time. Indeed, because of these numerous difficulties, the impact of holding elections seems even more salient. Even the contrived ethnic rivalries that developed into major divides in Ghana, Kenya, Senegal, and elsewhere seem to be losing their appeal. This is an important lesson, contradicting the claims voiced by African leaders like Daniel A. Moi in Kenya, Jerry J. Rawlings in Ghana, and Joseph Museveni in Uganda that multiparty politics would destroy the social fabric of African societies. The evidence from Africa so far seems to be that over a few electoral cycles mistrust between groups is moderated rather than exacerbated. Certainly this has not always been the case; in the Republic of Congo, elections accompanied by "ninjas" and other paramilitary forces have been used almost exclusively to further divide and rule. But in the greater number of countries tensions have been managed and channeled into electoral politics rather than through the power of the gun. While it may be a little early to pass definitive judgments on more long-term social processes such as these, this is the picture we get if we can judge by the regime survival rates, acceptance of electoral results, and increasing collaboration between opposition parties presented here.

It is quite likely that by participating in an ordered, or relatively ordered, framework for political competition and participation, political actors as well as large portions of the populations learn to replace fear and mistrust with a growing but somewhat cautious acceptance and coexistence. The choices and actions of elites are certainly important in many cases at critical junctures. Yet, over a longer period the incentive structures of electoral institutions tend to pull elites together rather than divide or disperse them. In short, many elites in different countries and contexts have made similar choices, and that should prompt us to qualify the actor-centered explanations.

Opposition Parties

Over three decades ago, Dahl (1971) suggested that the level of political competition to a large degree determines how democratic a regime is. Discussing Africa's opposition groups in a recent contribution, van de Walle (2002) similarly suggested that in Africa the quality of competition and the power of the opposition could go a long way to explaining the levels of democracy. Thus, opposition behavior should be particularly important in electoral regimes where the attainment of democracy is still in question. This study reaffirms that the role of opposition parties is crucial, and in addition it shows that even flawed elections can further the long-term goal of democracy, if opposition parties are willing, in the face of stolen verdicts, to fight another day. Of course, opposition participation is far more likely when at least minimal requirements for freedom and fairness of elections and relative peacefulness of campaigns are instituted (Lindberg forthcoming). This finding calls for more involvement by both domestic and international actors in policing the rules of the game. The presence or absence of authoritarian "big men" and their associates seems not so important in first and following elections; rather, efforts should be made to encourage opposition participation and support the conditions for free and fair and peaceful elections that are in place.

The literature on democratization seems to assume that opposition groups and parties are always prodemocratic actors. This reification of political opposition needs to be revisited, both in Africa and far beyond its borders. While established democracies in the West have reoccurring experiences with fascist and other forms of openly antidemocratic parties, in new democracies the problem is more the presence of less-than-democrats in disguise. The behavior of the new opposition parties in Africa's presidential elections is illustrative. Even in the free and fair elections, losing parties endorsed the results immediately in only 40 percent of the cases. In an additional 44 percent of cases it took up to three months for parties that lost elections to accept the result, a figure that is not encouraging. Losing parties use disputation of elections results, thereby questioning the legitimacy of the process and of the winning candidate's access to executive office, all too often. Efforts to discredit a legitimate and democratic process are a form of undemocratic behavior, and in this light, many opposition parties in Africa do not come across as genuinely prodemocratic. There is little to suggest that African opposition groups and parties should be a special case, since the same phenomena can be found in the postcommunist parties in Eastern Europe and some groups in Latin American countries, such as Bolivia, Chile, and Honduras. Once more, the empirical realities point to the need for institutions that work not thanks to but despite some of the actors. This gives credence to Dahl's (1971, 1989) pleas for polyarchy. It is not so much the quality of opposition parties and leaders that matters but the institutional incentives (guarantees) that constitute the actors and structure their actions along more democratic principles. But more research is needed on the interaction in newly democratizing countries between constitutions and regulations and among individuals within political parties in general and opposition parties in particular. We know too little about how individuals in these elites—especially the often less cooperative disguised nondemocrats—reason and react to new electoral institutions and rules and how their thinking as individuals translates into behavior in a new political environment. Researching this area will require qualitative data of a different kind from that which this study has generated, and producing such data would be a very valuable contribution to our understanding of the mechanisms of democratization.

Civil Society

The transition paradigm in general and the literature on Africa in particular has also posited the centrality of civil society in democratization processes. But it is telling that the more comprehensive reviews of the field, such as Bunce (2000), do not identify any big or even bounded generalizations on which a consensus has been formed with regards to civil society's role and functions. There are certainly many scholars working at extending Almond and Verba's (1963) pioneering work on attitudinal orientations and how organizations influence political processes (e.g., Diamond 1993; cf. Pye 2000). This study does not negate the argument that, once activated and empowered with formal rights, liberties, and a democratization agenda, civil society actors can be catalysts for furthering political development. Yet, Diamond, Linz, and Lipset (1989), for example, argued for the importance of a plural-istic, autonomous, and organized associational life as an instigator of democratiza-tion, and Bratton and van de Walle charged that political mass protests were instru-mental in triggering political transformation in many countries in Africa in the early 1990s. As has been shown elsewhere (e.g., Lindberg 2002, 126), protests were in fact as frequent in African countries that did not democratize, which questions the rele-vance of protests as a causal factor. In the multiple regression analysis in the previ-ous chapter the argument was corroborated when the number of popular protests could be shown to have no impact on the level of democratic qualities in society. Africanists pleading for the importance of civil society also frequently ignore the fact that protests were as common in the 1960s, '70s, and '80s, long before most of these transitions started (Bayart 1991, Wiseman 1990). The analysis presented here instead supports a theory that a strong and active civil society is the outcome of liberaliza-tion and electoral practice and not their cause. As noted in Chapter 6, the expansion of civil liberties, indicating more of an expanded arena for civil society, occurred as a consequence of, rather than in advance of, two-thirds of all first elections.

Meanwhile, as Joseph notes (1999, 454), gains made in freedom and reallocation of power—the dispersion of power through granting of procedural rights (cf. Dahl 1989)—in Africa should not be underestimated. That empowered civil societies legally and procedurally organize and assert themselves more openly now than at any time before represents a historic change. Students, professional organizations, workers and peasant groups, religious and ethnic associations, local development groups, and political parties have all benefited from both positive and negative ex-periences with elections and from the ensuing rise in civil liberties. Electoral activ-ities have tended to stretch boundaries of freedoms and to make them more elastic, and the civil society actors have probably had a role in transferring rights, procedures, and liberties to the societal sphere. Detailed research on the perceptions of such changes among actors in civil society during the formal redistribution of power is an-other underresearched area, not only for Africa but also for many other parts of the world. One hopes that the coming years will bring exciting new research on the processes of diffusion of the awareness, knowledge, and capabilities that translate ex-periences with national electoral rules and processes to other spheres of society.

The same hope for further research pertains to the study of local politics (as sug-gested by one of the causal links discussed in Chapter 5). One of the few attempts so far to probe this area corroborates these extensions of learning from national to lo-cal realms of society. Finkel's (2003) study shows significant effects of civic educa-tion programs in the Dominican Republic, Poland, and South Africa, on political participation and competence in local politics and in local civil life. Voter education programs and the training of election functionaries and administrators are likely to have similar effects, along the lines suggested in the causal links examined in Chapter 5, as the empirical analysis with accompanying examples from various countries hinted. Further research on the translation of engineered new capabilities to localized efforts is needed. Such research could focus in particular on the translation from national electoral politics of new ways of thinking and behaving to political processes governed by local structures and local traditional authorities and councils. Research efforts are under way on women's local empowerment, and it would be interesting to include in such studies a look at how new political procedures are linked to national-level electoral processes. My hunch is that the more continuous experience with competitive and participatory elections on a national level, the more the ideas of political equality and choice for both men and women are spread in praxis at the local political level and in the social and private spheres.

If religious associations and institutions are also seen as part of civil society, the multiple regression analysis in Chapter 6 provides further food for thought. Larger shares of the population adhering to Islam proved not to have a negative impact on the level of democratic qualities in society. This is a significant finding, since so much concern in the present global situation is focused on the Muslim countries' lack of democracy and since many therefore assume Islam to be incompatible with democracy. On this subject, Africa might point the way to the possible and provide lessons to be built upon in supporting the development of democratic practices in these regions.

CORRUPTION AND DEMOCRATIZATION

A pressing issue regarding governance in many developing countries is corruption. Even if it is easy to show a negative global correlation between corruption and democracy and/or freedom — however measured — the exact nature and direction of the relationship is still ill-defined. There are two main and contradictory hypotheses in the democratization literature. The first posits that democratization will lead to a decrease in corruption, and the second argues that corruption will undermine and perhaps reverse democratization. These hypotheses build on mutually exclusive theories, and sorting out which one is true remains an important puzzle. Africa seems to be an excellent field for renewed research efforts on this subject. While this book cannot provide anything more than indirect and suggestive evidence, the findings in Chapter 6 seem to support the first hypothesis.

Corruption indicators could not be included in the multivariate analysis. Of the two existing alternatives — Transparency International's Corruption Perception Index and the World Bank's Control of Corruption measure—TI's index is not comparable over the years and is available for only 13 to 16 countries (depending on the year) while the World Bank's measure is based to a large extent on the existence of electoral institutions and guarantees, which would make the analysis circular if we measured the relationship to elections. Although the World Bank's measure (for 2002) covers 48 African countries, the collinearity problem prevents its use in the multiregression analysis in Chapter 6. We can, however, measure the correlation between civil liberties and incidence of corruption in Africa; it is strong and negative (from Spearman's $-.648$ to $-.822$, $p = .000$, depending on the year of measure); and if elections improve civil liberties, it seems that, at the very least, possibilities for actors to contravene corrupt practices should increase.

Such a relationship would support the idea that corruption is the result of "unrestrained" state power, as is asserted by the World Bank, donors, and some scholars. According to this interpretation, unrestrained power is rule on which there are few or no constraints in terms of horizontal and vertical accountability (Schedler, Diamond, and Plattner 1999) and weak pressures for transparency. Combating corruption therefore appears to need democratization, because the horizontal controls of modern democratic institutions limit discretionary actions of individuals in official positions. In addition, vertical accountability presumably plays a role, since voters do not want to return corrupt leaders to office. The latter seems supported by the fact that anticorruption slogans have been prominent in many winning parties' campaigns during recent elections in South Africa, Ghana, Kenya, Zambia, and other countries. Thus, for two reasons democracy could be a recipe for limiting corruption, and this seems to be the orthodoxy of the day in the international community. Democracy is promoted not only as a positive feature in itself but also as a means to control corruption.

The second hypothesis is that if political corruption is systemic and endemic, voters, intimidated by vote buying and similar practices, are deprived of choices. Political competition puts pressure on the political patronage and clientelism that feed into corruption, both petty and grand. Corruption further undermines the rule of law if courts and judges are involved, making the entire system work inefficiently, with poor delivery of public safety, human rights, public health, schooling, and so on, and it delegitimatizes leaders (e.g., Diamond, Linz, and Lipset 1989). If voters have only corrupt leaders to choose among, democracy as an idea for a good self-government is endangered.

The well-known "big man" syndrome coincides with high degrees of continuity among elites in Africa. The numerous new opposition figures also tend to be dependent on patronage networks, and elections may spur political clientelism similar to America's "Chicago politics." My own research in Ghana on political clientelism (Lindberg 2003) suggests that even in a good case of democratization the dynamics of increasing political patronage and corruption play a detrimental role. Wantchekon's (2003) study in neighboring Benin also corroborates the second and more pessimistic of the hypotheses. Yet, these studies are single-country case studies. Large-N studies seem to lend more support to the first and more positive hypothesis, and this remains a contradiction to be resolved, perhaps by acknowledging that there are different types of corruption. Some kinds, such as grand spoils of politically managed contracts and siphoning-off of resources from the state, might be reduced by the introduction of democratic politics while others, such as political clientelism, may well feed from it. It should also be noted, however, that electoral politics, especially when there are presidential term limits in use, has usually undermined neopatrimonial rule (althoughnot diminished clientelism) and that might be one of its biggest achievements so far.[2] First Moi and now Kibaki in Kenya, similarly Rawlings and now Kufour in Ghana, Chiluba and now Mwanawasa in Zambia, Mpkapa in Tanzania, Museveni in Uganda, and so on, have been or are prevented from staying in office for too long. In sum, as far as the analyses in this book show, if elections improve civil liberties — including the rule of law, transparency, and civic associational life — repetitive elections could be building a bulwark against some types of corruption. At the very least, the institutions of electoral regimes do provide means to fight corruption. Who will make use of such means and under which circumstances remains to be clarified in future research.

STATENESS AND SOCIAL CITIZENSHIP

The notion of "stateness" has been (re-)introduced into democratization studies recently. It is a widely shared belief that a fair measure of empirical, as opposed to judicial, statehood[3] consists in a feeling of unity, a belief in that "we" are a "people" belonging to a state (Buzan 1991, Rustow 1970). An emerging consensus in comparative democratization seems to reaffirm Rustow's argument that successful democratization requires settling the issues of how to form the idea of a single nation and how to agree on the legitimacy of the territorial state. To the extent that the data in this study can speak to the subject of nationhood as expressed during electoral processes, the present analysis questions that widely held belief.

Historically, nation building and state creation in the West, from 1500 to the 1930s, was the outcome of intense war and the accompanying need for increasing taxation (Hall 1986; Hall 1998; Herbst 1989, 1990; Mann 1986). Increases in representation and its democratic qualities seem to have been side effects of a protracted bargaining process rather than a cause of state creation (e.g., North 1990, Tilly 1990). Once established in the European states, however, the increased influence over government that came with representation contributed to building perceptions of citizenship and societal loyalty. In effect, this is Rustow's claim turned on its head: representative government (epitomized in electoral processes that grew out of the demands for representation that followed wider imposition of taxes) contributed to stateness by forging citizenship. This raises a question: If democratization can induce a sense of belonging to a state and create a perception of a community of citizens, could it counteract disengagement and alienation from the state?

In Africa, the question of stateness is closely tied to the issue of social citizenship. It has been claimed that the failure of African states since the 1960s has resulted in an "uncaptured peasantry" (Hyden 1980) and a "disengagement" from the state by the citizens (e.g., Azarya and Chazan 1987, Chazan 1988). The resulting "two publics" (Ekeh 1974) weakened the state even further, making it irrelevant to many of its citizens. There are many descriptive and causal theories about African "predatory states" that contribute little positive to people's lives. In Africa, in response to such states, the informal sphere and affective personalistic networks of support and communication deepened as people sought to safeguard and secure livelihoods and other kinds of securities. This "economy of affection" (Hyden 1983, 2000) is thriving, even under the new democratic era and regardless of level of education. A recent study provides evidence that even modern, urban, and highly educated Ghanaians are actively reproducing these personalized networks that serve to strengthen the informal, as opposed to the formal, state arena (Pankani 2004). What needs to be investigated further is how electoral politics and a promotion of democratic rights and freedoms interact with such trends. It would be interesting to find out if electoral institutions and democratic rights and freedoms help "bring people back in," making them feel and be concerned, legitimate citizens. Will electoral processes, bringing the effects on party collaboration across divides and social organization in civil societies discussed above, contribute to increased stateness by strengthening social citizenship?

Given that development practitioners perceive economies of affection to be an obstacle to development, this is a pressing research issue. The limited—and indeed tentative—contribution the present study can make to this question is based on the data indicating a reduction in violence and electoral disputes and an increase in voter participation, regime survival, and—crucially—civil liberties such as interorganizational acceptance as countries gain more experience with elections. This suggests that electoral practices might contribute to bringing people closer to shared beliefs of citizenship and the rights, obligations, and benefits of collective action in both the political and the societal spheres. The symbolic power of such acts as people united by the voting experience, as one people making a collective decision on who shall govern, should not be underestimated. Other actions related to electoral practices, such as leaders of antagonistic factions converging in peaceful talks and even coalitions, probably have real effects on people's acceptance of each other as citizens of one country.

The argument that the symbolism of electoral processes is as important as its concrete workings could certainly be made, although it would be difficult to collect hard evidence to support it. Further research on the effects electoral politics and the exercise of democratic rights might have on notions of citizenship and identity is warranted. Narrative life histories and political and anthropological mapping of such outcomes will be invaluable in such future research on African politics. An approach like the one in this study can do only so much; these processes must be investigated by other means. Such research is needed not only for its inherent value but also to build a foundation for more general theories.

LESSONS ON CONSOLIDATION

Transition to and consolidation of democracy are typically considered as two analytically distinct phases with specific characteristics and causes. Although primarily concerned with elections, this study suggests two things to students of consolidation: to focus on empirical referents of stabilization of regimes, and to disaggregate their dependent variable. Regarding the first issue, there is an inherent but not unsolvable problem with the projection in the mainstream literature of consolidation as expected regime stability (e.g., O'Donnell 1996, Valenzuela 1992), making consolidation an inference rather than an empirically observable phenomenon (Sartori 1984, 24; Schedler 2001a, 67–68). The operationalization of such a dependent variable is inherently difficult and fraught with questions about how a dependent variable that is no longer an object but an expectation is to be measured. Methodologically, the analysis employed here suggests a focus on evidenced records to indicate stability of a regime. In Africa, electoral regimes tend not to break down after two or three electoral cycles, and that sort of indication of consolidation and stabilization would probably be preferable.

Secondly, the fact that many of the countries in Africa cannot be labeled liberal democracies, and some not even electoral democracies (Lindberg forthcoming), testifies that stabilization of "bundled wholes" such as democracy is not one coherent process. Different parts—partial regimes—may be stabilized through distinct processes with different starts and endings in time. The electoral partial regime may be consolidated—stabilized—at a much earlier stage than, say, the civilian control and democratic accountability of the military. Stabilization of such distinct parts of democracy may also have different causes and effects. People's attitudes, civil society's strength, the level of economic development, and so on—any of these may be the reason for stabilization in some but not other partial regimes. Elections are self-reinforcing and self-improving once they continue, and when that electoral regime has stabilized it becomes an independent variable in its own right, with effects on another part of the consolidation of democracy, namely, citizens' attitudes and elites' behavior. Structuring incentives for elites to behave more democratically and creating lock-in effects, repetitive elections contribute to manifest behavior. But they also seem to be able to affect citizens' belief in and valuation of elections and of democracy and, by repetition and habituation, to create expectations or discounts of the future that contribute to the consolidation of democracy. In short, this study calls on "consolidologists" to study *de facto* rather than expected regime stability and to disaggregate their inherently complex and multifaceted dependent variable. It should be investigated as a set of variables each with its own theoretical specification and existing empirical referents rather than being treated as an ontologically coherent inference, which has arguably never existed. More research on the consolidation or stabilization of constituent parts of regimes is an agenda worth pursuing. It would also open up the possibility for empirical questions about possible causal relationships between the stabilization of partial regimes rather than assuming that they make one coherent whole.

POLICY IMPLICATIONS

While the findings of this study relate to several important theoretical discussions in academia, they also have a few policy implications. Social science should, when it has the opportunity, provide guidance for practical action. In 1971, Dahl avowed that foreign aid should not be used to establish polyarchy in other parts of the world, because too little was known about the complex processes of political development (1971, 213–214). Since the end of the Cold War, democracy promotion has become a core goal of not only the United States' but most other Western countries' foreign policy (e.g., Burgess 2001). The question remains today: Exactly how much do we know about political development? This study's conclusion—that elections are not merely reflections of the level of democracy but that the power of elections is self-reinforcing and self-improving and causes democratic qualities in society to expand and deepen—provides a strong case for the continuation of aid and support for electoral processes in developing countries. At least in Africa, international support for elections has facilitated a move towards better and more stable polyarchies, as it were, contributing to the experience of greater freedoms for a greater number of people. In this regard, it is not support to activities in already democratized countries for inferred "consolidation" that is mostly needed. Rather, countries that have not yet made it to democracy should be assisted. Support is most needed in countries where opposing forces are still fighting over the rules of the game, where election results are disputed, elections are sometimes flawed, where opposition groups operate under less than free and fair conditions and the communications media are constrained, and where authoritarian tendencies are still strong but elections are being held. The findings also point to a need for the international community to sustain support to transitioning countries over an extended period of time, typically 12 to 15 years.

Empirical evidence also challenges pessimists about the export of institutions, such as Moss (1995, 208), who argue that exporting Western institutions and values is likely to fail and that elected regimes in non-Western countries will not be stable. The export and import of electoral institutions have most often turned out well, and most electoral regimes in Africa have remained stable over a decade or more. Foreign aid and policy pressure to bring about an electoral regime is an important external intervention in promoting the spread of democracy and freedom. Once started, efforts should be directed at securing the regime against breakdown over the first two, three, or four electoral cycles. If countries come that far, the level of freedom will generally have increased significantly and the habituation or socialization into the new institutional incentives for prodemocratic behavior will have gone far enough in most cases for the elections to take on their own self-reinforcing power.

The international focus during the 1990s on support of elections and election-related activities of civil society, the media, and opposition groups was therefore not misguided. Calls to reduce such support in favor of other activities are standing on shaky empirical ground. At the same time, the international community's support to (so-called) civil society organizations in Africa should be carefully calibrated. We know that many of these supposedly independent organizations are far from independent. Many have been initiated by individuals in or closely associated with political parties and leadership. Supporting them may risk undermining the assumed function of civil society in Africa as a counterbalancing power and independent agenda setter in the democratization process. International support for such organizations also risks creating artificial civil society associations (Boussard 2003). When funds for the support of organizations are announced, societal entrepreneurs are generally quick to see the potential for a good source of income. Briefcase NGOs and small profit-making firms in the civil society mix are well-known features in Africa.

Too much financial and programmatic dependence on international aid, diplomatic missions, and international NGOs can be a source of discomfort for well-meaning civil society organizations.

In the same way that aid has been seen to undermine the accountability and autonomy of governments (e.g., Brautigham 1992, 11; Friedman 1958; Karl 1997, 57, 190; Moore 1998; Tilly 1990), dependence risks undermining the autonomy and legitimacy of civil society organizations, both in the eyes of the people and in relation to government. U.S. foreign policy is clearly intent on using the leverage over civil society organizations to further its foreign policy agenda on a number of issues, including opposition to abortion and support of military interventions and war. This creates a dilemma. On the one hand, everyone who has worked in Africa knows that many organizations are in dire need of organizational, programmatic, strategic, and financial support; and foreign countries have a legitimate right to further their interests and goals, to a certain extent. There is no reason, for example, for Swedish, U.S., or U.K. taxpayers to support antidemocratic organizations or think tanks or media actors supporting violations of the rights of women. On the other hand, too much conditional aid risks undermining authentic civil society organizations and creating artificial associations that may not perform the expected functions.[4]

THE POWER OF ELECTIONS IN UNFAVORABLE CONDITIONS

The outlook presented in this book may seem excessively optimistic if read the wrong way. I certainly do not advocate a lowering of the standards of assessment and analysis of democratic qualities in Africa, for instance, a *démocratie tropicalisée*, or tropicalized version of democratic practices. While refraining from idealizing what democracy is or can be, using ideal types that no country has ever or will ever attain, I also do not see any point in measuring African politics by different standards than those applied to the rest of the world. Some indicators are more specifically interesting in the case of new rather than established democracies—such as participation of opposition parties—but that is not to say that partial boycotts or violence is acceptable.

Countries with a turbulent present and where the future seems unpredictable need *de jure* participatory, competitive, and legitimate elections to provide a possible means and mechanism for democratization. Elections have provided more than just an arena for political contest. The institutional ramifications of elections have ushered in new (semi-)independent bodies within the state that can provide ways for individuals and groups to pursue their own goals. The process of holding competitive elections can make actors adapt and change their strategies, as well as transfer democratic norms to other parts of society. Yet, it is a process that can, and does, fail. Democratization has always involved a struggle over political power, however. The struggle concerns fundamental rules of the game, and such struggles sometimes involve even life-and-death combat. Nevertheless, the message of this book's analysis is that just because things start off badly there is no reason to believe that the struggle will be lost.

An underlying assumption of this book is that liberal democracy is a desirable state for countries in Africa, as well as in the rest of the world. I have not—and will not at this late stage—argue that point. It should be obvious that I deem this to be a possible outcome for countries in Africa. I do not share the culturalist view that liberal democracy is an inherently misguided choice for African countries because of peculiarities in their societies and cultures. African electoral regimes and democracies are and will continue to be different from Western, Japanese, or Indian democracies in certain ways. Africa is not only distinguished from other parts of the world, but the variety of cultures, historical experiences, and societal institutions within Africa is equally diverse. African democracies and electoral regimes will therefore continue to be different among themselves as well as being distinct from the rest of the world. This is no different from the great divide that exists between the way democracy functions and is perceived in the universalistic welfare states of Scandinavia and in Anglo-Saxon counterparts, not to mention countries such as Italy, Greece, and heterogeneous Switzerland (where women achieved suffrage in the last semi-independent region only in 1994). The United States' democracy is itself a unique one, which in Sartori's words (1987) works in complex ways no thanks to but in spite of its constitution. If the world of established democracies can span such dissimilar countries and contexts, why should it be impossible or unsuitable in the diversity of Africa?

This study has not deduced factors lacking in Africa; it is based exclusively on Africa's own experiences with electoral procedures and practices. When scholars posit that the growth of an urban middle class, formation of pacted transitions, or establishment of parliamentary rather than presidential systems, for example, furthers democratic development, such advice is based on assumptions of causal equivalence and spatially constant effects. It is sometimes assumed that Europe's and Latin America's experiences will be had by Africa in the twenty-first century. This may or may not prove true. The same applies to the main theoretical contribution of this study, the democratizing power of elections. It may be a factor we have simply neglected to study in democratization processes in general—and it should be possible to go back and test it for Europe, Latin America, and Japan—or it may turn out to be a unique feature of African transitions in the late twentieth and early twenty-first centuries.

Dahl (1971) concluded his study by positing that countries with political conditions unfavorable to democracy—which includes most African nations—are unlikely to transform into stable polyarchies in the near future. This prediction has been borne out for more than 30 years now, but the present study has surveyed a blind spot in Dahl's and many others' reasoning. Exercising and improving democratic procedures in the partial regime of elections tends to have positive effects on democratic qualities in society. These freedoms and rights are undoubtedly of fundamental value in and of themselves. If all humans are born equal, we either have equal rights to participate in the self-government by the people or have equally no right to rule at all. I prefer the former. Holding repetitive elections is the mechanism we know to work best (or least bad) in translating self-government into effective government in a modern state. It is by no means an unfailing mechanism, but it is the best we have. It furthers a level of freedom and a set of rights and liberties that relatively few people in human history have experienced. What this book shows is that elections in and of themselves further the spread and depth of such fundamental freedoms. It seems that it is no small or insignificant thing to vote.

Appendix 1. Annual Overview
of Elections in Africa, 1989–2003

TABLE 18 *Overview of elections in Africa, by year*

	–1989	1990	1991	1992	1993	1994	1995	1996	1997	1998	1999	2000	2001	2002	2003	Total
Presidential	7	3	5	9	11	4	2	14	6	5	8	5	9	7	2	97
Parliamentary	19	3	5	12	11	8	9	9	9	8	11	7	6	14	4	135
Total	26	6	10	21	22	12	11	23	15	13	19	12	15	21	6	232
Free and fair	42%	33%	90%	43%	64%	92%	46%	44%	33%	54%	84%	50%	60%	57%	50%	56%
	11	2	9	9	14	11	5	10	5	7	16	6	9	12	3	119
Participation																
Voter turnout	67%	60%	57%	49%	60%	77%	62%	59%	53%	60%	66%	62%	64%	60%	57%	61%
	24	6	10	20	20	12	11	23	15	12	19	11	15	20	5	223
Full opposition participation	81%	17%	90%	62%	72%	100%	64%	30%	67%	77%	90%	67%	87%	67%	83%	70%
	21	1	9	13	16	12	7	7	10	10	17	8	13	14	5	163
Autocrats gone	19%	33%	0%	10%	9%	8%	18%	9%	20%	8%	16%	17%	20%	10%	17%	13%
	5	2	—	2	2	1	2	2	3	1	3	2	3	2	1	31
Competition																
Winner's % of votes	73%	53%	70%	47%	52%	54%	77%	56%	65%	64%	53%	60%	51%	59%	60%	57%
	6	3	5	8	11	4	2	14	6	5	8	5	9	7	2	95
Largest party's % of seats	76%	77%	56%	57%	58%	56%	58%	69%	72%	62%	60%	61%	66%	62%	57%	63%
	19	3	5	12	10	8	9	9	8	6	11	7	6	14	4	131
2nd party's % of seats	12%	6%	19%	9%	12%	28%	11%	8%	9%	10%	14%	14%	12%	18%	12%	13%
	19	3	5	12	10	8	9	8	8	6	11	7	6	14	4	130
Turnover of power*	15%	0%	80%	24%	46%	33%	27%	17%	7%	0%	42%	50%	40%	19%	17%	28%
	4	—	8	5	10	4	3	4	1	—	8	6	6	4	1	66

Legitimacy															
Losers accepted	42%	0%	70%	29%	27%	42%	18%	17%	27%	39%	33%	32%	27%	43%	33%	32%
	10	–	7	6	6	5	2	4	4	5	4	6	4	9	2	74
Peaceful process	29%	0%	30%	5%	9%	33%	18%	30%	13%	23%	8%	26%	40%	29%	50%	23%
	7	–	3	1	2	4	2	7	2	3	1	5	6	6	3	52
Regime survived	100%	83%	90%	62%	68%	75%	73%	74%	87%	85%	95%	83%	100%	100%	100%	85%
	26	5	9	13	15	9	8	17	13	11	18	10	15	21	6	196

[a] These figures combine "half" and "full" turnovers (see Chapter 3). Half turnovers make up 35% (N = 23) of the total, while full turnovers constitute a majority of cases, at 65% (N = 43).

Note: All data are compiled in 48 country files. The specification of the source for each data entry in the data set is found in these country files. The country files can be obtained from the author upon request but the general references are found below.

Sources: Africa South of Sahara 2003; Badu and Larvie 1996; Baker 2002; Bratton 1998; Bratton and van de Walle 1996; Burnell 2002; Clark and Gardiner 1997; Derbyshire and Derbyshire 1996; Di Lorenzo and Sborgi 2001; Galvan 2001; Lodge 2002; May and Massey 2001; Nohlen, Krennerich, and Thibaut 1999; Olukoshi 1998; Smith 2001; Uwechue 1996. Adam Carr's Election Archive, Agora Election Data; AllAfrica.com, various dates; BBC News Online, various dates; BBC World News, various dates; (Accra, Ghana) Daily Graphic; East African Standard, various dates; Freedom House Country Reports, various countries; Elections Around the World; Electionsworld.org (Netherlands); Election Watch, Journal of Democracy 1990–2003; Electionsworld.org IFES Elections Statistics; Independent Election Commission, various countries; International IDEA, News and Voter Turnout Project; IPU Chronicle of Parliamentary Elections; IPU Parline; Keesing's Record of World Events; Mampilly (graphed report), 2001; News from Nordic Africa Institute, various issues; NDI Elections Observation Reports, various issues; Pan African News Agency, various dates; UN IRIN News Reports; U.S. Department of State Background Notes, various countries and issues.

Appendix 2. Changes in Civil Liberties Rankings

Figures 6 and 7, in Chapter 6, chart changes in civil liberties over election periods. The outcomes matrices from the empirical analysis of the results displayed in those figures are presented below in Tables 19 and 20. The first matrix is based on an analysis of how many units of change in CL ranking are associated with each set of elections and the periods between them. Thus, if 10 first elections resulted in a positive change (more or better civil liberties) of two units on the CL scale each, that would make a total positive change of 20. If among first elections there were also 5 elections that each resulted in a negative unit change (less or worse civil liberties) of one unit, that would make a total negative change of 5. The balance (20 − 5) would accordingly be a total of +15. The second matrix is based on an analysis of how many of the elections (expressed as shares) in each electoral cycle are associated with changes in CL scores, either independently of the elections or dependent on them.

TABLE 19 *Unit changes of ranking in civil liberties over electoral periods (data for Fig. 6)*

	1st Period		2nd Period		3rd Period		4th+ Period	
	Pre-election (A)	1st Election Effects	Non-election (B)	2nd Election Effects	Non-election (C)	3rd Election Effects	Non-election (D)	4th+ Election Effects
Positive changes	23	62	8	17	1	5	1	2
Negative changes	−10	−3	−11	−4	−1	−1	−1	−4
Balance	13	59	−3	13	0	4	0	−2

TABLE 20 *Percentage of elections followed by changes in civil liberties (data for Fig. 7)*

	1st Period		2nd Period		3rd Period		4th+ Period	
	Pre-election (A)	1st Election Effects	Non-election (B)	2nd Election Effects	Non-election (C)	3rd Election Effects	Non-election (D)	4th+ Election Effects
Positive change (%)	26	47	13	28	3	10	5	10
Negative change (%)	11	4	18	7	3	3	5	14
No change (%)	63	49	68	66	93	87	91	76
Total %	100	100	99	101	99	100	101	100
Total N	70	70	60	61	30	30	21	21

Table 21 gives the unit changes in CL scores for each country's elections up to four electoral cycles, where that many have occurred. Selection of cases was the same as in Chapter 6. The countries have been coded as "Yes" when it fully corroborates the main hypothesis, as set out in Chapter 5, "(Yes)" when there was a slight deviation but the country's track record overall corroborates the hypothesis, or "No" when the country's track record does not support the hypothesis, either contradicting it or providing inconclusive evidence.

Changes in civil liberties occurring as a result of the election are measured as changes in civil liberties according to the operationalization in Chapter 6. A few deviations have been necessary, however, for various reasons. A few countries in Africa run presidential and parliamentary elections at different intervals. In these circumstances, the period of measurement has been adjusted in the data set to capture years unaffected by elections, as per the specification of election-related changes above. In some instances, coups and premature legislative elections have made the equation impossible. The full list of adjustments that had consequences for the coding is as follows:

Burkina Faso, 2nd presidential election, 1998
 Period: 1992–1996 reduced to 1993–1994 due to the parliamentary elections in 1992 and 1995.
 Change: 1993 record a ranking of "4" instead of "5" in 1992.

Chad, 2nd presidential election, 2001
 Period: 1997–1999 reduced to 1998–1999 due to the parliamentary election in 1997.
 Change: 1998 record a ranking of "4" instead of "5" in 1997.

Djibouti, 3rd parliamentary election, 2003
 Period: 1998–2001 reduced to 2000–2001 due to the presidential election in 1999.
 Change: 2000 record a ranking of "5" instead of "6" in 1998.

Gabon, 1st presidential election, 1993
 Period: 1989–1991 changed to 1991–1992 due to the parliamentary election in 1990.
 Change: 1991 record a ranking of "3" instead of "5" in 1989, and 1992 ranked "4" instead of "3" in 1991.

Gambia, 1st presidential election, 1996
 Period: 1992–1994 reduced to 1994–1995 due to coup in 1994.
 Change: 1992 ranked "2," but after the coup in 1994 it was given a ranking of "6."

Mauritania, 3rd parliamentary election, 2001
 Period: 1997–1999 reduced to 1998–1999 due to general elections 1997.
 Change: 1997 was ranked "6" instead of "5" in 1998.

Mauritius, 3rd parliamentary election, 1983
 Period: 1979–1981 equation impossible due to the parliamentary election in 1982. Coded as "missing."

TABLE 21 Unit changes in civil liberties over successive elections, by country

Country	Country Support Hypothesis?	Type of Election	Initial Ranking	Pre-election (A)	1st Election Effects	Non-election (B)	2nd Election Effects	Non-election (C)	3rd Election Effects	Non-election (D)	4th+ Election Effects
Benin	Yes	Pres.	7	—	+4	—	+1	—	—	—	—
		Parl.	7	—	+4	—	+1	—	—	—	—
Botswana	Yes	Parl.	4	—	+1	—	—	—	—		
Burkina Faso	No	Pres.	6	+1	—	—	—	—			
		Parl.	6	+1	—	—	—	—	+1		
Cameroon	Yes	Pres.	6	—	+1	—	—	—	—		
		Parl.	6	—	+1	—	—	-1	—		
Cape Verde	(Yes)*	Pres.	6	+1	+2	—	—	—	—		
		Parl.	6	+1	+2	—	—	—	—		
Chad	No	Pres.	5	—	—	-1	-1	—	—		
		Parl.	5	—	—	-1	—	—			
Djibouti	No	Pres.	5	—	-1	—	—				
		Parl.	5	—	-1	—	—				
Eql. Guinea	Yes	Pres.	7	—	—	—	+1	—	—		
		Parl.	7	—	—	—	—				
Ethiopia	No	Parl.	5	—	—	+1	-1				
Gabon	(Yes)*	Pres.	5	+1	—	—	-1				
		Parl.	6	—	+3	—	—				
Gambia	Yes	Pres.	4	-2	—	—	—				
		Parl.	4	-2	—	—	+1				
Ghana	Yes	Pres.	5	-1	+2	—	+1	—	—		
		Parl.	5	-1	+2	—	+1	—	—		
Guinea	No	Pres.	5	—	—	—	—				
		Parl.	5	—	—	—					
Kenya	Yes	Pres.	6	—	—	—	+1	—	+2		
		Parl.	6	—	—	—	+1	—	+2		
Madagascar	(Yes)*	Pres.	6	—	+1	+1	+1	—	—	—	—
		Parl.	6	—	—	+1	+1	—	—	—	+1
Malawi	Yes	Pres.	6	-1	+4	—	—	—			
		Parl.	6	-1	+4	—	—				

Country	Elections								
Mali	(Yes)*	Pres.	6	+1	+2	–	–	–	–
		Parl.	6	+1	+2	–	–	–	–
Mauritania	Yes	Pres.	6	–	–	–	–	–	–
		Parl.	6	–	–	–	–	–	–
Mauritius	Yes	Pres.	2	–	–	-1	+1	–	–
Mozambique	No	Parl.	6	+2	–	-1	+1	–	–
		Pres.	6	+2	–	–	–	–	–
Namibia	No	Parl.	6	+1	–	–	+1	–	–
		Pres.	3	NA	-1	–	-1	+1	–
		Parl.	3	NA	NA	–	-1	+1	–
Nigeria	Yes	Pres.	6	–	+3	-1	+1	–	–
		Parl	6	–	+3	-1	+1	–	–
Sao Tome & Principe**	No	Pres.	7	+2	+2	+1	+1	–	–
		Parl.	7	+2	+2	+1	+1	–	–
Senegal	No	Pres.	6	+2	+1	–	–	+1	-2
		Parl.	6	+2	+1	–	–	+1	-2
Seychelles	(Yes)*	Pres.	6	–	+2	–	–	–	–
		Parl.	6	–	+2	–	–	–	–
South Africa	Yes	Parl.	4	–	+1	–	–	–	–
Sudan	No	Pres.	7	–	–	–	–	–	–
		Parl.	7	–	–	–	–	–	–
Swaziland	Yes	Parl.	5	–	–	+1	–	–	–
Tanzania	No	Pres.	5	–	+1	–	–	–	–
		Parl.	5	–	+1	–	–	–	–
Togo	No	Pres.	6	+1	–	–	–	–	–
		Parl.	6	+1	–	–	–	–	–
Uganda	Yes	Pres.	5	–	+1	-1	–	–	–
		Parl.	5	–	+1	-1	–	–	–
Zambia	Yes	Pres.	5	–	+2	-1	–	-1	–
		Parl.	5	–	+2	-1	–	+1	–
Zimbabwe	(Yes)*	Pres.	6	+1	+1	-1	-1	+1	-1
		Parl.	5	–	+1	–	–	–	–

*These countries also in part disfavor the hypothesis, but their record in large part corroborates it.

**The development for Sao Tome and Principe has been calculated from 1991 when multiparty elections were introduced and disregarding the brief attempted coup in August 1995.

Namibia, 1st parliamentary election, 1989
  Period: 1985–1987 equation impossible due to missing values.
  Coded as "missing."

Nigeria, 1st presidential election, 1993
  Period: 1989–1991 reduced to 1989–1990 due to the parliamentary election in
    1992.
  Change: 1991 ranked "4" and 1990 ranked "5."

Sao Tome and Principe, 2nd parliamentary election, 1994
  Period: 1990–1992 reduced to 1991–1992 due to the parliamentary election in
    1991.
  Change: 1990 ranked "5" and 1991–1992 ranked "3."

Appendix 3. About the Freedom House Civil Liberties Index

Freedom House is a nonprofit, nonpartisan organization led by a board of trustees composed of political, business, and labor leaders, former senior government officials, scholars, writers, and journalists. Since 1972, it has published an annual assessment of the state of freedom in 192 countries and 18 territories, based on questions derived largely from the Universal Declaration of Human Rights. The survey's methodology is reviewed periodically by an advisory committee, which over the years has made modest methodological changes to adapt to evolving ideas about political rights and civil liberties. The time-series data are not revised retroactively, and any changes to the methodology are introduced incrementally, in order to ensure the comparability of the rating from year to year.

Freedom House rates each country on two main scales, one measuring political rights and one assessing other civil liberties. The latter includes freedom to express opinions, establish civil institutions, and have personal autonomy without interference from the state. This is crucial in distinguishing the CL index from state-provided aspects of democracy, such as elections, although the existence of civil liberties naturally is also dependent on the permissiveness or facilitation of the state and regime.

The survey does not rate governments but tries to evaluate real-world rights and freedoms enjoyed by individuals as enabled by both state and nongovernmental actors. The survey's methodology has changed a little over the years, but data are comparable. From 1972 to 1988, the survey was conducted by Raymond Gastil, but in 1989 a large team of analysts was created. The team reportedly uses a broad range of sources, including foreign and domestic news reports, nongovernmental organizations' publications, think tank and academic analyses, individual professional contacts, and visits to each region. Country ratings are reviewed on a comparative basis by more than 30 analysts and consultants. Each country is evaluated on 15 indicators of 4 dimensions (see list below). For each indicator, the country is awarded from zero (lowest) to four (highest) raw points, which are then added. The highest possible score for civil liberties is 60 raw points. Neither the raw points total nor raw points for each indicator are made public by Freedom House. However, the correspondence between raw points and the final rating is:

Total Raw Scores	CL Rating
60–53	1
52–44	2
43–35	3
34–26	4
25–17	5
16–8	6
0–7	7

DIMENSIONS AND INDICATORS OF CIVIL LIBERTIES

The following are word-for-word quotations of the dimensions and indicators of civil liberties used by Freedom House in their annual survey.

A. Freedom of Expression and Belief
   1. Are there free and independent media and other forms of cultural expression? (In cases where the media are state-controlled but offer pluralistic points of view, the survey gives the system credit.)
   2. Are there free religious institutions, and is there free private and public religious expression?
   3. Is there academic freedom, and is the educational system free of extensive political indoctrination?
   4. Is there open and free private discussion?

B. Associational and Organizational Rights
   1. Is there freedom of assembly, demonstration, and open public discussion?
   2. Is there freedom of political or quasi-political organization? (Note: this includes political parties, civic organizations, ad hoc issue groups, etc.)
   3. Are there free trade unions and peasant organizations or equivalents, and is there effective collective bargaining? Are there free professional and other private organizations?

C. Rule of Law
   1. Is there an independent judiciary?
   2. Does the rule of law prevail in civil and criminal matters? Are police under direct civilian control?
   3. Is there protection from police terror, unjustified imprisonment, exile, or torture, whether by groups that support or oppose the system? Is there freedom from war and insurgencies?
   4. Is the population treated equally under the law?

D. Personal Autonomy and Individual Rights
   1. Is there personal autonomy? Does the state control travel, choice of residence, or choice of employment? Is there freedom from indoctrination and excessive dependency on the state?

2. Do citizens have the right to own property and establish private businesses? Is private business activity unduly influenced by government officials, the security forces, or organized crime?

3. Are there personal social freedoms, including gender equality, choice of marriage partners, and size of family?

4. Is there equality of opportunity and the absence of economic exploitation?

Appendix 4. A Data Set on Elections in Africa

A Data Set on Elections in Africa

Country	Type of Election	Number of Election	Date of Election	Electoral System	Free and Fair?	Turn-out (%)	Opposition Participate?	Autocrats Gone?	Winner's % Votes/ Seats	2nd's % Votes/ Seats	Turn-over?	Losers Accept?	Peaceful?	Regime Survive?	Date of Breakdown	Cands./ Parties Participate	Cands./ Parties Boycott	Parties in Lower House
Angola	Pres.	1st	30 Sep 1992	—	Yes, somewhat	91	Yes, all	No	50	40	No	No, none	Isolated incidents	No, civil war	01 Jan 1993	12	1	—
	Parl.	1st	30 Sep 1992	PR	Yes, somewhat	91	Yes, all	No	59	32	No	No, none	Yes	No, civil war	01 Jan 1993	18	0	12
Benin	Pres.	1st	24 Mar 1991	—	Yes, somewhat	64	Yes, all	No	36	27	Half	Yes, all immediately	Yes	Yes	—	13	0	—
	Pres.	2nd	18 Mar 1996	—	Yes, entirely	88	Yes, all	No	34	37	Half	Some/later	Yes	Yes	—	7	0	—
	Pres.	3rd	18 Mar 2001	—	No, irregularities affected outcome	70	Partial boycott	No	47	29	No	Some/later	Yes	Yes	—	17	0	—
	Parl.	1st	17 Feb 1991	PR/ small MMCs	Yes, somewhat	53	Yes, all	No	19	14	Half	Yes, all immediately	Yes	Yes	—	14	0	12
	Parl.	2nd	28 Mar 1995	PR/ small MMCs	Yes, somewhat	76	Yes, all	No	25	23	Half	Some/later	Yes	Yes	—	31	0	18
	Parl.	3rd	30 Mar 1999	PR/ small MMCs	Yes, somewhat	70	Yes, all	No	33	13	Half	Yes, all immediately	Yes	Yes	—	35	0	20
	Parl.	4th	30 Mar 2003	PR/ small MMCs	Yes, somewhat	52	Yes, all	No	38	18	Yes	Yes, all immediately	Yes	Yes	—	14	0	11
Botswana	Parl.	1st	18 Oct 1969	Plurality SMC	Yes, somewhat	55	Yes, all	Yes	77	10	No	Yes, all immediately	Yes	Yes	—	4	0	4
	Parl.	2nd	01 Oct 1974	Plurality SMC	Yes, somewhat	31	Yes, all	Yes	84	6	No	Yes, all immediately	Yes	Yes	—	4	0	4

(continued)

A Data Set on Elections in Africa (continued)

Country	Type of Election	Number of Election	Date of Election	Electoral System	Free and Fair?	Turn-out (%)	Opposition Participate?	Autocrats Gone?	Winner's % Votes/ Seats	2nd's % Votes/ Seats	Turn-over?	Losers Accept?	Peaceful?	Regime Survive?	Date of Breakdown	Cands/ Parties Participate	Cands/ Parties Boycott	Parties in Lower House
	Parl.	3rd	01 Oct 1979	Plurality SMC	Yes, entirely	58	Yes, all	Yes	91	6	No	Yes, all immediately	Yes	Yes	—	4	0	3
	Parl.	4th	01 Oct 1984	Plurality SMC	Yes, entirely	78	Yes, all	Yes	82	15	No	Yes, all immediately	Yes	Yes	—	5	0	3
	Parl.	5th	07 Oct 1989	Plurality SMC	Yes, entirely	68	Yes, all	Yes	91	9	No	Yes, all immediately	Yes	Yes	—	7	0	2
	Parl.	6th	15 Oct 1994	Plurality SMC	Yes, entirely	70	Yes, all	Yes	68	33	No	Yes, all immediately	Yes	Yes	—	9	0	2
	Parl.	7th	16 Oct 1999	Plurality SMC	Yes, entirely	77	Yes, all	Yes	83	15	No	Yes, all immediately	Yes	Yes	—	7	0	3
Burkina Faso	Pres.	1st	01 Dec 1991	—	No, irregularities affected outcome	27	Boycott	No	99	1	No	No, none	Isolated incidents	Yes	—	1	2	—
	Pres.	2nd	15 Nov 1998	—	No, irregularities affected outcome	56	Partial boycott	No	88	7	No	Some/later	Isolated incidents	Yes	—	3	5	—
	Parl.	1st	24 May 1992	PR/ small MMCs	No, not at all	34	Yes, all	No	73	12	No	Some/later	Isolated incidents	Yes	—	29	0	10
	Parl.	2nd	11 May 1997	PR/ small MMCs	No, irregularities affected outcome	44	Yes, all	No	90	5	No	Some/later	Isolated incidents	Yes	—	13	0	4
	Parl.	3rd	05 May 2002	PR	Yes, somewhat	64	Yes, all	No	51	15	No	Yes, all immediately	Yes	Yes	—	30	0	13
Burundi	Pres.	1st	01 Jun 1993	—	Yes, somewhat	97	Yes, all	No	66	33	Yes	No, none	Isolated incidents	No, civil war	01 Jul 1996	4	0	—
	Parl.	1st	30 Jun 1993	PR	Yes, somewhat	91	Yes, all	No	80	20	Yes	No, none	Isolated incidents	No, civil war	01 Jul 1996	6	0	2

Cameroon	Pres.	1st	11 Oct 1992	—	No, irregularities affected outcome	72	Partial boycott	No	40	36	No	No, none	Isolated incidents	Yes	—	6	0	—
	Pres.	2nd	12 Oct 1997	—	No, irregularities affected outcome	81	Boycott	No	93	3	No	No, none	Isolated incidents	Yes	—	3	4	—
	Parl.	1st	01 Mar 1992	Majority SMC/MMC	No, irregularities affected outcome	61	Partial boycott	No	49	36	No	No, none	Isolated incidents	Yes	—	32	4	4
	Parl.	2nd	17 May 1997	Majority SMC/MMC	No, irregularities affected outcome	76	Yes, all	No	64	24	No	Some/later	Isolated incidents	Yes	—	45	0	7
	Parl.	3rd	15 Sep 2002	Majority SMC/MMC	No, irregularities affected outcome	70	Yes, all	No	83	12	No	No, none	Yes	Yes	—	46	1	5
Cape Verde	Pres.	1st	17 Feb 1991	—	Yes, somewhat	61	Yes, all	No	74	26	Yes	Yes, all immediately	Isolated incidents	Yes	—	2	0	—
	Pres.	2nd	18 Feb 1996	—	Yes, somewhat	44	Partial boycott	Associates participate	92	1	No	Yes, all immediately	Yes	Yes	—	1	0	—
	Pres.	3rd	25 Feb 2001	—	Yes, somewhat	49	Yes, all	Associates participate	47	46	Yes	Some/later	Yes	Yes	—	4	0	—
	Parl.	1st	13 Jan 1991	PR/small MMCs	Yes, somewhat	75	Yes, all	No	71	29	Yes	Yes, all immediately	Isolated incidents	Yes	—	2	0	2
	Parl.	2nd	17 Dec 1995	PR/small MMCs	Yes, somewhat	76	Yes, all	Associates participate	69	29	No	Yes, all immediately	Isolated incidents	Yes	—	5	0	3
	Parl.	3rd	14 Jan 2001	PR/small MMCs	Yes, somewhat	55	Yes, all	Associates participate	56	42	Yes	Yes, all immediately	Yes	Yes	—	5	0	3
CAR	Pres.	1st	25 Oct 1992	—	No, not at all	—	Partial boycott	No	—	—	No	No, none	No, not at all	No, other	01 Nov 1992	—	—	—
	Pres.	1st	19 Sep 1993	—	Yes, somewhat	69	Yes, all	No	37	22	Half	Some/later	Isolated incidents	Yes	—	8	0	—

(continued)

A Data Set on Elections in Africa (continued)

Country	Type of Election	Number of Election	Date of Election	Electoral System	Free and Fair?	Turn-out (%)	Opposition Participate?	Autocrats Gone?	Winner's % Votes/Seats	2nd's % Votes/Seats	Turn-over?	Losers Accept?	Peaceful?	Regime Survive?	Date of Breakdown	Cands/Parties Participate	Cands/Parties Boycott	Parties in Lower House
	Pres.	2nd	19 Dec 1999	–	Yes, somewhat	56	Yes, all	No	52	19	No	Some/later	Isolated incidents	No, civil war	01 Mar 2003	10	0	–
	Parl.	1st	19 Sep 1993	Majority SMC/MMC	Yes, somewhat	68	Yes, all	No	40	15	Half	Yes, all immediately	Isolated incidents	Yes	–	15	0	12
	Parl.	2nd	13 Dec 1998	Majority SMC/MMC	Yes, somewhat	59	Yes, all	No	43	18	Half	Yes, all immediately	No, not at all	No, civil war	01 Mar 2003	29	0	11
Chad	Pres.	1st	03 Jul 1996	–	No, irregularities affected outcome	68	Yes, all	No	44	12	No	Some/later	Isolated incidents	Yes	–	15	0	–
	Pres.	2nd	27 May 2001	–	No, irregularities affected outcome	61	Yes, all	No	63	16	No	Some/later	Isolated incidents	Yes	–	7	0	–
	Parl.	1st	23 Feb 1997	Mixed	No, irregularities affected outcome	46	Yes, all	No	52	23	No	Some/later	Isolated incidents	Yes	–	38	0	10
	Parl.	2nd	21 Apr 2002	Mixed	No, irregularities affected outcome	53	Yes, all	No	73	46	No	Yes, all immediately	Isolated incidents	Yes	–--	40	2	15
Comoros*	Pres.	1st	11 Mar 1990	–	No, irregularities affected outcome	64	Yes, all	No	23	24	No	No, none	No, not at all	No, coup	01 Sep 1995	8	0	–
	Pres.	1st	16 Mar 1996	–	Yes, somewhat	64	Partial boycott	Associates participate	21	16	Yes	No, none	No, not at all	No, coup	01 Jan 1999	6	0	–
	Pres.	1st	14 Apr 2002	–	No, irregularities affected outcome	76	Partial boycott	No	40	16	No	No, none	Isolated incidents	Yes	–	7	2	–

Country	Type	Round	Date	System	Irregularities affected outcome		Boycott	Associates										
	Parl.	1st	29 Nov 1992	Majority SMC/MMC	No, irregularities affected outcome	48	Partial boycott	No	17	7	No	No, none	No, not at all	Yes	—	22	2	12
	Parl.	1st	08 Dec 1996	Majority SMC/MMC	No, irregularities affected outcome	20	Boycott	Associates participate	84	7	No	No, none	Isolated incidents	No, coup	01 Jan 1999	2	8	2
	Parl.	2nd	26 Dec 1993	Majority SMC/MMC	No, irregularities affected outcome	—	Partial boycott	No	68	10	No	No, none	No, not at all	No, coup	01 Sep 1995	10	2	9
Djibouti	Pres.	1st	15 May 1993	—	No, irregularities affected outcome	51	Partial boycott	No	61	22	No	No, none	Isolated incidents	Yes	—	5	1	—
	Pres.	2nd	12 Apr 1999	—	Yes, somewhat	56	Yes, all	Associates participate	74	26	Half	Some/later	Yes	Yes	—	2	0	—
	Parl.	1st	18 Dec 1992	Plurality SMC	No, irregularities affected outcome	49	Partial boycott	No	99	1	No	No, none	Isolated incidents	Yes	—	3	3	1
	Parl.	2nd	19 Dec 1997	Plurality SMC	Yes, somewhat	57	Yes, all	No	99	1	No	Yes, all immediately	Isolated incidents	Yes	—	4	2	1
	Parl.	3rd	10 Jan 2003	Plurality SMC	Yes, somewhat	48	Yes, all	Associates participate	99	1	No	Some/later	Yes	Yes	—	8	0	1
DRC[+]	Pres.	NA																
	Parl.	NA																
Eql. Guinea	Pres.	1st	25 Feb 1996	—	No, not at all	80	Boycott	No	98	1	No	No, none	Isolated incidents	Yes	—	3	2	—
	Pres.	2nd	15 Dec 2002	—	No, not at all	—	Boycott	No	99	1	No	No, none	Isolated incidents	Yes	—	1	4	—
	Parl.	1st	21 Nov 1993	PR/small MMCs	No, not at all	68	Partial boycott	No	85	8	No	No, none	Isolated incidents	Yes	—	6	8	4
	Parl.	2nd	07 Mar 1999	PR/small MMCs	No, irregularities affected outcome	95	Yes, all	No	94	5	No	No, none	Isolated incidents	Yes	—	13	0	3

(continued)

A Data Set on Elections in Africa (continued)

Country	Type of Election	Number of Election	Date of Election	Electoral System	Free and Fair?	Turn-out (%)	Opposition Participate?	Autocrats Gone?	Winner's % Votes/ Seats	2nd's % Votes/ Seats	Turn-over?	Losers Accept?	Peaceful?	Regime Survive?	Date of Breakdown	Cands./ Parties Participate	Cands./ Parties Boycott	Parties in Lower House
Eritrea†	Pres.	NA																
	Parl.	NA																
Ethiopia	Parl.	1st	07 May 1995	Plurality SMC	No, irregularities affected outcome	94	Partial boycott	Associates participate	32	24	No	No, none	Isolated incidents	Yes	—	44	3	44
	Parl.	2nd	14 May 2000	Plurality SMC	No, irregularities affected outcome	90	Yes, all	Associates participate	32	24	No	Some/later	Isolated incidents	Yes	—	50	0	26
Gabon	Pres.	1st	05 Dec 1993	—	Yes, somewhat	88	Yes, all	No	51	27	No	No, none	No, not at all	Yes	—	13	0	--
	Pres.	2nd	06 Dec 1998	—	No, irregularities affected outcome	54	Yes, all	No	67	17	No	No, none	Isolated incidents	Yes	—	8	0	—
	Parl.	1st	04 Nov 1990	PR	No, irregularities affected outcome	88	Partial boycott	No	52	17	No	No, none	Isolated incidents	Yes	—	36	—	8
	Parl.	2nd	29 Dec 1996	PR	No, irregularities affected outcome	54	Partial boycott	No	71	8	No	Some/later	Isolated incidents	Yes	—	36	0	13
	Parl.	3rd	09 Dec 2001	PR	No, irregularities affected outcome	44	Partial boycott	No	72	7	No	Some/later	Isolated incidents	Yes	—	33	3	5
Gambia*	Pres.	1st	05 May 1982	—	No, irregularities affected outcome	56	Yes, all	No	—	—	No	No, none	Isolated incidents	Yes	—	2	0	—

Pres.	1st	26 Sep 1996	—	No, irregularities affected outcome	80	Partial boycott	No	56	33	No	Some/later	Isolated incidents	Yes	—	4	0	—
Pres.	2nd	05 May 1987	—	No, irregularities affected outcome	80	Yes, all	No	59	28	No	No, none	Yes	Yes	—	3	0	—
Pres.	2nd	18 Oct 2001	—	Yes, somewhat	90	Yes, all	No	53	33	No	Some/later	Isolated incidents	Yes	—	5	0	—
Pres.	3rd	29 Apr 1992	—	Yes, somewhat	56	Yes, all	No	58	22	No	Yes, all immediately	Isolated incidents	No, coup	01 Jul 1994	5	0	—
Parl.	1st	05 May 1982	Plurality SMC	No, irregularities affected outcome	57	Yes, all	No	77	9	No	No, none	Isolated incidents	Yes	—	2	0	2
Parl.	1st	02 Jan 1997	Plurality SMC	No, irregularities affected outcome	73	Yes, all	No	69	15	No	Some/later	Yes	Yes	—	4	0	4
Parl.	2nd	05 May 1987	Plurality SMC	No, irregularities affected outcome	80	Yes, all	No	89	14	No	No, none	Yes	Yes	—	3	0	2
Parl.	2nd	17 Jan 2002	Plurality SMC	No, irregularities affected outcome	57	Partialt boycott	No	94	4	No	Some/later	Yes	Yes	—	3	3	3
Parl.	3rd	29 Apr 1992	Plurality SMC	Yes, somewhat	56	Yes, all	No	61	9	No	Yes, all immediately	Isolated incidents	No, coup	01 Jul 1994	5	0	3
Ghana Pres.	1st	03 Nov 1992	—	No, irregularities affected outcome	50	Yes, all	No	59	30	No	Some/later	Isolated incidents	Yes	—	5	0	—
Pres.	2nd	07 Dec 1996	—	Yes, somewhat	77	Yes, all	No	57	40	No	Yes, all immediately	Yes	Yes	—	5	0	—
Pres.	3rd	28 Dec 2000	—	Yes, somewhat	60	Yes, all	Associates participate	48	44	Yes	Yes, all immediately	Isolated incidents	Yes	—	7	0	—

(continued)

A Data Set on Elections in Africa (continued)

Country	Type of Election	Number of Election	Date of Election	Electoral System	Free and Fair?	Turn-out (%)	Opposition Participate?	Autocrats Gone?	Winner's % Votes/ Seats	2nd's % Votes/ Seats	Turn-over?	Losers Accept?	Peaceful?	Regime Survive?	Date of Breakdown	Cands./ Parties Participate	Cands./ Parties Boycott	Parties in Lower House
	Parl.	1st	29 Dec 1992	Plurality SMC	Yes, somewhat	29	Boycott	No	98	4	No	No, none	Isolated incidents	Yes	–	3	3	3
	Parl.	2nd	07 Dec 1996	Plurality SMC	Yes, somewhat	77	Yes, all	No	67	31	No	Yes, all immediately	Yes	Yes	–	5	0	4
	Parl.	3rd	07 Dec 2000	Plurality SMC	Yes, somewhat	70	Yes, all	Associates participate	50	46	Yes	Yes, all immediately	Isolated incidents	Yes	–	7	0	4
Guinea	Pres.	1st	19 Dec 1993	–	No, irregularities affected outcome	79	Yes, all	No	52	20	No	No, none	Isolated incidents	Yes	–	4	4	–
	Pres.	2nd	14 Dec 1998	–	No, irregularities affected outcome	70	Yes, all	No	54	25	No	No, none	No, not at all	Yes	–	5	0	–
	Parl.	1st	11 Jun 1995	Mixed	Yes, somewhat	62	Partial boycott	No	62	17	No	Some/later	Isolated incidents	Yes	–	21	2	9
	Parl.	2nd	30 Jun 2002	Mixed	No, irregularities affected outcome	72	Partial boycott	No	75	18	No	Some/later	No, not at all	Yes	–	12	6	6
Guinea-Bissau	Pres.	1st	07 Aug 1994	–	Yes, somewhat	89	Yes, all	No	46	22	No	Some/later	Isolated incidents	No, coup	01 Jun 1998	8	0	–
	Pres.	1st	28 Nov 1999	–	Yes, somewhat	72	Yes, all	Associates participate	39	23	Yes	Yes, all immediately	Isolated incidents	Yes	–	11	0	–
	Parl.	1st	03 Jul 1994	PR/ small MMCs	Yes, somewhat	89	Yes, all	No	62	19	No	Some/later	Isolated incidents	No, coup	01 Jun 1998	12	0	5
	Parl.	1st	28 Nov 1999	PR/ small MMCs	Yes, somewhat	80	Yes, all	Associates participate	37	27	Yes	Yes, all immediately	Isolated incidents	Yes	–	11	0	8
Ivory Coast*	Pres.	1st	28 Oct 1990	–	Yes, somewhat	69	Partial boycott	No	82	18	No	Some/later	No, not at all	Yes	–	2	0	–

Pres.	1st	22 Oct 2000	—	No, irregularities affected outcome	37	Partial boycott	No	59	33	Yes	Some/later	No, not at all	No, civil war	01 Sep 2002	5	2	—
Pres.	2nd	22 Oct 1995	—	No, irregularities affected outcome	56	Partial boycott	Associates participate	95	4	No	No, none	No, not at all	No, coup	01 Dec 1999	3	2	—
Parl.	1st	25 Nov 1990	Plurality SMC	No, irregularities affected outcome	40	Partial boycott	No	93	5	No	Some/later	No, not at all	Yes	—	17	0	3
Parl.	1st	10 Dec 2000	Plurality SMC	No, irregularities affected outcome	33	Partial boycott	Associates participate	43	42	Yes	Some/later	No, not at all	No, civil war	01 Sep 2002	6	4	6
Parl.	2nd	26 Nov 1995	Plurality SMC	No, irregularities affected outcome	30	Yes, all	No	85	7	No	Some/later	Isolated incidents	No, coup	01 Dec 1999	10	0	3
Kenya Pres.	1st	29 Dec 1992	—	No, irregularities affected outcome	66	Yes, all	No	36	26	No	Some/later	No, not at all	Yes	—	8	0	—
Pres.	2nd	30 Dec 1997	—	No, irregularities affected outcome	65	Yes, all	No	40	31	No	Some/later	Isolated incidents	Yes	—	15	0	—
Pres.	3rd	27 Dec 2002	—	Yes, somewhat	57	Yes, all	Associates participate	62	31	Half	Yes, all immediately	Isolated incidents	Yes	—	5	0	—
Parl.	1st	29 Dec 1992	Plurality SMC	No, irregularities affected outcome	68	Yes, all	No	56	16	No	Some/later	No, not at all	Yes	—	8	0	6
Parl.	2nd	30 Dec 1997	Plurality SMC	No, irregularities affected outcome	64	Yes, all	No	51	18	No	Some/later	Isolated incidents	Yes	—	22	0	10

(continued)

A Data Set on Elections in Africa (continued)

Country	Type of Election	Number of Election	Date of Election	Electoral System	Free and Fair?	Turn-out (%)	Opposition Participate?	Autocrats Gone?	Winner's % Votes/ Seats	2nd's % Votes/ Seats	Turn-over?	Losers Accept?	Peaceful?	Regime Survive?	Date of Breakdown	Cands./ Parties Participate	Cands./ Parties Boycott	Parties in Lower House
	Parl.	3rd	27 Dec 2002	Plurality SMC	Yes, somewhat	57	Yes, all	Associates participate	60	31	Half	Yes, all immediately	Isolated incidents	Yes	—	40	0	19
Lesotho	Parl.	1st	28 Mar 1993	Plurality SMC	Yes, somewhat	72	Yes, all	Associates participate	99	1	Yes	No, none	Isolated incidents	No, coup	01 Aug 1994	3	0	1
	Parl.	1st	23 May 1998	Plurality SMC	Yes, somewhat	72	Yes, all	Associates participate	99	1	No	No, none	Isolated incidents	Yes	01 Sep 1998	12	0	2
	Parl.	1st	25 May 2002	Mixed	Yes, somewhat	68	Yes, all	Associates participate	65	18	No	Some/later	Isolated incidents	Yes	—	19	0	10
Liberia	Pres.	1st	09 Jul 1997	—	Yes, somewhat	83	Yes, all	No	75	10	No	Yes, all immediately	Isolated incidents	No, civil war	01 Jun 2003	13	0	—
	Parl.	1st	19 Jul 1997	PR	Yes, somewhat	89	Yes, all	No	76	11	No	Yes, all immediately	Isolated incidents	No, civil war	01 Jun 2003	16	0	6
Madagascar	Pres.	1st	07 Oct 1982	—	No, irregularities affected outcome	87	Partial boycott	No	80	20	No	No, none	Isolated incidents	Yes	—	2	0	—
	Pres.	2nd	06 Apr 1989	—	No, irregularities affected outcome	81	Yes, all	No	62	20	No	Some/later	Isolated incidents	Yes	—	4	0	—
	Pres.	3rd	10 Feb 1993	—	Yes, somewhat	74	Yes, all	No	45	29	Yes	Yes, all immediately	No, not at all	Yes	—	8	0	—
	Pres.	4th	02 Jan 1997	—	Yes, somewhat	58	Yes, all	No	37	23	Yes	Yes, all immediately	Isolated incidents	Yes	—	15	0	—
	Pres.	5th	16 Dec 2001	—	No, irregularities affected outcome	58	Yes, all	No	52	36	Yes	No, none	Isolated incidents	Yes	—	6	0	—

Parl.	1st	28 Aug 1983	Plurality SMC	No, irregularities affected outcome	73	Partial boycott	No	86	6	No	No, none	Isolated incidents	Yes	—	7	1	4
Parl.	2nd	06 Apr 1989	Plurality SMC	No, irregularities affected outcome	74	Yes, all	No	87	5	No	Some/later	Isolated incidents	Yes	—	8	0	5
Parl.	3rd	16 Jun 1993	PR/small MMCs	Yes, somewhat	55	Yes, all	No	33	11	Yes	Yes, all immediately	No, not at all	Yes	—	121	0	23
Parl.	4th	17 May 1998	Mixed	Yes, somewhat	60	Yes, all	No	42	11	Half	Yes, all immediately	Isolated incidents	Yes	—	151	0	9
Parl.	5th	17 Dec 2002	Mixed	Yes, somewhat	60	Partial boycott	Associates participate	64	14	No	Yes, all immediately	Yes	Yes	—	40	1	7
Malawi																	
Pres.	1st	17 May 1994	—	Yes, somewhat	80	Yes, all	No	47	34	Half	Yes, all immediately	Isolated incidents	Yes	—	4	0	—
Pres.	2nd	15 Jun 1999	—	Yes, somewhat	93	Yes, all	Associates participate	52	45	No	No, none	Isolated incidents	Yes	—	5	0	—
Parl.	1st	17 May 1994	Plurality SMC	Yes, somewhat	80	Yes, all	No	48	32	Half	Yes, all immediately	Isolated incidents	Yes	—	8	0	3
Parl.	2nd	15 Jun 1999	Plurality SMC	Yes, somewhat	93	Yes, all	Associates participate	48	34	No	No, none	Isolated incidents	Yes	—	11	0	4
Mali																	
Pres.	1st	26 Apr 1992	—	Yes, somewhat	23	Yes, all	Yes	45	14	Yes	Yes, all immediately	Isolated incidents	Yes	—	9	0	—
Pres.	2nd	11 May 1997	—	Yes, somewhat	29	Partial boycott	Yes	84	4	No	No, none	No, not at all	Yes	—	2	8	—
Pres.	3rd	28 Apr 2002	—	Yes, somewhat	38	Yes, all	Associates participate	29	21	Yes	Some/later	Isolated incidents	Yes	—	24	0	—
Parl.	1st	08 Mar 1992	Majority SMC/MMC	Yes, somewhat	21	Yes, all	Yes	65	8	Yes	Yes, all immediately	Isolated incidents	Yes	—	12	0	10
Parl.	2nd	13 Apr 1997	Majority SMC/MMC	No, not at all	20	Partial boycott	Yes	—	—	No	No, none	No, not at all	Yes	—	36	24	—
Parl.	3rd	03 Aug 1997	Majority SMC/MMC	No, irregularities affected outcome	21	Partial boycott	Yes	87	5	No	Some/later	Isolated incidents	Yes	—	17	18	8

(continued)

A Data Set on Elections in Africa (continued)

Country	Type of Election	Number of Election	Date of Election	Electoral System	Free and Fair?	Turn-out (%)	Opposition Participate?	Autocrats Gone?	Winner's % Votes/Seats	2nd's % Votes/Seats	Turn-over?	Losers Accept?	Peaceful?	Regime Survive?	Date of Breakdown	Cands/Parties Participate	Cands/Parties Boycott	Parties in Lower House
	Parl.	4th	14 Jul 2002	Mixed	Yes, somewhat	21	Yes, all	Associates participate	31	31	Half	Some/later	Isolated incidents	Yes	—	—	—	—
Mauritania	Pres.	1st	24 Jan 1992	—	No, irregularities affected outcome	47	Yes, all	No	63	33	No	Some/later	Isolated incidents	Yes	—	4	0	—
	Pres.	2nd	12 Dec 1997	—	No, irregularities affected outcome	75	Partial boycott	No	90	7	No	No, none	Yes	Yes	—	5	5	—
	Parl.	1st	13 Mar 1992	Majority SMC/MMC	No, irregularities affected outcome	39	Partial boycott	No	85	1	No	No, none	Isolated incidents	Yes	—	8	6	3
	Parl.	2nd	18 Oct 1996	Majority SMC/MMC	No, irregularities affected outcome	52	Partial boycott	No	89	1	No	Some/later	Isolated incidents	Yes	—	11	1	3
	Parl.	3rd	19 Oct 2001	Majority SMC/MMC	Yes, somewhat	55	Yes, all	No	79	5	No	Yes, all immediately	Yes	Yes	—	16	0	7
Mauritius	Parl.	1st	01 Jul 1976	Plurality SMC	No, irregularities affected outcome	88	Partial boycott	No	49	40	Half	Some/later	Isolated incidents	Yes	—	16	0	3
	Parl.	2nd	01 Jul 1982	Plurality SMC	Yes, somewhat	90	Yes, all	No	91	3	No	Some/later	Isolated incidents	Yes	—	18	0	4
	Parl.	3rd	01 Jul 1983	Plurality SMC	Yes, somewhat	84	Yes, all	No	66	31	Half	Yes, all immediately	Isolated incidents	Yes	—	15	0	5
	Parl.	4th	01 Jul 1987	Plurality SMC	Yes, somewhat	88	Yes, all	Associates participate	63	34	No	Yes, all immediately	Isolated incidents	Yes	—	22	0	8
	Parl.	5th	15 Sep 1991	Plurality SMC	Yes, somewhat	84	Yes, all	Associates participate	85	11	No	Some/later	Yes	Yes	—	15	0	5

Mozambique	Parl.	6th	20 Dec 1995	Plurality SMC	Yes, entirely	78	Yes, all	Yes	90	3	Half	Yes, all immediately	Yes	Yes	–	23	0	6
	Parl.	7th	11 Sep 2000	Plurality SMC	Yes, entirely	81	Yes, all	Yes	81	11	Half	Yes, all immediately	Yes	Yes	–	20	0	7
	Pres.	1st	29 Oct 1994	–	Yes, somewhat	88	Yes, all	No	53	34	No	Some/later	Isolated incidents	Yes	–	12	0	–
	Pres.	2nd	05 Dec 1999	–	Yes, somewhat	70	Yes, all	No	52	48	No	No, none	Yes	Yes	–	3	0	–
	Parl.	1st	29 Oct 1994	PR	Yes, somewhat	88	Yes, all	No	52	45	No	Some/later	Isolated incidents	Yes	–	15	0	3
	Parl.	2nd	05 Dec 1999	PR	Yes, somewhat	63	Yes, all	No	53	47	No	No, none	Yes	Yes	–	15	0	2
Namibia	Pres.	1st	08 Dec 1994	–	Yes, somewhat	76	Yes, all	Associates participate	75	24	No	Some/later	Yes	Yes	–	3	0	–
	Pres.	2nd	01 Dec 1999	–	Yes, somewhat	63	Yes, all	Yes	77	10	No	Some/later	Isolated incidents	Yes	–	4	0	–
	Parl.	1st	11 Nov 1989	PR	Yes, somewhat	97	Yes, all	No	57	29	Yes	Yes, all immediately	Isolated incidents	Yes	–	10	0	7
	Parl.	2nd	08 Dec 1994	PR	Yes, somewhat	76	Yes, all	Associates participate	74	21	No	Some/later	Yes	Yes	–	8	0	5
	Parl.	3rd	01 Dec 1999	PR	Yes, somewhat	63	Yes, all	Yes	76	10	No	Some/later	Isolated incidents	Yes	–	8	0	5
Niger°	Pres.	1st	27 Mar 1993	–	Yes, somewhat	33	Yes, all	No	27	34	Yes	No, none	Isolated incidents	No, coup	01 Jan 1996	8	0	–
	Pres.	1st	08 Jul 1996	–	No, irregularities affected outcome	66	Partial boycott	No	52	20	No	No, none	Yes	No, coup	01 Apr 1999	4	0	–
	Pres.	1st	24 Nov 1999	–	Yes, somewhat	43	Yes, all	Associates participate	32	22	Yes	Some/later	Isolated incidents	Yes	–	7	0	–
	Parl.	1st	14 Feb 1993	Mixed	Yes, somewhat	33	Yes, all	No	35	26	Yes	Yes, all immediately	Isolated incidents	Yes	–	14	0	9
	Parl.	1st	23 Nov 1996	Mixed	No, irregularities affected outcome	39	Partial boycott	No	70	13	No	No, none	Isolated incidents	No, coup	01 Apr 1999	4	8	4

(continued)

A Data Set on Elections in Africa (continued)

Country	Type of Election	Number of Election	Date of Election	Electoral System	Free and Fair?	Turn-out (%)	Opposition Participate?	Autocrats Gone?	Winner's % Votes/Seats	2nd's % Votes/Seats	Turn-over?	Losers Accept?	Peaceful?	Regime Survive?	Date of Breakdown	Cands./Parties Participate	Cands./Parties Boycott	Parties in Lower House
	Parl.	1st	24 Nov 1999	Mixed	Yes, somewhat	43	Yes, all	Associates participate	46	20	Yes	Yes, all immediately	Isolated incidents	Yes	—	19	0	5
	Parl.	2nd	12 Jan 1995	Mixed	Yes, somewhat	35	Yes, all	Associates participate	35	29	Yes	Some/later	Isolated incidents	No, coup	01 Jan 1996	12	0	9
Nigeria	Pres.	1st	12 Jun 1993	—	No, irregularities affected outcome	37	Partial boycott	Yes	52	48	Yes	No, none	No, not at all	No, coup	01 Nov 1993	352	0	—
	Pres.	1st	27 Feb 1999	—	No, irregularities affected outcome	52	Partial boycott	No	63	37	Yes	No, none	Isolated incidents	Yes	—	2	0	—
	Pres.	2nd	19 Apr 2003	—	No, irregularities affected outcome	68	Yes, all	No	62	32	No	No, none	No, not at all	Yes	—	20	0	—
	Parl.	1st	04 Jul 1992	Plurality SMC	No, irregularities affected outcome	44	Partial boycott	Associates participate	54	46	Half	Some/later	Isolated incidents	No, coup	01 Nov 1993	2	—	2
	Parl.	1st	01 Apr 1998	Plurality SMC	No, not at all	—	Boycott	No	—	—	No	No, none	Isolated incidents	No, other	01 May 1998	—	—	—
	Parl.	1st	20 Feb 1999	Plurality SMC	Yes, somewhat	41	Yes, all	No	61	20	Half	Some/later	Isolated incidents	Yes	—	3	0	3
	Parl.	2nd	12 Apr 2003	Plurality SMC	No, irregularities affected outcome	50	Yes, all	No	67	27	No	Some/later	No, not at all	Yes	—	30	0	8
RoC*	Pres.	1st	16 Aug 1992	—	Yes, somewhat	60	Yes, all	No	36	20	Yes	Yes, all immediately	Isolated incidents	No, other	01 May 1997	16	0	—
	Pres.	1st	10 Mar 2002	—	No, irregularities affected outcome	69	Partial boycott	No	89	3	No	Some/later	Yes	Yes	—	7	3	—

Parl.	1st	21 Jul 1992	Majority SMC/MMC	Yes, somewhat	50	Yes, all	No	31	23	Yes	Yes, all immediately	Isolated incidents	No, other	—	40	0	19
Parl.	1st	23 Jun 2002	Majority SMC/MMC	Yes, somewhat	65	Yes, all	No	39	22	No	Some/later	No, not at all	Yes	—	100	0	32
Parl.	2nd	06 Oct 1993	Majority SMC/MMC	No, irregularities affected outcome	—	Yes, all	No	38	22	No	No, none	No, not at all	No, civil war	01 May 1997	20	0	12
Rwanda[†]																	
NA																	
NA																	
Sao Tome & Principe[°]																	
Pres.	1st	03 Mar 1991	—	Yes, somewhat	60	Yes, all	Associates participate	82	—	Half	Some/later	Isolated incidents	No, coup	01 Aug 1995	3	0	—
Pres.	1st	21 Jul 1996	—	Yes, somewhat	77	Yes, all	No	41	38	No	Yes, all immediately	Yes	Yes	—	5	0	—
Pres.	2nd	29 Jul 2001	—	Yes, somewhat	62	Yes, all	Yes	56	39	Yes	Yes, all immediately	Isolated incidents	Yes	—	5	0	—
Parl.	1st	20 Jan 1991	PR/small MMCs	Yes, somewhat	77	Yes, all	No	60	38	Yes	Yes, all immediately	Isolated incidents	Yes	—	4	0	3
Parl.	1st	08 Nov 1998	PR/small MMCs	Yes, somewhat	64	Yes, all	Associates participate	56	29	No	Yes, all immediately	Yes	Yes	—	8	0	3
Parl.	2nd	02 Oct 1994	PR/small MMCs	Yes, somewhat	52	Yes, all	No	49	26	Yes	Yes, all immediately	Yes	No, coup	01 Aug 1995	8	0	3
Parl.	2nd	03 Mar 2002	PR/small MMCs	Yes, somewhat	67	Yes, all	Yes	44	42	No	Yes, all immediately	Yes	Yes	—	9	0	9
Parl.	3rd	03 Mar 2003	PR/small MMCs	Yes, somewhat	—	Yes, all	Yes	42	42	No	Yes, all immediately	Yes	Yes	—	—	0	8
Senegal																	
Pres.	1st	01 Jan 1978	—	No, irregularities affected outcome	—	Partial boycott	No	83	18	No	—	—	Yes	—	—	—	—

(continued)

A Data Set on Elections in Africa (continued)

Country	Type of Election	Number of Election	Date of Election	Electoral System	Free and Fair?	Turnout (%)	Opposition Participate?	Autocrats Gone?	Winner's % Votes/Seats	2nd's % Votes/Seats	Turnover?	Losers Accept?	Peaceful?	Regime Survive?	Date of Breakdown	Cands./Parties Participate	Cands./Parties Boycott	Parties in Lower House
	Pres.	2nd	27 Feb 1983	–	No, irregularities affected outcome	56	Yes, all	Associates participate	83	15	No	No, none	Isolated incidents	Yes	–	5	0	–
	Pres.	3rd	28 Feb 1988	–	No, irregularities affected outcome	58	Yes, all	Associates participate	73	26	No	No, none	Isolated incidents	Yes	–	4	0	–
	Pres.	4th	21 Feb 1993	–	Yes, somewhat	51	Yes, all	Associates participate	58	32	No	Some/later	Isolated incidents	Yes	–	9	0	–
	Pres.	5th	19 Mar 2000	–	Yes, somewhat	62	Yes, all	Associates participate	41	30	Yes	Yes, all immediately	Isolated incidents	Yes	–	8	0	–
	Parl.	1st	01 Jan 1978	PR/ small MMCs	No, irregularities affected outcome	–	Partial boycott	No	82	18	No	–	–	Yes	–	–	–	2
	Parl.	2nd	01 Jul 1983	PR/ small MMCs	No, irregularities affected outcome	56	Yes, all	Associates participate	92	7	No	No, none	Isolated incidents	Yes	–	14	0	3
	Parl.	3rd	01 Jul 1988	PR/ small MMCs	No, irregularities affected outcome	58	Yes, all	Associates participate	86	14	No	No, none	Isolated incidents	Yes	–	14	0	2
	Parl.	4th	09 May 1993	Mixed	Yes, somewhat	41	Yes, all	Yes	70	22	No	Some/later	Isolated incidents	Yes	–	14	0	6
	Parl.	5th	24 May 1998	Mixed	Yes, somewhat	39	Yes, all	Yes	66	16	No	Some/later	Isolated incidents	Yes	–	18	0	11
	Parl.	6th	01 Apr 2001	Mixed	Yes, somewhat	67	Yes, all	Yes	64	8	Yes	Yes, all immediately	Isolated incidents	Yes	–	61	0	49
Seychelles	Pres.	1st	23 Jul 1993	–	Yes, somewhat	86	Yes, all	No	60	37	No	Yes, all immediately	Yes	Yes	–	3	0	–
	Pres.	2nd	22 Mar 1998	–	Yes, somewhat	84	Yes, all	No	67	20	No	Yes, all immediately	Yes	Yes	–	3	0	–

	Pres.	3rd	02 Sep 2001	—	Yes, somewhat	84	Yes, all	No	54	45	No	Some/later	Yes	Yes	—	3	0	—
	Parl.	1st	25 Jul 1993	Mixed	Yes, somewhat	86	Yes, all	No	82	15	No	Yes all immediately	Yes	Yes	—	5	0	3
	Parl.	2nd	22 Mar 1998	Mixed	Yes, somewhat	87	Yes, all	No	88	9	No	Yes, all immediately	Yes	Yes	—	5	0	3
	Parl.	3rd	06 Dec 2002	Mixed	Yes, somewhat	85	Yes, all	No	68	32	No	Yes, all immediately	Isolated incidents	Yes	—	4	0	2
Sierra Leone	Pres.	1st	26 Feb 1996	—	Yes, somewhat	83	Yes, all	Associates participate	36	23	Yes	Some/later	No, not at all	No, coup	01 Mar 1997	15	0	—
	Pres.	1st	14 May 2002	—	Yes, somewhat	50	Yes, all	No	70	22	No	Yes, all immediately	Isolated incidents	Yes	—	9	0	—
	Parl.	1st	26 Feb 1996	PR	Yes, somewhat	50	Yes, all	Associates participate	33	21	Yes	No, none	No, not at all	No, coup	01 Mar 1997	15	0	6
	Parl.	1st	14 May 2002	PR/ small MMCs	Yes, somewhat	83	Yes, all	No	74	24	No	Yes, all immediately	Isolated incidents	Yes	—	10	0	3
Somalia†	NA																	
	NA																	
South Africa	Parl.	1st	26 Apr 1994	PR	Yes, somewhat	86	Yes, all	No	63	20	Yes	Yes, all immediately	Isolated incidents	Yes	—	19	0	7
	Parl.	2nd	02 Jun 1999	PR	Yes, somewhat	89	Yes, all	Associates participate	66	10	No	Yes, all immediately	Isolated incidents	Yes	—	16	0	13
Sudan	Pres.	1st	17 Mar 1996	—	No, irregularities affected outcome	69	Partial boycott	No	76	24	No	No, none	No, not at all	Yes	—	41	10	—
	Pres.	2nd	20 Dec 2000	—	No, irregularities affected outcome	69	Partial boycott	No	86	10	No	No, none	Isolated incidents	Yes	—	5	—	—
	Parl.	1st	06 Mar 1996	Majority SMC/ MMC	No, irregularities affected outcome	55	Partial boycott	No	90	8	No	No, none	No, not at all	Yes	—	0	—	—

(continued)

A Data Set on Elections in Africa (continued)

Country	Type of Election	Number of Election	Date of Election	Electoral System	Free and Fair?	Turn-out (%)	Opposition Participate?	Autocrats Gone?	Winner's % Votes/ Seats	2nd's % Votes/ Seats	Turn-over?	Losers Accept?	Peaceful?	Regime Survive?	Date of Breakdown	Cands/ Parties Participate	Cands/ Parties Boycott	Parties in Lower House
	Parl.	2nd	20 Dec 2000	Majority SMC/MMC	No, irregularities affected outcome	–	Partial boycott	No	99	1	No	No, none	Isolated incidents	Yes	–	2	6	2
Swaziland	Parl.	1st	11 Oct 1993	Plurality SMC	No, not at all	61	Partial boycott	No	–	–	No	No, none	Isolated incidents	Yes	–	0	–	–
	Parl.	2nd	24 Oct 1998	Plurality SMC	No, not at all	60	Partial boycott	No	–	–	No	No, none	Isolated incidents	Yes	–	0	–	–
Tanzania	Pres.	1st	29 Oct 1995	–	No, irregularities affected outcome	77	Yes, all	Associates participate	62	28	No	No, none	Isolated incidents	Yes	–	4	0	–
	Pres.	2nd	29 Oct 2000	–	Yes, somewhat	84	Yes, all	Associates participate	75	17	No	Some/later	Isolated incidents	Yes	–	4	0	–
	Parl.	1st	29 Oct 1995	Plurality SMC	No, irregularities affected outcome	77	Yes, all	No	78	10	No	No, none	Isolated incidents	Yes	–	13	0	4
	Parl.	2nd	29 Oct 2000	Plurality SMC	Yes, somewhat	84	Yes, all	Associates participate	91	6	No	Some/later	Isolated incidents	Yes	–	13	0	5
Togo	Pres.	1st	25 Aug 1993	–	No, not at all	36	Partial boycott	No	96	3	No	No, none	No, not at all	Yes	–	3	3	–
	Pres.	2nd	21 Jun 1998	–	No, not at all	39	Yes, all	No	52	34	No	No, none	Isolated incidents	Yes	–	6	0	–
	Pres.	3rd	01 Jun 2003	–	No, irregularities affected outcome	72	Partial boycott	No	58	34	No	No, none	Isolated incidents	Yes	–	6	0	–
	Parl.	1st	20 Feb 1994	Majority SMC/MMC	No, irregularities affected outcome	65	Yes, all	No	43	42	No	No, none	No, not at all	Yes	–	20	0	4

Country			Date	System	Irregularities affected outcome		Boycott	Participation					Turnover	Violence					
	Parl.	2nd	21 Mar 1999	Majority SMC/MMC	No, irregularities affected outcome	66	Partial boycott	No	98	2	No	No, none	Isolated incidents	Yes	—	3	8	1
	Parl.	3rd	27 Oct 2002	Majority SMC/MMC	No, irregularities affected outcome	67	Partial boycott	No	89	4	No	Some/later	Isolated incidents	Yes	—	16	9	5
Uganda	Pres.	1st	09 May 1996	—	Yes, somewhat	73	Partial boycott	No	74	24	No	Some/later	Isolated incidents	Yes	—	3	0	—
	Pres.	2nd	12 Mar 2001	—	Yes, somewhat	70	Yes, all	No	69	28	No	Some/later	Yes	Yes	—	6	0	—
	Parl.	1st	27 Jun 1996	Plurality SMC	Yes, somewhat	61	Partial boycott	No	56	—	No	Some/later	Yes	Yes	—	0	—	—
	Parl.	2nd	26 Jun 2001	Plurality SMC	Yes, somewhat	70	Yes, all	No	80	9	No	Some/later	Isolated incidents	Yes	—	0	—	—
Zambia	Pres.	1st	31 Oct 1991	—	Yes, somewhat	46	Yes, all	No	76	24	Yes	Yes, all immediately	Isolated incidents	Yes	—	2	0	—
	Pres.	2nd	18 Nov 1996	—	No, irregularities affected outcome	58	Partial boycott	Yes	73	13	No	No, none	Isolated incidents	Yes	—	5	0	—
	Pres.	3rd	27 Dec 2001	—	No, irregularities affected outcome	68	Yes, all	Yes	28	27	No	No, none	Isolated incidents	Yes	—	15	0	—
	Parl.	1st	31 Oct 1991	Plurality SMC	Yes, somewhat	46	Yes, all	No	83	17	Yes	Yes, all immediately	Isolated incidents	Yes	—	5	0	2
	Parl.	2nd	18 Nov 1996	Plurality SMC	No, irregularities affected outcome	58	Partial boycott	Associates participate	88	3	No	No, none	Isolated incidents	Yes	—	11	6	4
	Parl.	3rd	27 Dec 2001	Plurality SMC	No, irregularities affected outcome	68	Yes, all	Associates participate	49	31	Half	No, none	Isolated incidents	Yes	—	15	0	7

(continued)

A Data Set on Elections in Africa (continued)

Country	Type of Election	Number of Election	Date of Election	Electoral System	Free and Fair?	Turn-out (%)	Opposition Participate?	Autocrats Gone?	Winner's % Votes/Seats	2nd's % Votes/Seats	Turn-over?	Losers Accept?	Peaceful?	Regime Survive?	Date of Breakdown	Cands./Parties Participate	Cands./Parties Boycott	Parties in Lower House
Zimbabwe	Pres.	1st	28 Mar 1990	—	Yes, somewhat	54	Partial boycott	Yes	78	16	No	Some/later	No, not at all	Yes	—	2	0	—
	Pres.	2nd	17 Mar 1996	—	No, irregularities affected outcome	32	Boycott	Yes	92	5	No	No, none	No, not at all	Yes	—	3	0	—
	Pres.	3rd	09 Mar 2002	—	No, not at all	60	Yes, all	Yes	56	42	No	No, none	No, not at all	Yes	—	5	0	—
	Parl.	1st	28 Feb 1980	Plurality SMC	Yes, somewhat	56	Yes, all	No	57	20	Yes	Yes, all immediately	Isolated incidents	Yes	—	4	0	4
	Parl.	2nd	28 Mar 1985	Plurality SMC	Yes, somewhat	54	Yes, all	Associates participate	64	15	No	Yes, all immediately	No, not at all	Yes	—	4	0	4
	Parl.	3rd	28 Mar 1990	Plurality SMC	No, irregularities affected outcome	53	Partial boycott	Yes	96	3	No	Some/later	No, not at all	Yes	—	5	3	3
	Parl.	4th	09 Apr 1995	Plurality SMC	No, irregularities affected outcome	57	Partial boycott	Yes	98	2	No	Some/later	Isolated incidents	Yes	—	7	4	3
	Parl.	5th	25 Jun 2000	Plurality SMC	No, not at all	49	Yes, all	Yes	61	38	No	No, none	No, not at all	Yes	—	7	0	3

Key: Pres. = presidential, Parl. = parliamentary, MMC = multimember constituency, PR = proportional representation, CAR = Central African Republic, DRC = Democratic Republic of Congo, NA = not available, RoC = Republic of Congo.

[a] For countries that had held a series of elections that was interrupted by a coup or civil war, after which competitive elections were reinstated, the dates of first elections held as part of the renewed series, and third elections may precede those of first elections held as part of the renewed series, and third elections may precede first and second chronologically. Dates shown are correct for the elections indicated.

[b] These four countries did not hold any *de jure* competitive and participatory elections during the period studied.

Notes

CHAPTER 1: INTRODUCTION

1. For a good discussion on this point, see Gibson (2002). Similar problems seem to have developed in the study of democratization in Eastern Europe and Latin America; see Munck (2001b).

2. Recently, many have argued for variations on the theme of structuration theory, following the lead of Giddens (1984, 1993). While structures and actors obviously interact and both play important roles in every form of social change (Sztompka, 1993), good thinking may also be produced by separating the two and assessing their distinct contributions at different points. This is often the main task of historians (Carr, 1961/1990).

3. All these sub-Saharan countries are states in the formal juridical sense of the term, although several of them have recently had or still have significant problems of state implosion (Villalón and Huxtable 1998), for example Democratic Republic of Congo (DRC), Liberia, and Somalia. The last is presently *de facto* three states: Somalia, Somaliland, and Puntland. Elections were recently held in Somaliland, but I have decided to classify them as regional elections, rather than national ones because of the unresolved sovereignty, and hence, uncertainty of statehood.

4. An exception to typical history is Botswana, which inaugurated its democracy upon gaining independence in 1969 and has persisted in it. Another special case is Liberia, which gained independence in 1847 but has been under autocratic rule or civil war for most of its existence.

5. This finding led Barkan (1995) to declare that a proportional system of representation would not really make much difference in agrarian societies and that a single-member district plurality system is equally good in ensuring a distribution of seats in parliament that reflects the total vote.

6. In the literature the first election after a period of autocratic rule is often referred to as a "founding" election, meaning that its occurrence is considered foundational of a democratic regime. This is one of the notions that the present study refutes.

7. Separation of this group is restricted to Table 2. In the empirical analysis in Chapters 3 and 4 all cases of elections are included. The latter part of Chapter 4 presents a panel-group comparison necessarily restricted to a subset of elections in countries that have held two or more successive elections as of June 2003. In Chapter 6, the same subset is used for the analysis for similar methodological reasons.

8. It is important to note here that the measure of alternation in power is not influenced by any constitutional limit on the number of presidential terms. An alternation in power is coded as a turnover *only* if there is both a change of person and a change in the party affiliation of the president or the majority in parliament. In other words, if a president steps down after the second term because of a constitutional requirement and his successor is the candidate from the very same party, it is not counted as a turnover.

CHAPTER 2: ON DEMOCRACY AND ELECTIONS

1. This recognition has led to efforts at simplifying the conceptual constructs, in order to facilitate more valid measurement and analysis. This is particularly true of complex, multidimensional phenomena like democracy (e.g., Bollen 1990, Coppedge 2003, Munck and Verkuilen 2003). But this is a separate discussion. For some particularly useful—even if by no means unproblematic—criticism of positivism, see Bourdieu (1977), Dreyfus and Dreyfus (1967/1986), Flyvbjerg (1991), Garfinkel (1984), and Giddens (1982, 1984)

2. The terminologies they use are slightly different. Peirce referred to these concepts as sign, object, and interpretant; Ogden and Richards talked about symbol, referent, and reference; while de Saussure worked with signifier, signified, and referent.

3. Even if a political system would reach the theoretical maximum on all specified indicators of democratic attributes, it would not make democracy the object. Objectification is a matter of conceptual analysis, not empirical conclusion. If we study water and its qualities, for example, finding it to be yellowish or pure does not render the color yellow or purity our object of study.

4. There are also dangers associated with this approach. One of them is the importance ascribed to the cut-off point. If the distribution of cases is ∪-shaped, the share of classification error is reduced, as most cases are distributed towards the ends of the thought continuum. The effects of a particular cut-off point are relatively small, since there are few "grey-zone" cases. But with a distribution that is normal or even ∩-shaped, the selection of cut-off point naturally plays a greater role in producing the results. Even a small change in classificatory criteria will then result in rearrangement of a large number of cases. Elkins (1999) and Coppedge (1997), among others, have demonstrated that significantly different results emerge depending on which cut-off point is used to classify countries as either democracies or nondemocracies. We must guard against overstating the degree to which defining attributes cohere to define democracy, as this leads to reification.

5. This reasoning partly avoids the more technical discussion of random and systematic errors. Alvarez et al. (1996) argue, correctly, that the bulk of errors resulting from classification of so-called borderline cases are systematic and their effect can therefore be measured and corrected for. They also argue that polychotomous scales generate smaller but more numerous errors, while dichotomous scales generate larger ones but fewer of them. The latter, however, is dependent on the distribution of cases as discussed above, which cannot be known unless a graded measure is used first.

6. Sartori (1984, 1991) refers to it as the ladder of abstraction. I agree, however, with Collier and Mahon (1993, 853, n. 5) that the term *abstraction* is misleading since *abstract* is com-

monly understood as the opposite of real or concrete. Hence, I prefer Collier and Mahon's suggestion of renaming it "ladder of generality."

7. This discussion applies to various forms of less-than-full subtypes that Collier and Levitsky's (1997) labels diminished as well as to full-but-suboptimal subtypes such as O'Donnell's (1994) "delegative democracy." However, it does not apply to the classical subtypes of democracy like the division into presidential and parliamentary democracies (e.g., Lijphart 1977), or different kinds of electoral systems (e.g., Powell 1982; Sartori 1991), because these are not graduations in terms of more or less democracy.

8. With nominal variables, on the other hand, there is only a difference between categories, no ranking.

9. The difference between additive and multiplicative formulas is methodologically and conceptually important, however. A multiplicative scale implies that all characteristics are necessary conditions: if one scores zero, the total will also be nil. An additive scale involves no such logic, with the implication that none of the characteristics is necessary. For example, such an index if it includes full suffrage could end up classifying a country with no suffrage as a democracy if it scored high enough on other indicators. This is a highly questionable strategy. (Cf. Munck and Verkuilen 2002.)

10. A difficult and unresolved issue is how to combine multidimensional measures into a single index of democracy. While Coppedge and Reinicke (1990) claim to have proven that democracy, understood as polyarchy, is unidimensional, Dahl (1971, 1989), Bollen and Jackman (1989), Hadenius (1992), and Vanhanen (1997), among others, find democracy to consist of two or more dimensions. The methodological implications are many and complex. Most important, perhaps, is that if democracy has two or more dimensions, the formula for combining these has to be established if we search for a single scale. For example, do we use simple addition or multiplication of indicators? Metaphorically, are we measuring using meters or square meters; is democracy a long line or an area? If three or more dimensions are involved, the possible geometric formulas increase to include a range of geometric figures. For excellent discussions of this and other intricate problems of measuring democracy, see Coppedge (2003), and Munck (2001a, 2001b).

11. Naturally, this does not apply if the study is on how ordinary people think of democracy, for example. But given that the study is concerned with finding out if democracy is present or not, perhaps also raising issues of causes and effects, it is necessary to define democracy first.

12. In Locke's time, of course, "men" meant only free males, excluding the vast majority of the population. Without any intention of downplaying the significance of the resulting exclusion, the difference is a matter of citizenship, not democratic principle, and hence is not central to the discussion here.

13. For a good discussion of the notion of how "the people" can be conceived, see Dahl 1989, ch. 9. The scope of this study does not allow for exploration of the point here.

14. Political participation in the decision-making process may indeed take many forms in a democracy, ranging from localized and indulgent deliberations among friends to national and cross-national advocacy; but in terms of democracy as a political system of national self-rule, it is the selection of representatives for the execution of power that is a necessary component and hence the focus here.

15. That is a conceptual point. In empirical terms, the realization of equal participation may vary.

16. Even "participatory" democracy as a formula for decision making translates into a representative form, as only the few can in practice lead, speak, and contribute to mass meetings, or the meetings would be endless, while the many are confined to listening, evaluating, and voting just as in a representative democracy proper (e.g., Dahl 1989, 277). There are indeed other venues for participatory approaches of inclusion that can feed into a policy process before the decision-point, but that renders participatory approaches a supplement, as opposed to alternative, to representative democracy.

17. While more competition is often better in terms of democratic freedom of choice, too much competition can create problems. Too many parties in the legislature, for example, make a fragmented party system (Sartori 1968) that deters governability and thus effective representation. In certain respects, then, there is such a thing as too much democratic quality (cf. Coppedge 2003).

18. It is quite possible to make the argument that the level of competition in any political system is also dependent on the character of political parties, not only their number. Political parties based on ethnicity, class, or another differentiation that applies more or less automatically would make for less competition than programmatic parties. One cannot choose which ethnic group, family, or class one is born into, and social mobility is typically highly constrained. If parties and voting are based on such belongingness rather than on policy positions, few voters could or would change their party affiliation or voting behavior. Competition is thereby reduced.

19. Weber's (1958) rational-legal legitimacy is closest to democratic legitimacy as defined here. The interested reader can compare Weber's classification to Bobbio (1989, 83–86), who discusses six different kinds of legitimacy where only one is dependent on the will of the people.

20. There is one exception to this. In the last two of the five empirical tests in Chapter 6, the unit is changed to country, for reasons of double-checking the validity of the findings.

21. This operationalization allows for inclusion of a borderline case: Uganda. While political parties have been allowed to exist in Uganda, they have only very recently been allowed to officially support and campaign for candidates. In practice, the difference has not been all that dramatic, though, as candidates' party and policy affiliations have generally been known to voters. This is further evidenced by the fact that it has even been possible to calculate seat shares in the legislature, despite the official no party, movement policy. It is clear that Uganda's electoral processes have been endowed with a substantial share of democratic qualities, and much more of such than several other countries on the continent who officially operate multiparty systems, for example, Togo and Zimbabwe.

22. Botswana, Ethiopia, Lesotho, Mauritius, and South Africa.

23. The countries using proportional representation in medium to large multimember constituencies are South Africa, Angola, Namibia, Mozambique, Liberia, Burundi, and Sierra Leone. An additional six countries operate proportional representation systems in small multimember constituencies. These systems have a strong majoritarian effect, so the reasoning about the effects of such systems does not apply.

24. For a variant of the argument with an emphasis on a bounded uncertainty, see Schmitter and Karl (1991).

25. The Afro-Barometer, engineered by Michael Bratton at Michigan State University, fills a very important function in this regard. The first survey was completed in 1999, but its scope was only ten countries; so it is of limited use in the present study. The second and third rounds increased the number of countries, but this resource does not yet provide coverage over a long enough sequence of years to be useful to the present study.

26. The data set also provides the date of the breakdowns.

27. Specific information on exactly which sources have been used to code these indicators can be found in Appendix 1.

28. Cases were coded in two major batches. All cases until 31 December 2001 were coded in one sweep in February–March 2002. This initial set of cases was analyzed and used in Lindberg (2004a). The remaining cases, dating from 1 January 2002 to 30 June 2003 were coded in October 2003. During that process, the initial data set was reviewed to check for consistency of coding; in the process, very few errors were found and have been corrected. The final set is the basis for three publications (Lindberg 2004b, 2005, and 2006) in addition to the present book.

29. Only one kind of theory or hypothesis could be tested in an $N = 1$ study. Such a theory would claim to (a) have identified a truly determinate rather than probabilistic causal relationship, (b) be complete in the sense of including all variables needed to explain all variation, and (c) have full information on all variables, measured without error, including noise possibly induced by interpretation of the researcher. Like Munck and Verkuilen (Munck 2005; Munck and Verkuilen 2004), I do not think there is such a theory.

CHAPTER 3: ELECTIONS IN AFRICA OVER TIME

1. Gambia inaugurated its long-lasting democracy by declaring independence in 1965. The regime's success was interrupted briefly by a coup in late July 1980. Gambia had no military forces at the time and so called on neighboring Senegal, who intervened and restored the regime in early August. A confederation announced on 21 August 1980 by the two countries took effect on 1 February 1982 and lasted until September 1989.

2. There are also numerous frequently cited case studies and small-N comparisons, for example Barkan (2000), Clapham and Wiseman (1995), Joseph (1999), Sandbrook (1996), Sisk and Reynolds (1998), Young (1993), Wiseman (1992, 1993). The work of Bratton and colleagues remains the most influential large-N study on elections and democratization in Africa.

3. Bratton (1997, 1998), Bratton and Posner (1999), and Bratton and van de Walle (1996, 1997).

4. See second half of Chapter 2. The detailed sources on each illustration based on the country files are not given in the following text, for practical reasons. Most of the events referred to are uncontroversial, but the sources in the country files documenting them are very numerous, and listing them would only impair readability. They are available from the author.

5. Elections before 1990 and those held in 2003 have been excluded from Figure 1 because it reports on N rather than percentages, hence, pre-1990 elections and the half-year only of 2003 would distort the trend.

6. The first round of Madagascar's fourth presidential election took place on 3 November 1996, while the second round, which Ratsiraka won by a narrow margin over the impeached former opposition leader, Albert Zafy, was held on 2 January 1997.

7. Ratsiraka and some loyal forces took up arms and engaged government troops for nine months, mainly from one of the provinces. The dangerous process was resolved with international mediation and premature legislative elections on 15 December 2002 in which Ravalomanana's party scored a landslide, winning 64 percent of the seats in the parliament.

8. There are a few works on specific aspects, such as ethnicity and voting (Mozaffar, Scarritt, and Galaich 2003), electoral management bodies (Mozaffar 2002), party systems and dominant parties (Bogaards 2000, 2003, 2004), women's legislative representation (Yoon 2001), and my work preliminary to this study (Lindberg 2002, 2004a, 2004b, 2005).

CHAPTER 4: THE SELF-REINFORCING POWER OF ELECTIONS

1. This improvement in democratic quality also opened up the field for new prospectors to become double-gain free riders. For example, two of President Diouf's closest allies, Moustapha Nissé and Djibou Ká, defected from the ruling Parti Socialiste, of which Nissé was one of the founding members.

2. There has been some debate about this point, but this is how current evidence reads. For further details on these two elections and the one in 2000, see Boahen (1995), Green (1998), Gyimah-Boadi (1998, 1999, 2001), Jeffries (1998), Lindberg (2003), Lyon (1997), Ninsin (1998), Nugent (2001), Quaye (1995), and Sandbrook and Ouelbaum (1999).

3. Although, as Lisa Laakso pointed out to me, the reinstatement of Kérèkou was preceded by amazingly open and democratic public and parliamentary debate on the economic policy of the government.

CHAPTER 5: THE CAUSAL EFFECTS OF ELECTIONS

1. For a description of these 15 criteria and a brief note on the methodology employed to rank countries, see Appendix 3 of this volume.

2. One recent analysis (Gleditsch and Ward 1997) concludes that only one of the components of Polity IV is a valid measure of democracy; the others simply add noise.

3. Among other failings of the various measures, it is charged that comparisons based on qualitative data mismatch the indexing and that intersubjective assessment of the rationales for country ratings are severely restricted (McHenry 2000). There seems also to be an overdependence on subjective judgment in assignment of values to indicators (Bollen 1993) and inadequate data sources (Bollen 1990, 17; Shin 1994, 147).

4. Causality is always an analytical construction and cannot be evidenced as such if it is referred to as causal chain, link, or mechanism. It is not an empirical observation but an argument, which should be guided by logical consistency and empirical reference.

5. Students of democratic consolidation have now improved their knowledge about the different routes that "slow deaths" of democracies might take. Those routes include reassertion of military supremacy by a progressive diminution of opportunities for civilian control; state weakness that subverts the rule of law; the rise of hegemonic parties, suffocating electoral competition; decay of electoral institutions, affecting the fairness of voting; incumbents' use of state resources and media to violate civil and political rights; introduction of exclusionary citizenship laws, circumventing democratic inclusion (Schedler 1998, 98).

6. Schedler provides an excellent overview and analysis of the manifold meanings of democratic consolidation, depending on the empirical contexts and normative goals. Yet, I disagree with him and subscribe to Sartori's claim that collective semantic confusion among scholars should be avoided. Phenomena that are different in kind ought to be identified by different terms (Sartori 1984, 1991, 243-257).

7. Consolidation can occur and be measured as stability without necessarily making any predictive inferences. It remains quite possible to say that, so far as certain institutions are in place and the major actors evidently play by the rules and accept the outcomes of the democratic game over an extended period of time, at least *at this point* there is an amount of stability of the democratic regime. As long as those conditions prevail, democracy remains stable. If the conditions change, democracy may destabilize. Such an approach does not make unnecessary predicative judgments and inferences, a form of "qualified guessing" on shaky grounds. Another advantage of this approach is that consolidation becomes an empirically observable phenomenon. It does not give the dependent variable ontological status by inference based on prospective reasoning and intersubjective judgments of future developments, which, as Schedler has correctly noted (2001a, 67) many consolidation studies do.

8. Determined autocrats, of course, are likely to try to circumvent official rules and regulations, constitutive or not, in order to hold on to power.

9. This study, like many in the rational choice vein, does not explain why and how institutions emerge. This omission should be insignificant, since the study is not concerned with how or why states institute elections but with what happens after their introduction. Yet, some rational actor theorists would certainly object to being labeled institutionalists on the claim that they work from methodological individualism. I cannot see, however, how the game theoretical approach can be conceived of other than as an institutional framework where the incentives, in the form of rules, to a large extent produce the outcome. For a good discussion of explanations of how and why institutions emerge, see, for example, Pierson (2000).

10. Giddens (1979, 199) knows, and I agree with him, that there is hardly any sensible way to speak of continuity other than over time. Sociologists like Sztompka (1993, 41) and Sorokin (1937, 156) have correctly noted that time—as temporal variance—cannot be conceived of apart from concepts like change, process, motion, and becoming; but they argue that continuity and "being" are not related to time. This seems to me senseless.

11. This behavior by some of these groups has already been substantiated empirically by Bratton and van de Walle (1997). In their study, they found that the military in Africa intervened to sustain or reinstate democratic processes more often than to subvert them.

CHAPTER 6: DEMOCRATIZATION BY ELECTIONS?

1. Such categorizations often combine the CL rating with the PR (political rights) rating, of which the average should be 2.5, or 3 on one indicator and 2 on the other.

2. Another interesting and unexplored issue in the debate on constitutional engineering is to what extent are attempts to democratize dependent on the length of electoral cycles? Although not pursued here, it is an area worthy of inquiry.

3. For a list of such adjustments, see Appendix 2.

4. For each subperiod all recorded changes in CL have been added. For example, if the

first election period in one country resulted in a changed rating from 6 to 4, that equals a +2 unit change; but if in another country the change was from 4 to 5, that equals a −1 unit change and the net result is a total gain of +1.

5. For three countries for which values were missing from the 1989 WBDI data, figures were found from adjacent years: Djibouti from 1995, Eritrea from 1992, and Mali from 1990.

CHAPTER 7: COMPARATIVE PERSPECTIVES AND REFLECTIONS

1. Bratton and van de Walle refer to Madagascar's as a relatively long period of transition by African standards, then totaling only 22 months which they saw as starting in the early 1990s. Scrutinizing the background on Madagascar we find that the process actually started in 1982 to 1983 when a partial liberalization took place as a consequence of the decision to hold the first competitive elections with several parties.

2. I am grateful to Joel Barkan for pointing this out to me.

3. The distinction between empirical and judicial statehood (Clapham 1996) is echoed in similar concepts, such as positive and negative statehood (Jackson 1990), internal and external (Herbst 1989), and functional and constitutive (Thompson 1995).

4. For a good discussion of this dilemma and other problems with aid, see Knack (2004).

References

Africa South of Sahara 2003. 32nd ed. London: Europa Publications.

Ake, Claude. 1993. "The Unique Case of African Democracy." *International Affairs* 69:239–244.

———. 1996. *Democracy and Development in Africa*. Washington, DC: Brookings Institution.

———. 2000. *The Feasibility of Democracy in Africa*. Dakar, Senegal: CODRESIA.

Akinrinade, Sola. 1998. "The Re-Democratization Process in Africa: Plus ça change, plus c'est la même chose." In S. Akinrinade and A. Sesay, *Africa in the Post–Cold War International System*. London: Pinter.

Allison, Lincoln. 1994. "On the Gap between Theories of Democracy and Theories of Democratization." *Democratization* 1 (1): 8–26.

Almond, Gabriel, and James Coleman, eds. 1960. *Politics in Developing Countries*. Princeton: Princeton University Press.

Almond, Gabriel A., and Sidney Verba. 1963. *The Civic Culture*. Princeton: Princeton University Press.

Altman, David, and Anibal Pérez-Linán. 2002. "Assessing the Quality of Democracy: Freedom, Competitiveness and Participation in Eighteen Latin American Countries." *Democratization* 9 (2): 85–100.

Alvarez, Mike, José A. Cheibub, Fernando N. Limongi, Adam Przeworski. 1996. "Classifying Political Regimes." *Studies in International Comparative Development* 31 (2): 3–36.

Ansprenger, Franz. 1997. *Politische Geschichte Afrikas in 20. Jahrhundert*. 2nd ed. Munich: Beck.

Arat, Zehra F. 1988. "Democracy and Economic Development: Modernization Theory Revisited." *Comparative Politics* 21:21–36.

Archer, Ronald P. 1995. "Party Strength and Weakness in Colombia's Besieged Democracy." In Scott Mainwaring and Timothy R. Scully, eds. *Building Party Systems in Latin America*. Stanford, CA: Stanford University Press.

Arrow, Kenneth. 1951. *Social Choice and Individual Values*. New York: John Wiley & Sons.

Austin, Dennis. 1975. "Introduction." In Dennis Austin and Robin Luckham, eds., *Politicians and Soldiers in Ghana, 1966–1972*. London: Frank Cass.

Axelrod, Robert. 1984. *The Evolution of Cooperation*. New York: Basic Books.

Ayittey, George. 1992. *Africa Betrayed*. New York: St. Martin's Press.

Azarya, Victor, and Naomi Chazan. 1987. "Disengagement from the State in Africa: Reflections on the Experience of Ghana and Guinea." *Comparative Studies in Society and History* 29 (1): 106–131.

Badu, Kwesi A., and John Larvie. 1996. *Election in Ghana*. Accra, Ghana: Friedrich Ebert Foundation.

Baker, Bruce. 1998. "The Class of 1990: How Have the Autocratic Leaders of Sub-Saharan Africa Fared under Democratisation?" *Third World Quarterly* 19 (1): 115–127.

———. 2002. "When to Call Black White: Zimbabwe's Electoral Reports." *Third World Quarterly* 23 (6): 1145–1158.

Barkan, Joel D. 1995. "Elections in Agrarian Societies." *Journal of Democracy* 6:106–116.

———. 1998. "Rethinking the Applicability of Proportional Representation for Africa." In Andrew Reynolds and Timothy D. Sisk, eds., *Elections and Conflict Management in Africa*. Washington, DC: United States Institute of Peace Press.

———. 2000. "Protracted Transitions among Africa's New Democracies." *Democratization* 7 (3): 227–243.

Bates, Robert H. 1981. *Markets and States in Tropical Africa*. Berkeley: University of California Press.

———. 1989. *Beyond the Miracle and the Market: The Political Economy of Agrarian Development in Kenya*. Cambridge: Cambridge University Press.

Bateson, G. 1972. "Space, Time, Space-Time and Society." *Sociological Inquiry* 63 (4): 406–424.

Bayart, Jean-François. 1991. "La problématique de la démocratie en Afrique noire." *Politique Africaine* 43 (October).

BBC News OnLine. http://www.bbc.co.uk. News stories with various dates.

Beetham, David. 1991. *The Legitimation of Power*. London: Macmillan.

Bernhard, Michael. 1999. "Institutional Choice and the Failure of Democracy: The Case of Interwar Poland." *East European Politics and Societies* 13 (1): 34–70.

Blume, Marshall E. 1974. "Unbiased Estimators of Long-Run Expected Rates of Return." *Journal of the American Statistical Association* 69 (347): 634–638.

Boahen, Adu. 1995. "A Note on the Ghanaian Elections." *African Affairs* 94:277–280.

Bobbio, Noberto. 1989. *Democracy and Dictatorship*. Cambridge, England: Polity Press.

Bogaards, Matthijs. 2000. "Crafting Competitive Party Systems: Electoral Laws and the Opposition in Africa." *Democratization* 7 (4): 163–190.

———. 2003. "Electoral Choices for Divided Societies: Multi-Ethnic Parties and Constituency Polling in Africa." *Journal of Commonwealth and Comparative Politics* 41 (3): 59–80.

———. 2004. "Counting Parties and Identifying Dominant Party Systems in Africa." *European Journal of Political Research* 43:173–197.

Bogdanor, Vernon, and David Butler, eds. 1983. *Democracy and Elections*. Cambridge: Cambridge University Press.

Bollen, Kenneth. 1979. "Political Democracy and the Timing of Development." *American Sociological Review* 44 (4): 527–587.

———. 1990. "Political Democracy: Conceptual and Measurement Traps." *Studies in Comparative International Development* 25 (1): 7–25.

———. 1993. "Liberal Democracy: Validity and Method Factors in Cross-National Measures." *American Political Science Review* 37 (4): 1207–1230.

Bollen, Kenneth, and Robert W. Jackman. 1989. "Democracy, Stability and Dichotomies." *American Sociological Review* 54:612–621.

Bourdieu, Pierre. 1977. *An Outline of a Theory of Practice*. Cambridge: Cambridge University Press.

Boussard, Caroline. 2003. "Crafting Democracy: Civil Society in Post-Transitional Honduras." PhD diss., Lund University.

Brady, Henry E., and David Collier, eds. 2004. *Rethinking Social Inquiry: Diverse Tools, Shared Standards*. Oxford: Rowman & Littlefield.

Bratton, Michael. 1994. "Economic Crisis and Political Realignment in Zambia." In Jennifer A. Widner, ed. *Economic Change and Political Liberalization in Sub-Saharan Africa*. Baltimore: Johns Hopkins University Press.

———. 1997. "Deciphering Africa's Divergent Transitions." *Political Science Quarterly* 112 (1): 67–93.

———. 1998. "Second Elections in Africa." *Journal of Democracy* 9 (3): 51–66.

Bratton, Michael, and Daniel N. Posner. 1999. "A First Look at Second Elections in Africa." In Richard Joseph, ed., *State, Conflict, and Democracy in Africa*. Boulder, CO: Lynne Rienner.

Bratton, Michael, and Nicholas van de Walle. 1996. *Political Regimes and Regime Transitions in Africa, 1910–1994*. Computer file. ICPSR version. File no. 6996. Michigan: Inter-University Consortium for Political and Social Research.

———. 1997. *Democratic Experiments in Africa: Regime Transitions in a Comparative Perspective*. Cambridge: Cambridge University Press.

Brautigam, Deborah A. 1992. "Governance, Economy, and Foreign Aid." *Studies in Comparative International Development* 27 (3): 3–25.

Burkhart, Ross, and Michael Lewis-Beck. 1994. "Comparative Democracy: The Economic Development Thesis." *American Political Science Review* 88 (4): 903–910.

Bunce, Valerie. 2000. "Comparative Democratization." *Comparative Political Studies* 33 (6–7): 703–735.

Burgess, Adam. 2001. "Universal Democracy, Diminished Expectation." *Democratization* 8 (3): 51–74.

Burnell, Peter. 2002. "Zambia's 2001 Elections." *Third World Quarterly* 23 (6): 1103–1120.

Buzan, Barry. 1991. *People, States and Fear*. New York: Harvester Wheatsheaf.

Buzan, Barry, Charles Jones, and Richard Little. 1993. *The Logic of Anarchy: Neo-Realism to Structural Realism*. New York: Columbia University Press.

Carey, John M. 2000. "Parchment, Equilibria, and Institutions." *Comparative Political Studies* 33 (6–7): 735–761.

Carothers, Thomas. 1997. "Democracy without Illusions." *Foreign Affairs* 76:85–99.

———. 1998. "The Rule-of-Law Revival." *Foreign Affairs* 77:95–106.

———. 2002a. "The End of the Transition Paradigm." *Journal of Democracy* 13 (1): 5–20.

———. 2002b. "A Reply to My Critics." *Journal of Democracy* 13 (3): 33–38.

Carr, Edward H. 1961/1990. *What Is History?* London: Penguin Books.

Chabal, Patrick. 1998. "A Few Considerations on Democracy in Africa." *International Affairs* 74 (2): 289–303.

Chabal, Patrick, and Jean-Paul Daloz. 1999. *Africa Works: Disorder as Political Instrument*. Bloomington: Indiana University Press.

Chandra, Kanchan. 2004. *Why Ethnic Parties Succeed*. Cambridge: Cambridge University Press.

Chazan, Naomi. 1979. "A Re-Examination of the Role of Elections in African Politics." *Journal of Commonwealth and Comparative Politics* 14 (2): 169–190.

——. 1988. "Patterns of State-Society Incorporation and Disengagement in Africa." In Donald Rothchild and Naomi Chazan, eds. *The Precarious Balance: State and Society in Africa*. Boulder, CO: Westview Press.

Chege, Michael. 1996. "Between Africa's Extremes." In Larry Diamond and Marc Plattner, eds. *The Global Resurgence of Democracy*. 2nd ed. Baltimore: Johns Hopkins University Press. Also published, in an earlier version, in *Journal of Democracy* 6:44–51.

Cheibub, José A., and Fernando N. Limongi. 2002. "Democratic Institutions and Regime Survival: Parliamentary and Presidential Democracies Reconsidered." *Annual Review of Political Science* 5:151–179.

Cheibub, José A., Adam Przeworski, Fernando N. Limongi, and Michael M. Alvarez. 1996. "What Makes Democracies Endure?" *Journal of Democracy* 7 (1): 39–55.

Clapham, Christopher. 1996. *Africa and the International System: The Politics of State Survival*. Cambridge: Cambridge University Press.

——. 1998. "Discerning the New Africa." *International Affairs* 74 (2): 263–269.

Clapham, Christopher, and John A. Wiseman. 1995. "Conclusion: Assessing the Prospects for the Consolidation of Democracy in Africa." In John A. Wiseman, ed. *Democracy and Political Change in Sub-Saharan Africa*. London: Routledge.

Clark, Elisabeth S. 2000. "Why Elections Matter." *Washington Quarterly* 23 (3): 27–40.

Clark, John F. 1998. "Zaire: The Bankruptcy of the Extractive State." In Leonardo A. Villalón and Philip A. Huxtable, eds. *The African State at a Critical Juncture*. Boulder, CO: Lynne Rienner.

Clark, John F., and David E. Gardiner. 1997. *Political Reform in Francophone Africa*. Boulder, CO: Westview Press.

Cliffe, Lionel. 1967. *One Party Democracy in Tanzania*. Nairobi, Kenya: East African Publishing House.

Coleman, James. 1990. *Foundations of Social Theory*. Cambridge: Harvard University Press.

Collier, David, and Robert Adcock. 1999. "Democracy and Dichotomies: A Pragmatic Approach to Choices about Concepts." *Annual Review of Political Science* 2:537–565.

Collier, David, and Steven Levitsky. 1995. "Democracy with Adjectives: Strategies to Avoid Conceptual Stretching." Paper presented at the annual meeting of the Latin American Studies Association, Washington, DC. Revised version published 1997 as "Democracy with Adjectives: Conceptual Innovation in Comparative Research." *World Politics* 49:430–451.

Collier, David, and James E. Mahon Jr. 1993. "Conceptual 'Stretching' Revisited: Adapting Categories in Comparative Analysis." *American Political Science Review* 84 (4): 845–855.

Collier, Ruth B. 1982. *Regimes in Tropical Africa: Changing Forms of Supremacy, 1945–1975*. Berkeley: University of California Press.

Coppedge, Michael. 1997. "Modernization and Thresholds of Democracy: Evidence for a Common Path and Process." In Manus I. Mildarsky, ed. *Inequality, Democracy, and Economic Development*. New York: Cambridge University Press.

———. 2002. "Democracy and Dimensions: Comments on Munck and Verkuilen." *Comparative Political Studies* 35 (1): 35–39.

———. 2003. "Party Systems, Governability, and the Quality of Democracy in Latin America." Paper presented at the conference Diagnosing Democracy: Methods of Analysis, Findings, and Remedies, in Santiago, Chile, 11–13 April 2003.

———. 2005. "Thickening Thin Concepts: Issues in Large-N Data Generation." In Gerardo Munck, ed., *Regimes and Democracy in Latin America.* Vol. 2, *Methods and Data.* Oxford: Oxford University Press.

Coppedge, Michael, and Wolfgang H. Reinicke. 1990. "Measuring Polyarchy." *Studies in Comparative International Development* 25 (1): 51–73.

Cowen, Michael, and Liisa Laakso, eds. 2002. *Multiparty Elections in Africa.* Oxford: James Currey.

Cox, Gary W. 1997. *Making Votes Count: Strategic Coordination in the World's Electoral Systems.* Cambridge: Cambridge University Press.

Cutright, Phillips. 1963. "National Political Development: Measurement and Analysis." *American Sociological Review* 28 (2): 253–264.

Dahl, Robert. 1971. *Polyarchy: Participation and Opposition.* New Haven: Yale University Press.

———. 1989. *Democracy and Its Critics.* New Haven: Yale University Press.

Datton, Kenneth, John S. Greenies, and Kenneth J. Stewart. 1998. "Incorporating a Geometric Mean Formula into the CPI." *Monthly Labor Review* (October): 3–7.

Dawes, Robyn. 1995. "The Nature of Human Nature: An Empirical Case for Withholding Judgment — Perhaps Indefinitely." *Political Psychology* 16 (1).

Derbyshire, Denis J., and Ian Derbyshire. 1996. *Political Systems of the World.* Edinburgh: Chambers.

de Saussure, François. 1915/1974. *Course in General Linguistics.* London: Fontana.

Diamond, Larry. 1990. "Three Paradoxes of Democracy." *Journal of Democracy* 5 (3): 48–61.

———. 1993. "Political Culture and Democracy." In Larry Diamond, ed. *Political Culture and Democracy in Developing Countries.* Boulder, CO: Lynne Rienner.

———. 1996. "Democracy in Latin America: Degrees, Illusions, and Directions for Consolidation." In Tom J. Farer, ed. *Beyond Sovereignty: Collectively Defending Democracy in the Americas.* Baltimore: Johns Hopkins University Press.

———. 1997. "Prospects for Democratic Development in Africa." Essays in Public Policy 74, Hoover Institution on War, Revolution and Peace, Stanford University, Stanford, CA.

———. 1999. *Developing Democracy: Toward Consolidation.* Baltimore: Johns Hopkins University Press.

———. 2002. "Elections without Democracy: Thinking about Hybrid Regimes." *Journal of Democracy* 13 (2): 21–35.

Diamond, Larry, and Marc Plattner, eds. 1999. *Democratization in Africa.* Baltimore: Johns Hopkins University Press.

Diamond, Larry, Juan J. Linz, and Seymour M. Lipset. 1989. *Comparing Experiences with Democracy: Democracy in Developing Countries.* Boulder, CO: Lynne Rienner.

Di Lorenson, A., and E. Sborgi. 2001. "The 1999 Presidential and Legislative Elections in Niger." *Electoral Studies* 3: 470–476.

Di Palma, Giuseppe. 1990. *To Craft Democracies: An Essay in Democratic Transition.* Berkeley: University of California Press.

Downs, Anthony. 1957. *An Economic Theory of Democracy.* New York: Harper.

Dreher, Axel. 2003. "The Influence of Elections on IMF Programme Interruptions." *Journal of Development Studies* 39 (6): 101–120.

Dreyfus, Hubert, and Stuart Dreyfus. 1967/1986. *Mind over Machine: The Power of Human Intuition and Expertise in the Era of the Computer.* New York: Free Press.

Duverger, Maurice. 1954. *Les Partis Politiques.* Paris: Colin.

Easter, Gerald M. 1997. "Preferences for Presidentialism: Postcommunist Regime Change in Russia and the NIS." *World Politics* 49 (2): 184–211.

Eisenstadt, Todd. 2004. *Courting Democracy in Mexico: Party Strategies and Electoral Institutions.* Cambridge: Cambridge University Press.

Ekeh, Peter P. 1974. "Colonialism and the Two Publics in Africa: A Theoretical Statement." *Comparative Studies in Society and History* 17 (1): 91–112.

Elections around the World. Agorà Telematica. http://www.agora.stm.it/elections. (Country statistics.)

Election Watch. 1990–2001. *Journal of Democracy* 1–12.

Elkins, Zachary. 1999. "Gradations of Democracy: Empirical Tests of Alternative Conceptualizations." Paper presented at Seminar on Democratization, Institute of International Studies, 21 January. Stanford, CA: Stanford University. Later version published in *American Journal of Political Science* 44 (2): 287–294.

Elklit, Jörgen, and Palle Svensson. 1997. "What Makes Elections Free and Fair?" *Journal of Democracy* 8 (3): 32–46.

Ellingsen, Tanja. 2000. "Colorful Community or Ethnic Witches' Brew? Multiethnicity and Domestic Conflict during and after the Cold War." *Journal of Conflict Resolution* 44 (2): 228–249.

Elster, Jon. 1982. "The Case for Methodological Individualism." *Theory and Society* 11 (4): 453–482.

Elster, Jon, Claus Offe, and U. K. Preuss, with F. Boenker, U. Goetting, and F. W. Rueb. 1998. *Institutional Design in Post-Communist Societies: Rebuilding the Ship at Sea.* Cambridge: Cambridge University Press.

Finkel, Steven E. 2003. "Can Democracy Be Taught?" *Journal of Democracy* 14 (4): 137–151.

Fishman, Robert M. 1990. "Rethinking State and Regime: Southern Europe's Transition to Democracy." *World Politics* 42 (3): 422–440.

Flyvbjerg, Berndt. 1991. *Rationalitet og Magt: Det konkretes videnskap.* Copenhagen: Akademisk Forlag.

Fomunyoh, Christopher. 2001. "Democratization in Fits and Starts." *Journal of Democracy* 12 (3): 37–50.

Fosu, Augustin K. 2002. "Transforming Economic Growth to Human Development in Sub-Saharan Africa: The Role of Elite Political Instability." *Oxford Development Studies* 30 (1): 9–19.

Foweraker, Joe, and Todd Landmann. 2002. "Constitutional Design and Democratic Performance." *Democratization* 9 (2): 43–66.

Freedom House. 2004. *Annual Survey of Freedom Country Scores, 1972–73 to 2003–2004.* Ratings on political rights and civil liberties. Data file at http://www.freedomhouse.org.

Friedman, Milton. 1958. "Foreign Economic Aid: Means and Objectives." *Yale Review* 47 (4): 500–516.

Galvan, Dennis. 2001 "Political Turnover and Social Change in Senegal." *Journal of Democracy* 12 (3): 51–62.

Garfinkel, Harold. 1984. *Studies in Ethnomethodology.* Cambridge, England: Polity Press.

Gasiorowski, Mark. 1995. "Economic Crisis and Political Regime Change: An Event History Analysis." *American Political Science Review* 89 (4): 882–897.

Gasiorowski, Mark J., and Timothy J. Power. 1998. "The Structural Determinants of Democratic Consolidation." *Comparative Political Studies* 31 (10): 740–772.

Geddes, Barbara. 1999. "What Do We Know about Democratization after Twenty Years?" *Annual Review of Political Science* 2:115–144.

Gellner, Ernest. 1988. *Plough, Sword and Book: The Structure of Human History.* Chicago: University of Chicago Press.

Gibson, Clark C. 2002 "Of Waves and Ripples: Democracy and Political Change in Africa in the 1990s." *Annual Review of Political Science* 5:201–221.

Giddens, Anthony. 1979. *Central Problems in Social Theory.* London: Macmillan.

——. 1982. *Profiles and Critiques in Social Theory.* Berkeley: University of California Press.

——. 1984. *The Constitution of Society.* Cambridge, England: Polity Press.

——. 1993. *Sociology.* 2nd ed. Cambridge, England: Polity Press.

Gleditsch, Kristian, and Michael D. Ward. 1997. "Double-Take: A Re-examination of Democracy and Autocracy in Modern Polities." *Journal of Conflict Resolution* 41 (3): 361–384.

Goffman, Erving. 1969. *Strategic Interaction.* Philadelphia: University of Pennsylvania Press.

Green, Daniel. 1998. "Ghana: Structural Adjustment and State (Re)Formation." In Leonardo A. Villalón and Philip A. Huxtable, eds. *The African State at a Critical Juncture.* Boulder, CO: Lynne Rienner.

Günther, Richard, Nikiforos P. Diamandouros, and Hans-Jürgen Puhle. 1995. *The Politics of Democratic Consolidation: Southern Europe in a Comparative Perspective.* Baltimore: Johns Hopkins University Press.

Gyimah-Boadi, Emmanuel. 1998. "Managing Electoral Conflicts: Lessons from Ghana." In Timothy D. Sisk and Andrew Reynolds, eds. *Elections and Conflict Management in Africa.* Washington, DC: United States Institute of Peace Press.

——. 1999. "Six Years of Constitutional Rule in Ghana: An Assessment and Prospects of the Executive and Legislature." In *Six Years of Constitutional Rule in Ghana.* Accra, Ghana: Friedrich Ebert Foundation and Ghana Academy of Arts and Sciences.

——. 2001. "A Peaceful Turnover in Ghana." *Journal of Democracy* 12 (1): 103–104.

Haan, Jakob de, and Jan-Egbert Sturm. 2003. "Does More Democracy Lead to Greater Economic Freedom? New Evidence for Developing Countries." *European Journal of Political Economy* 19:547–563.

Hadenius, Axel. 1992. *Democracy and Development.* Cambridge: Cambridge University Press.

——. 2001. *Institutions and Democratic Citizenship.* Oxford: Oxford University Press.

Hägerstrand, Torsten. 1973. "The Domain of Human Geography." In R. J. Chorley, ed. *Directions in Geography.* London: Methuen.

Haggard, Stephan, and Robert Kaufman. 1997. "The Political Economy of Democratic Transitions." *Comparative Politics* 29:263–283.

Hall, John A. 1986. *Power and Liberties: The Causes and Consequences of the Rise of the West.* London: Penguin Books.

Hall, Martin. 1998. "International Political Economy Meets Historical Sociology." *Cooperation and Conflict* 33 (3): 257–277.

Hanusheck, Eric A., and Jackson, John E. 1997. *Statistical Methods for Social Scientists.* San Diego, CA: Academic Press.

Hartlyn, Jonathan. 2004. "'Free and Fair' Enough? Assessing Electoral Manipulation in Democratizing Contexts." Paper prepared for the conference Democratization by Elections? The Dynamics of Electoral Authoritarianism. Organized by the Centro de Investigación y Docencia Económica (CIDE) and the International Forum for Democratic Studies, Mexico City, 2–3 April.

Hayward, Fred, ed. 1987. *Elections in Independent Africa.* Boulder, CO: Westview Press.

Herbst, Jeffrey. 1989. "The Creation and Maintenance of National Boundaries in Africa." *International Organization* 43 (4): 673–692.

——. 1990. "War and the State in Africa." *International Security* 14 (4): 117–139.

——. 2000a. "Understanding Ambiguity during Democratization in Africa." In James F. Hollifield and Calvin Jillson, eds. *Pathways to Democracy: The Political Economy of Democratic Transitions.* New York: Routledge.

——. 2000b. *States and Power in Africa: Comparative Lessons in Authority and Control.* Princeton: Princeton University Press.

——. 2001. "Political Liberalization after Ten Years." *Comparative Politics* 34:357–375.

Hermet, Guy, Richard Rose, and Alain Rouquij, eds. 1978. *Elections without Choice.* London: Macmillan.

Hindess, Barry. 2000. "Representation Ingrafted upon Democracy?" *Democratization* 7 (2): 1–18.

Høyrup, Jens. 1995. *The Art of Knowing.* Filosofi og videnskapsteori på Roskilde Universitetscenter, 1. Raekke: Enkeltpublikationer, nr. 1, Institut for Sprog og Kultur, Roskilde, Denmark: Roskilde Universitetscenter. Revised version published in 2000 as *Human Sciences: Reappraising the Humanities through History and Philosophy.* New York: State University of New York Press.

Huntington, Samuel P. 1991. *The Third Wave: Democratization in the Late Twentieth Century.* Norman: University of Oklahoma Press.

Hyden, Goran. 1980. *Beyond Ujamaa in Tanzania.* Berkeley: University of California Press.

——. 1983. *No Shortcuts to Progress.* Berkeley: University of California Press.

——. 2000. "The Social Capital Crush in the Periphery: An Analysis of the Current Predicament in Sub-Saharan Africa." *Journal of Social Economics* 30:161–163.

——. 2005. *African Politics in Comparative Perspective.* Cambridge: Cambridge University Press.

Hyden, Goran, and Michael Bratton, eds. 1992. *Governance and Politics in Africa.* Boulder, CO: Lynne Rienner.

Hyden, Goran, and Colin Leys. 1972. "Elections and Politics in Single-Party Systems: The Case of Kenya and Tanzania." *British Journal of Political Science* 2 (4).

Hyden, Goran, Michel Leslie, and Folu F. Ogundimu, eds. 2002. *Media and Democracy in Africa.* New Brunswick, NJ: Transaction Publishers.

IFES Elections Statistics. International Foundation for Electoral Systems. http://www.ifes
.org/eguide. (Country statistics.) IPU. 1992–2000. *Chronicle of Parliamentary Elections* 25–
33. Geneva: IPU (Inter-Parliamentary Union).

IPU Parline. http://www.ipu.org/parline. (On-line database of parliamentary elections.)

Jackson, Robert H. 1990. *Quasi-States: Sovereignty, International Relations and the Third World.* Cambridge: Cambridge University Press.

Jefferson, Thomas. 1816/1903–1904. Letter to John Taylor, 28 May 1816. In *The Writings of Thomas Jefferson.* Memorial edition. Washington, DC.

Jeffries, Richard. 1998. "The Ghanaian Elections of 1996: Towards the Consolidation of De-mocracy?" *African Affairs* 97:189–208.

Jordan, Robert S. 1969. *Government and Power in West Africa.* London: Faber & Faber.

Joseph, Richard. 1987. *Prebendalism and Democracy in Nigeria.* Cambridge: Cambridge University Press.

———. 1992. "Africa: The Rebirth of Political Freedom." *Journal of Democracy* 2:11–25.

———. 1997. "Democratization in Africa after 1989: Comparative and Theoretical Perspec-tives." *Comparative Politics* 29 (3): 363–382.

———. 1998. "Africa, 1990–1997: From Abertura to Closure." *Journal of Democracy* 9 (2): 3–17.

———, ed. 1999. *State, Conflict and Democracy in Africa.* Boulder, CO: Lynne Rienner.

Karatnycky, Adrian. 1999. "The Decline of Illiberal Democracy." *Journal of Democracy* 10 (1): 112–125.

———. 2001. "The 2001 Freedom House Survey: Muslim Countries and the Democracy Gap." *Journal of Democracy* 13 (1): 99–112.

Karl, Terry L. 1986. "Imposing Consent: Electoralism and Democratization in El Salvador." In Paul W. Drake and Eduardo Silva, eds. *Elections and Democratization in Latin America, 1980–1985.* La Jolla: Center for Iberian and Latin American Studies, University of California, San Diego.

———. 1995. "The Hybrid Regimes of Latin America." *Journal of Democracy* 6 (3): 72–86.

———. 1997. *The Paradox of Plenty: Oil Booms and Petro-States.* Berkeley: University of California Press.

Keesing's Record of World Events. http://keesings.gvpi.net/keesings.

King, Gary, Robert O. Keohane, and Sidney Verba. 1994. *Designing Social Inquiry: Scientific Inference in Qualitative Research.* Princeton: Princeton University Press.

Knack, Stephen. 2004. "Does Foreign Aid Promote Democracy?" *International Studies Quarterly* 48:251–266.

Kritzer, Herbert M. 1996. "The Data Puzzle: The Nature of Interpretation in Quantitative Re-search." *American Journal of Political Science* 40 (1): 1–32.

Laakso, Maarku, and Rein Taagepera. 1979. "Effective Number of Parties: A Measure with Ap-plication to Western Europe." *Comparative Political Studies* 12:3–27.

Lehoucq, Fabrice. 2003. "Electoral Fraud: Types, Causes, and Consequences." *Annual Review of Political Science* 6:233–256.

Lemarchand, René. 1970. *Rwanda and Burundi.* New York: Praeger.

———. 1972. "Political Clientelism and Ethnicity in Tropical Africa: Competing Solidarities in Nation-Building." *American Political Science Review* 66 (1): 68–90.

Levi, Margareth. 1990. "A Logic of Institutional Change." In Karen Schweers Cook and Margareth Levi, eds. *The Limits of Rationality*. Chicago: University of Chicago Press.

Levitsky, Steven, and Robert Adcock. 1999. "Democracy and Dichotomies: A Pragmatic Approach to Choices about Concepts." *Annual Review of Political Science* 2:537–565.

Levitsky, Steven, and Lucan A. Way. 2002. "Elections without Democracy: The Rise of Competitive Authoritarianism." *Journal of Democracy* 13 (2): 51–65.

Li, Quan, and Rafael Reuveny. 2003. "Economic Globalization and Democracy: An Empirical Analysis." *British Journal of Political Science* 33:29–54.

Lijphart, Arendt. 1977. *Democracy in Plural Societies: A Comparative Exploration*. New Haven: Yale University Press.

——. 1984. *Democracies: Patterns of Majoritarian and Consensus Government in Twenty-One Countries*. New Haven: Yale University Press.

——. 1994. "Democracies: Forms, Performance and Constitutional Engineering." *European Journal of Political Research* 25 (1): 1–17.

——. 1999. *Patterns of Democracy: Government Forms and Performance in Thirty-Six Countries*. New Haven: Yale University Press.

Lijphart, Arendt, and Carl H. Waisman. 1996. "Institutional Design and Democratization." In Arendt Lijphart and Carl H. Waisman, eds. *Institutional Design in New Democracies: Eastern Europe and Latin America*. Boulder, CO: Westview Press.

Lindberg, Staffan I. 2001. "Forms of State, Governance and Regime: Reconceptualising the Prospects for Democratic Consolidation in Sub-Saharan Africa." *International Political Science Review* 22 (2): 173–199.

——. 2002. "Problems of Measuring Democracy: Illustrations from Africa." In Göran Hyden and Ole Elgstrom, eds. *Development and Democracy: What Have We Learned and How?* London: Routledge.

——. 2003. "It's Our Time to 'Chop': Do Elections in Africa Feed Neopatrimonialism Rather Than Counter-Act It?" *Democratization* 10 (2): 121–140.

——. 2004a. "The Democratic Quality of Multiparty Elections: Participation, Competition and Legitimacy in Africa." *Journal of Commonwealth and Comparative Studies* 42 (1): 61–104.

——. 2004b. "Democratization and Women's Empowerment: The Effects of Electoral Systems, Participation and Repetition in Africa." *Studies in Comparative International Development* 38 (1): 28–53.

——. 2005. "Consequences of Electoral Systems in Africa: A Preliminary Inquiry." *Electoral Studies* 24 (1): 41–64.

——. 2006. "When Do Opposition Parties Participate?" In Andreas Schedler, ed. *Electoral Authoritarianism*. Boulder, CO: Lynne Rienner.

Lindberg, Staffan I., and Minion K. C. Morrison. 2005. "Exploring Voter Alignments in Africa: Core and Swing Voters in Ghana." *Journal of Modern African Studies* 43 (4): 1–22.

Linz, Juan J. 1975. "Totalitarian and Authoritarian Regimes." In F. I. Greenstein and N. W. Polsby, eds. *Handbook of Political Science*. Vol. 3. Reading, MA: Addison-Wesley.

——. 1988. "Legitimacy of Democracy and the Socioeconomic System." In Mattei Dogan, ed. *Comparing Pluralist Democracies: Strains on Legitimacy*. Boulder, CO: Westview Press.

———. 1990. "The Perils of Presidentialism." *Journal of Democracy* 1 (1): 51–69.

———. 1994. "Presidential or Parliamentary Democracy: Does It Make a Difference?" In Juan J. Linz and Arturo Valenzuela, eds. *The Failure of Presidential Democracy*. Baltimore: Johns Hopkins University Press.

———. 1998. "Democracy's Time Constraints." *International Political Science Review* 19 (1): 19–37.

Linz, Juan J., and Alfred Stepan. 1978. *The Breakdown of Democratic Regimes*. 4 vols. Baltimore: Johns Hopkins University Press.

———. 1996. *The Problems of Democratic Transition and Consolidation: Southern Europe, South America and Post-Communist Europe*. Baltimore: Johns Hopkins University Press.

Lipset, Seymour M. 1959. "Some Social Requisites of Democracy: Economic Development and Political Legitimacy." *American Political Science Review* 53 (1): 69–105.

———. 1993. "The Social Requisites of Democracy Revisited." *American Sociological Review* 59 (February): 1–22.

Lipset, Seymour Martin, Kyoung-Ryung Seong, and John Charles Torres. 1993. "A Comparative Analysis of the Social Requisites of Democracy." *International Social Science Journal* 45:155–175.

Locke, John. 1689–90/1970. *Two Treatises of Government*. 2nd ed. Cambridge: Cambridge University Press.

Lodge, Tom. 2002. "The Namibian Elections of 1999." *Democratization* 8 (2): 191–230.

Londregan, John B., and Keith T. Poole. 1996. "Does High Income Promote Democracy?" *World Politics* 49 (1): 56–91.

Loveman, Brian. 1994. "'Protected Democracies' and Military Guardianship: Political Transition in Latin America, 1978–1993." *Journal of Interamerican Studies and World Affairs* 36 (Summer): 108–111.

Luckham, Robert. 1995. "Dilemmas of Military Disengagement and Democratization in Africa." *IDS Bulletin* 26:49–61.

Lyon, Terrence. 1997. "A Major Step Forward." *Journal of Democracy* 8 (2): 65–77.

MacKenzie, W. J. M., and K. Robinson. 1960. *Five Elections in Africa*. Oxford: Clarendon.

Macpherson, C. B. 1968. *Den mångtydiga demokratin*. Stockholm: Albert Bonniers.

Madison, James. 1789/1961. *The Federalist Papers*. No. 10. New York: Mentor.

Mahmud, S. S. 1996. "Africa's Democratic Transitions, Change, and Development." *Africa Today* 43:405–416.

Mainwaring, Scott. 1993. "Presidentialism, Multipartyism, and Democracy: The Difficult Combination." *Comparative Political Studies* 26:198–228.

Mainwaring, Scott, and Timothy Scully, eds. 1995. *Building Democratic Institutions: Party Systems in Latin America*. Stanford, CA: Stanford University Press.

Mair, Peter, ed. 1990. *The West European Party System*. Oxford: Oxford University Press.

Mamdani, Mahmood. 1996. *Citizen and Subject: Contemporary Africa and the Legacy of Late Colonialism*. Princeton: Princeton University Press.

Mampilly, Zachariah. 2001. "Ivory Coast." Paper presented to Parliamentarians for Global Action, New York, 20 February.

Mann, Michael. 1986. *The Sources of Social Power I: A History of Power from the Beginning to A.D. 1760*. Cambridge: Cambridge University Press.

March, James G., and Johan P. Olsen. 1989. *Rediscovering Institutions*. New York: Free Press.

Marcus, Richard. 2002. "Participation and the Poverty of Electoral Democracy in Madagascar." Paper presented at African Studies Association's annual meeting, Washington, DC, 5–8 December.

Marsh, David, and Gerry Stoker, eds. 2002. *Theory and Methods in Political Science*. 2nd ed. Hampshire: Palgrave Macmillan.

Marshall, Monty G., and Keith Jaggers. 2001. *Polity IV Project: Political Regime Characteristics and Transition, 1800–1999*. Retrieved from: http://www.bsos.umd.edu/cidcm/polity/.

May, Roy, and Simon Massey. 2001. "The 1996 and 1997 Elections in Chad." *Electoral Studies* 20 (1): 127–135.

Mbembe, A. 1995. "Complex Transformations in the Late Twentieth Century." *Africa Demos* 3:28–30.

McHenry, Dean E., Jr. 2000. "Quantitative Measures of Democracy in Africa: An Assessment." *Democratization* 7 (2): 168–185.

Medard, Jean-François. 1982. "The Underdeveloped State in Tropical Africa: Political Clientelism or Neo-Patrimonialism?" In Christopher Clapham, ed. *Private Patronage and Public Power: Political Clientelism in the Modern State*. London: Frances Pinter.

Merkel, Wolfgang. 1998. "The Consolidation of Post-Autocratic Democracies: A Multi-Level Model." *Democratization* 5 (3): 33–67.

Mill, John Stuart. 1861/1958. *Considerations on Representative Government*. Indianapolis: Bobbs-Merrill.

Moe, Ronald C. 1990. "Traditional Organizational Principles and the Managerial Presidency: From Phoenix to Ashes." *Public Administration Review* 50 (2): 129–140.

Molinar, J. 1991. "Counting the Number of Parties: An Alternative Index." *American Political Science Review* 85 (4): 1383–1391.

Monga, Celestine. 1995. "Civil Society and Democratisation in Francophone Africa." *Journal of Modern African Studies* 33 (3): 359–379.

Moore, Mick. 1995. "Democracy and Development in Cross-National Perspective." *Democratization* 2 (2): 1–19.

———. 1998. "Death without Taxes: Democracy, State Capacity, and Aid Dependence in the Fourth World." In Gordon White and Mary Robinson, eds. *Towards a Democratic Developmental State*. Oxford: Oxford University Press.

Morgenthau, Ruth S. 1964. *Political Parties in French-Speaking West Africa*. Oxford: Clarendon Press.

Moss, Todd J. 1995. "U.S. Policy and Democratisation in Africa: The Limits of Liberal Universalism." *Journal of Modern African Studies* 33 (2): 189–209.

Mozaffar, Shaheen. 2002. "Patterns of Electoral Governance in Africa's Emerging Democracies." *International Political Science Review* 23 (1): 85–101.

Mozaffar, Shaheen, James Scarritt, and Glen Galaich. 2003. "Electoral Institutions, Ethnopolitical Cleavages, and Party Systems in Africa's Emerging Democracies." *American Political Science Review* 97:379–390.

Munck, Gerardo L. 1994. "Democratic Transitions in Comparative Perspective." *Comparative Politics* 26:355–375.

——. 1998. "Canons of Research Design in Qualitative Analysis." *Studies in Comparative International Development* 33 (3): 18–45.

——. 2001a. "Democratic Consolidation." In Paul B. Clarke and Joe Foweraker, eds. *Encyclopedia of Democratic Thought*. London: Routledge.

——. 2001b. "The Regime Question: Theory Building in Democracy Studies." *World Politics* 54:119–144.

——. 2001c. "Game Theory and Comparative Politics: New Perspectives and Old Concerns." *World Politics* 53 (January): 173–204.

——. 2005. "Ten Fallacies about Qualitative Research." *Qualitative Methods* 3 (1): 2–5.

Munck, Gerardo L., and Jay Verkuilen. 2002. "Conceptualizing and Measuring Democracy: Evaluating Alternative Indices." *Comparative Political Studies* 35 (1): 5–34.

——. 2003. "The Democratic Regime Index: A Methodological Note." Paper presented at "Diagnosing Democracy: Methods of Analysis, Remedies and Findings," 11–13 April 2003, in Santiago de Chile, Chile, organized by Department of Political Science, Uppsala University, Sweden.

——. 2004. "Research Designs." *Encyclopedia of Social Measurement*. Oxford: Elsevier.

Nagel, Thomas. 1991. *Equality and Partiality*. New York: Oxford University Press.

NDI. Elections observation reports. http://www.ndi.org. Country reports.

Neumann, John von, and Oskar Morgenstern. 1994. *Theory of Games and Economic Behavior*. Princeton: Princeton University Press.

Ninsin, Kwame A. 1998. "Elections, Democracy and Elite Consensus." In Kwame A. Ninsin, ed. *Ghana: Transition to Democracy*. Dakar, Senegal: CODRESIA.

Nohlen, Dieter. 1996. "Electoral Systems and Electoral Reform in Latin America." In Arendt Lijphart and Carlos H. Waisman, eds. *Institutional Design in New Democracies: Eastern Europe and Latin America*. Boulder, CO: Westview Press.

Nohlen, Dieter, Michael Krennerich, and Bernhard Thibaut, eds. 1999. *Elections in Africa: A Data Handbook*. Oxford: Oxford University Press.

North, Douglass C. 1990. *Institutions, Institutional Change and Development*. Cambridge: Cambridge University Press.

Nugent, Paul. 2001. "Winners, Losers and Also-Rans: Money, Moral Authority and Voting Patterns in the Ghana 2000 Election." *African Affairs* 100 (400): 405–428.

O'Connell, James. 1970. "The Fragility of Stability: The Fall of the Nigerian Federal Republic." In Robert I. Rotberg and Ali Mazrui, eds. *Protest and Power in Black Africa*. New York: Oxford University Press.

O'Donnell, Guillermo. 1992. "Transitions, Continuities, and Paradoxes." In Scott Mainwaring, Guillermo O'Donnell, and J. Samuel Valenzuela, eds. *Issues in Democratic Consolidation: The New South American Democracies in Comparative Perspective*. Notre Dame, IN: University of Notre Dame Press.

——. 1994. "Delegative Democracy." *Journal of Democracy* 5 (1): 55–69.

——. 1996. "Illusions about Consolidation." *Journal of Democracy* 7 (2): 34–51.

O'Donnell, Guillermo, and Philippe C. Schmitter. 1986. *Transitions from Authoritarian Rule: Tentative Conclusions about Uncertain Democracies*. Baltimore: Johns Hopkins University Press.

Ogden, Charles K., and Ivor A. Richards. 1923. *The Meaning of Meaning: A Study of the Influence of Language upon Thought and of the Science of Symbolism.* London: Routledge.

Ogendo, H. W. O. Okoth. 1999. "The Quest for Constitutional Government." In Goran Hyden, H. W. O. Okoth Ogendo, and D. Olowu, eds. *African Perspectives on Governance.* Trenton, NJ: Africa World Press.

Olsen, Mancur. 1965. *The Logic of Collective Action.* Cambridge: Harvard University Press.

Olukoshi, Adebayo, ed. 1998. *The Politics of Opposition in Contemporary Africa.* Uppsala, Sweden: Nordic Africa Institute.

Ordershook, Peter. 1992. "Constitutional Stability." *Constitutional Political Economy* 3:137–175.

Osaghae, Eghosa E. 1995. "The Study of Political Transitions in Africa" *Review of African Political Economy* 64:183–197.

Ostrom, Elinor, Larry Schroeder, and Susan Wynne. 1993. *Institutional Incentives and Sustainable Development: Infrastructure Policies in Perspective.* Boulder, CO: Westview Press.

Pankani, Winifred V. 2004. "The Ties Still Bind: Changing Economies of Affection among Educated Ghanaians." MA thesis, University of Oregon.

Pedersen, M. N. 1980. "On Measuring Party System Change: A Methodological Critique and a Suggestion." *Comparative Political Studies* 12 (4): 387–403.

Peirce, C. S. 1958. *Collected Papers.* Cambridge: Harvard University Press.

Piaget, Jean. 1972. *Psychology and Epistemology.* London: Allen Lane.

Pierson, Paul. 2000. "Increasing Returns, Path Dependence, and the Study of Politics." *American Political Science Review* 84 (2): 251–267.

Polity IV Data Set. http://weber.ucsd.edu/~kgledits/Polity.html.

Popper, Karl. 1953/1999. *The Logic of Scientific Discovery.* London: Routledge.

——. 1963/2002. *Conjectures and Refutations: The Growth of Scientific Knowledge.* 4th ed. London: Routledge.

Posner, Dan. 2004. "Measuring Ethnic Fractionalization in Africa." *American Journal of Political Science* 48 (4): 849–864.

Powell, Bingham G. 1982. *Contemporary Democracies: Participation, Stability and Violence.* Cambridge: Harvard University Press.

——. 2000. *Elections as Instruments of Democracy.* New Haven: Yale University Press.

Price, J. H. 1967. *Political Institutions of West Africa.* London: Hutchinson.

Pridham, Geoffrey. 1991. "International Influences and Democratic Transition: Problems of Theory and Practice in Linkage Politics." In Geoffrey Pridham, ed. *Encouraging Democracy: The International Context of Regime Transition in Southern Europe.* Leicester: Leicester University Press.

Przeworski, Adam. 1986. "Some Problems in the Study of Transitions to Democracy." In Guillermo O'Donnell and Philippe Schmitter, eds. *Transitions from Authoritarian Rule: Prospects for Democracy.* Baltimore: Johns Hopkins University Press.

——. 1988. "Democracy as the Contingent Outcome of Conflict." In Jon Elster and Rune Slagstad, eds. *Constitutionalism and Democracy.* Cambridge: Cambridge University Press.

Przeworski, Adam, Michael Alvarez, José A. Cheibub, and Fernando Limongi. 1996. "What Makes Democracies Endure?" *Journal of Democracy* 7 (1): 39–55.

——. 2000. *Democracy and Development: Political Institutions and Well-Being in the World, 1950–1990.* Cambridge: Cambridge University Press.

Pye, Lucian W. 2000. "Democracy and Its Enemies." In James F. Hollifield and Calvin Jillson, eds. *Pathways to Democracy: The Political Economy of Democratic Transitions*. New
York: Routledge.

Quaye, Mike. 1995. "The Ghanaian Elections of 1992: A Dissenting View." *African Affairs*
94:259–275.

Rae, Douglas. 1971. *The Political Consequences of Electoral Laws*. New Haven: Yale University Press.

Reilly, Benjamin. 2001. *Democracy in Divided Societies: Electoral Engineering for Conflict
Management*. Cambridge: Cambridge University Press.

Remmer, Karen. 1996. "The Sustainability of Political Democracy: Lessons from South America." *Comparative Political Studies* 29 (6): 611–634.

Reno, William. 1998. *Warlord Politics and African States*. Boulder, CO: Lynne Rienner.

———. 1999. "Violence, Crime and State Making on the Margins of the Global Economy."
Paper presented at the International Studies Association's 40th annual convention, Washington, DC, 16–20 February.

Reynolds, Andrew, and Timothy D. Sisk. 1998. "Elections and Electoral Systems: Implications
for Conflict Management." In Timothy D. Sisk and Andrew Reynolds, eds. *Elections and
Conflict Management in Africa*. Washington, DC: United States Institute of Peace Press.

Ridley, Fredrick F. 1975. *The Study of Government*. London: Allen & Unwin.

Riker, William H. 1986. *The Art of Political Manipulation*. New Haven: Yale University Press.

Rosenberg, Shawn W. 1995. "Against Neoclassical Political Economy: A Political Psychological Critique." *Political Psychology* 16 (1): 99–136.

Ross, Michael. 2001. "Does Oil Hinder Democracy?" *World Politics* 53 (April): 325–361.

Rothstein, Bo. 1998. "Political Institutions: An Overview." In Robert E. Goodin and Hans-Dieter
Klingemann, eds. *A New Handbook of Political Science*. Oxford: Oxford University Press.

Rowen, Henry S. 1996. "The Tide underneath the 'Third Wave.'" In Larry Diamond and Marc
Plattner, eds. *The Global Resurgence of Democracy*. Baltimore: Johns Hopkins University
Press.

Rustow, Dankwart. 1970. "Transitions to Democracy: Toward a Dynamic Model." *Comparative Politics* 2:337–363.

Sandbrook, Richard. 1996. "Transition without Consolidation: Democratisation in Six African
Cases." *Third World Quarterly* 17 (1): 69–88.

Sandbrook, Richard, and Jay Ouelbaum. 1999. *Reforming the Political Kingdom: Governance
and Development in Ghana's Fourth Republic*. Accra, Ghana: Center for Democracy and
Development.

Sanders, David. 2002. "Behaviouralism." In David Marsh and Gerry Stoker, eds. *Theory and
Methods in Political Science*. Hampshire: Palgrave.

Sartori, Giovanni. 1968. "Political Development and Political Engineering." In J. D. Mont-
gomery and Albert O. Hirschman, eds. *Public Policy*. Cambridge: Cambridge University
Press.

———. 1984. "Guidelines for Conceptual Analysis." In Giovanni Sartori, ed. *Social Science
Concepts: A Systematic Analysis*. Beverly Hills, CA: Sage Publications.

———. 1986. "The Influence of Electoral Systems: Faulty Laws or Faulty Method?" In Bernard

Grofman and Arendt Lijphart, eds. *Electoral Laws and Their Political Consequences*. New York: Agathon Press.

——. 1987. *The Theory of Democracy Revisited*. Chatham: Chatham House.

——. 1991. "Comparing and Miscomparing." *Journal of Theoretical Politics* 3 (3): 243–257.

——. 1997. *Comparative Constitutional Engineering*. 2nd ed. New York: New York University Press.

——. 2001. "The Party Effects of Electoral Systems." In Larry Diamond and Richard Günther, eds. *Political Parties and Democracy*. Baltimore: Johns Hopkins University Press.

Scarritt, James, and Shaheen Mozaffar. 1999. "The Specification of Ethnic Cleavages and Ethnopolitical Groups for the Analysis of Democratic Competition in Contemporary Africa." *Nationalism and Ethnic Politics* 5 (1): 82–117.

Schedler, Andreas. 1998. "What Is Democratic Consolidation?" *Journal of Democracy* 9 (2): 91–107.

——. 1999. "Conceptualizing Accountability." In Andreas Schedler, Larry Diamond, and Marc F. Plattner, eds. *The Self-Restraining State: Power and Accountability in New Democracies*. Boulder, CO: Lynne Rienner.

——. 2001a. "Measuring Democratic Consolidation." *Studies in Comparative International Development* 36 (1): 66–92.

——. 2001b. "Taking Uncertainty Seriously: The Blurred Boundaries of Democratic Transition and Consolidation." *Democratization* 8 (4): 1–22.

——. 2002a. "Elections without Democracy: The Menu of Manipulation." *Journal of Democracy* 13 (2): 36–50.

——. 2002b. "The Nested Game of Democratization by Elections." *International Political Science Review* 23 (1): 103–122.

——, ed. 2006. *Electoral Authoritarianism*. Boulder, CO: Lynne Rienner.

Schedler, Andreas, Larry Diamond, and Marc F. Plattner, eds. 1999. *The Self-Restraining State: Power and Accountability in New Democracies*. Boulder, CO: Lynne Rienner.

Schedler, Andreas, and Javier Santiso. 1998. "Democracy and Time: An Invitation." *International Political Science Review* 19 (1): 5–18.

Schmitter, Philippe C. 1992. "The Consolidation of Democracy and Representation of Social Groups." *American Behavioral Scientist* 35 (4–5): 422–449.

Schmitter, Philippe C., and Terry L. Karl. 1991. "What Democracy Is . . . and Is Not." *Journal of Democracy* 3 (1): 75–88.

Schmitter, Philippe C., and Javier Santiso. 1998. "Three Temporal Dimensions to the Consolidation of Democracy." *International Political Science Review* 19 (1): 69–92.

Schumpeter, Joseph. 1947. *Capitalism, Socialism and Democracy*. 2nd ed. New York: Harper.

Seligson, Mitchell A., and J. A. Booth. 1995. *Elections and Democracy in Central America Revisited*. Chapel Hill: University of North Carolina Press.

Shin, Do Chull. 1994. "On the Third Wave of Democratization: A Synthesis and Evaluation of Recent Theory and Research." *World Politics* 47 (1): 135–170.

Sisk, Timothy D. and Andrew Reynolds. 1998. "Elections and Electoral Systems: Implications for Conflict Management." In Andrew Reynolds and Timothy E. Sisk, eds., *Elections and Conflict Management in Africa*. Washington, DC: United States Institute of Peace Press.

Sklar, Richard L. 1983. "Democracy in Africa." *African Studies Review* 26 (3): 11–24.

———. 1987. "Developmental Democracy." *Comparative Studies in Society and History* 29 (4): 686–714.

———. 1996. "Toward a Theory of Developmental Democracy." In Adrian Leftwich, ed. *Democracy and Development*. Cambridge, England: Polity Press.

Smith, Zeric K. 2001. "Mali's Decade of Democracy." *Journal of Democracy* 12 (3): 73–79.

Sorokin, Pitirim A. 1937. *Social and Cultural Dynamics*. Vol. 1. New York: American Book Company.

Stepan, Alfred, and Cindy Skach. 1993. "Constitutional Frameworks and Democratic Consolidation: Parliamentarianism versus Presidentialism." *World Politics* 46 (1): 1–22.

Sztompka, Piotr. 1993. *The Sociology of Social Change*. Oxford: Blackwell.

Taagepera, Rein. 1999. "Supplementing the Effective Number of Parties." *Electoral Studies* 18 (4): 497–504.

Taylor, Michael. 1987. *The Possibility of Cooperation*. Cambridge: Cambridge University Press.

Teorell, Jan, and Axel Hadenius. 2004. "Global and Regional Determinants of Democratization: Taking Stock of the Large-N Evidence." Paper presented at the conference Democratic Advancements and Setbacks: What Have We Learnt? Uppsala, Sweden, 11–13 June 2004.

Thibaut, Bernhard. 1998. "Prasidentielle, parlamentarische oder hybride Regierungssysteme? Institutionen und Demokratientwicklung in de dritten Welt und in den Transformationsstaaten Osteuropas." *Zeitschrift für Politikwissenschaft* 8 (1): 5–37.

Thompson, Janice E. 1995. "State Sovereignty in International Relations: Bridging the Gap between Theory and Empirical Research." *International Science Quarterly* 39:213–233.

Tilly, Charles. 1990. *Coercion, Capital and European States: AD 990–1992*. Oxford: Blackwell.

———. 1993. *European Revolutions 1492–1992*. Oxford: Blackwell.

Tsebelis, George. 1990. *Nested Games: Rational Choice in Comparative Politics*. Berkeley: University of California Press.

United Nations. *IRIN News Reports*. Various dates. Integrated Regional Information Networks. http://www.irinnews.org.

Uwechue, Raph, ed. 1996. *Africa Today*. 3rd ed. London: Africa Books.

Valenzuela, J. Samuel. 1992. "Democratic Consolidation in Post-Transitional Settings: Notion, Process, and Facilitating Conditions." In Scott Mainwaring, Guillermo O'Donnell, and J. Samuel Valenzuela, eds. *Issues in Democratic Consolidation: The New South American Democracies in Comparative Perspective*. Notre Dame, IN: University of Notre Dame Press.

Vanberg, Georg. 1998. "Abstract Judicial Review, Legislative Bargaining, and Policy Compromise." *Journal of Theoretical Politics* 10 (3): 299–346.

van de Walle, Nicholas. 2001. *African Economies and the Politics of Permanent Crisis, 1979–1999*. Cambridge: Cambridge University Press.

———. 2002. "Elections without Democracy: Africa's Range of Regimes." *Journal of Democracy* 13 (2): 66–80.

Vanhanen, Tatu. 1997. *Prospects of Democracy: A Study of 172 Countries.* London: Routledge.

Villalón, Leonardo A. 1998 "The African State at the End of the Twentieth Century." In Leonardo A. Villalón and Philip A. Huxtable, eds. *The African State at a Critical Juncture.* Boulder, CO: Lynne Rienner.

Villalón, Leonardo A., and Philip A. Huxtable, eds. 1998. *The African State at a Critical Juncture.* Boulder, CO: Lynne Rienner.

Waisman, Carlos H. 1989. "Argentina: Autarkic Industrialization and Illegitimacy." In Larry Diamond, Juan J. Linz, and Seymour M. Lipset, eds. *Democracy in Developing Countries: Latin America.* Boulder, CO: Lynne Rienner.

Wantchekon, Leonard. 2003. "Clientelism and Voting Behavior: A Field Experiment in Benin." *World Politics* 54:399–422.

Weber, Max. 1958. *From Max Weber: Essays in Sociology.* Translated, edited, and with an introduction by H. H. Gerth and C. Wright Mills. New York: Oxford University Press.

Weingast, Barry R. 1997. "The Political Foundations of Democracy and the Rule of Law." *American Political Science Review* 91 (2): 245–263.

Westebbe, Richard. 1994. "Structural Adjustment, Rent Seeking, and Liberalization in Benin." In Jennifer A. Widner, ed. *Economic Change and Political Liberalization in Sub-Saharan Africa.* Baltimore: Johns Hopkins University Press.

Whitehead, Lawrence, ed. 1996. *The International Dimension of Democratization.* Oxford: Oxford University Press.

Wilson, E. J. 1994. "Creating a Research Agenda for the Study of Political Change in Africa." In Jennifer A. Widner, ed. *Economic Change and Political Liberalization in Sub-Saharan Africa.* Baltimore: Johns Hopkins University Press.

Wiseman, John A. 1990. *Democracy in Black Africa: Survival and Revival.* New York: Paragon House.

———. 1992. "Early Post-Democratization Elections in Africa." *Electoral Studies* 11 (4): 279–291.

———. 1993. "Democracy and the New Political Pluralism in Africa: Causes, Consequences and Significance." *Third World Quarterly* 14 (3): 439–449.

———. 1999. "The Continuing Case for Demo-Optimism in Africa." *Democratization* 6 (2): 128–155.

Wolf, Tom. 2003. "Paying the Public, or Caring for Constituents?" Report for Transparency International (Kenya). Nairobi: Friedrich Ebert Stiftung.

World Bank Africa Database 2002. CD-ROM. Washington, DC: World Bank.

Yoon, Mi Young. 2001. "Democratization and Women's Legislative Representation in Sub-Saharan Africa." *Democratization* 8 (2): 169–190.

Young, Crawford. 1965. *Politics in the Congo.* Princeton: Princeton University Press.

———. 1982. *Ideology and Development in Africa.* New Haven: Yale University Press.

———. 1999. "The Third Wave of Democratization in Africa: Ambiguities and Contradictions." In Richard Joseph, ed. *State, Conflict and Democracy in Africa.* Boulder, CO: Lynne Rienner.

Young, Tom, ed. 1993. "Understanding Elections in Africa: Special Issue." *Africa* 63 (3): 299–418.

Zakaria, Fareed. 1997. "The Rise of Illiberal Democracy." *Foreign Affairs* 76:22–43.

Zerubavel, Eviatar. 1981. "Private-Time and Public Time." In John Hassard, ed. *The Sociology of Time*. London: Macmillan.

Zolberg, Aristide R. 1966. *Creating Political Order: The Party States in West Africa*. Chicago: Rand McNally.

Index

accountability, 153, 159

actors (in elections): attitudes, 19, 105, 111, 150, 157; behavior, 5, 96–97, 159; conceptualization, 109; incentives, 7, 110–111, 122; interests, 106

adaptation and learning, 19, 75, 107, 110, 147, 149, 159

African Union, 49

Afro-optimism, 4, 52

Afro-pessimism, 3–4, 57, 97, 143

aid. *See* foreign aid

alternation in power. *See* turnovers of power

analysis: large-N, 36, 50, 62, 115–116, 140, 154; small-N, 50, 125, 147; techniques, 116; unit of, 8, 35

Angola: breakdown, 53, 95; rejection of results, 60

armed forces. *See* military

authoritarian governments and regimes, 1, 3, 10, 24, 43, 96, 121, 133, 135, 145; rule, 93, 95

autocratic rulers: become democrats, 38–39, 73, 76, 93, 97; disappearing, 58, 71, 76–77; still present, 13, 64–66, 97

Barkan, Joel, 73, 106–107, 116

Benin: civil liberties, 127; clientelism, 154; democratic, 130; hybrid regime, 143; old autocrats, 76; one party, 10; previous regime, 146; turnovers, 52, 83

Botswana: democratic rule, 52, 130, 143; dominant party, 42; elections, 11, 70, 96

boycotts, 38, 58, 64, 66, 75–76, 87

Bratton, Michael, and Nicholas van de Walle: assumptions, 28, 32; data, 46, 134–136; on "founding" elections, 15, 72, 104; hypotheses and contradictory findings, 16, 19, 53–54, 56, 72–73, 81, 106, 145, 148, 150; measures used, 40,

60, 106; pioneering work, 2, 5; on second and later elections, 61–62, 72, 81

Brazzaville Conference, 9

breakdown of regimes. *See* regime survival

British colonies, 9

Burkina Faso, 124, 131

Burundi: elections, 10; peace process, 95; turnover, 83

Cameroon: façade regime, 148; one party, 11; stalled process, 53

Cape Verde, 130; elections, 123; turnovers, 76, 83; voter turnout, 64; voting behavior, 82

capital investments and democratization, 133

Carothers, Thomas, 38, 70, 119, 140

causal links, 111–118

Center for Democratic Development, 115

Central African Republic (CAR): breakdown, 68, 84–85; elections, 68; one party, 11; turnover, 83

Central America, elections and democratization in, 106

Chad: authoritarian, 143; civil liberties, 127; elections, 61; one party, 10; repressive regime, 53, 63, 74, 95

citizenship, 106–107, 111, 113, 155

civil liberties: institutionalization of, 2; rankings, 117–118, 120; spread and deepening of, 19, 100–101, 120–121, 140

civil society, 151, 157, 158; and individuals, 116, 150; organizations, 112–113, 123; and protest, 19, 136; reinvigorated, 107, 140

clientelism, 4, 11–13, 20, 24, 80–81, 134, 153–154

collective action, 76–77, 80–81, 96–97, 105, 155–156

Comoros: breakdown, 84–85, 95; dissolution of legislature, 54, 85; one party, 11; turnover, 83